THE TRADE HANDBOOK

W0060494

Arancha Gonzalez
with Yanis Bourgeois

THE TRADE HANDBOOK

Making trade work for
prosperity, people and planet

 **FEPS**
Handbook

This book has been produced with the financial support
of the European Parliament.

Bibliographical information of the German National Library
The German Library catalogues this publication in the
German National Bibliography; detailed bibliographic information
can be found on the internet at: *http://dnb.dnb.de.*

ISBN 978-3-8012-3103-3

Published by
Verlag J.H.W. Dietz Nachf. GmbH
Dreizehnmorgenweg 24, D-53175 Bonn

Published in association with the
Foundation for European Progressive Studies
www.feps-europe.eu
European Political Foundation – N° 4 BE 896.230.213

FEPS
Handbook

– Vol. 1

Cover design und typesetting: Rohtext, Bonn
Cover picture: shutterstock/brutto film.
Printing and processing: Bookpress, Olsztyn

Find us on the internet: *www.dietz-verlag.de*

Contents

Foreword   7

Preamble   11

Introduction   15

Part I:

why trade and economic integration matter   21

Setting the scene: the rationale for open trade   22

Trade, integration and related challenges: a question of narrative?   30

Trade and integration: processes with flaws and risks   33

The future of trade...   39

NextGen trade agreements and the EU: going beyond trade policy   51

Part II:

making trade possible – the trade opening and regulating agenda   57

The institutional foundation of the multilateral trading system   59

Principles of the multilateral trading system   74

Operating under the multilateral trading system: adapt and overcome   94

Part III:

making trade happen – mens sana in corpore sano   117

Trade needs a sound 'brain': promoting trade intelligence   118

The lifeblood of trade: inclusive trade finance and Aid for Trade   126

The backbone of trade: supportive and conducive infrastructure   135

Trade policy enforcement mechanisms with teeth and muscles   150

Part IV:

making trade work for all – ensuring long-term social gains   163

Managing the transition costs   165

Fair taxation to address inequalities and

power up the EU's 21st century transitions   169

Making trade work for the environment in the EU and beyond   179

Making trade advance decent work in the EU and beyond   200

Conclusion   **213**

The EU and global trade timeline   **219**

Glossary   **230**

List of abbreviations   **239**

List of figures   **244**

Bibliography   **246**

Reviews   **274**

About the Authors   **276**

Acknowledgements   278

Foreword

Disruption, upheaval and disorder are words commonly used to describe the times we are living in. The multitude of international conflicts, the weaknesses of multilateral institutions and the failure of global policy coordination keep the world economy functioning well below potential. And with the breakdowns of the economic system, our societies can achieve much less prosperity and equality than what would be first of all desired but most likely also possible. How much, under what conditions and what exactly is traded between nations and regions are critical factors that influence not only the conditions of material wealth but also whether people can live with each other in conflict or harmony. At the same time, the development of international trade rests on peace. Nations need to create an ecosystem supportive of production and mutually beneficial exchanges.

However, developing international trade is not simply about bringing down barriers but also establishing and maintaining a necessary infrastructure. Finance, for example, is an important system that serves as infrastructure for trade, and readers find fresh knowledge about this crucial connection in the book, together with issues that would not have popped up in books on trade just a few decades ago, like the impact on gender equality, or the efforts of European Union (EU) to protect its citizens and businesses from undesirable foreign investments.

Organising trade is also about setting, maintaining and developing standards. Not understanding this has resulted in vast misunderstandings about the single market of the EU, particularly in England which after the great financial crisis escalated anti-Brussels sentiments and eventually took Scotland, Wales and Northern Ireland also out of the EU. This is, however, just one recent example of trade disintegration leading to further grave consequences in economics and politics. One hundred years before, World War One marked the end of the golden age of free trade, when deglobalisation brought with itself the end of the classical form of liberal civilisation as well.

Globalisation and integration through trade in goods and services is supposed to bring more opportunities than a world full of hard borders and various trade barriers. For a long time after the end of the Cold War, countries of the world were converging on a shared platform of open cooperation. China became member of the World Trade Organisation (WTO) in 2001, and Russia became a WTO member in 2012. The first one happened thanks to the policy of Bill Clinton, and the second one thanks to Barack Obama. And in the years following the Great Recession of 2009, the EU and the United States were endeavouring in the establishment of a Transatlantic Trade and Investment Partnership (TTIP), which was a genuine exercise in interdependence, even if it ran into the sand after two rounds of negotiations.

The economic system of the European Union is extroverted. Importantly, it is much more outward looking than our main transatlantic partner, the US. Furthermore, the EU responded to the 2010-3 crisis of the Economic and Monetary Union (EMU) with a further push for more openness and outward orientation. Thus the subsequent experience of a polycrisis has particularly hurt Europe, since it can also be seen through the lense of trade and thus as a series of breakdowns in international economic relations.

Brexit represented a break-up of our Single Market and the four years of Donald Trump in the White House was an experiment with trade wars. The 2020-2 Covid-19 pandemic disrupted trade relations for completely different reasons but with a lasting effect, followed by the Russia—Ukraine war which launched a new era of economic warfare. Multilateral organisations like the WTO, but also the IMF, are facing an identity crisis.

Should this therefore be the time to give up on global cooperation? Should one give in to escalating economic warfare, friendshoring, and hidden and overt protectionism? Definitely not! This can also be the time for bold visions based on sound analysis of economic opportunities and attention to human needs. As Pedro Sanchez, Spanish prime minister and President of the Socialist International remarked when visiting China in 2023: "free, balanced and fair trade is essential if we want stability and prosperity for all".

This book written by Arancha Gonzalez and published by the Foundation for European Progressive Studies (FEPS) combines the approach of an introduction to the profession of international trade with the philosophy of progressive policy making. It serves the reader with not only up to date catalogue of trade relations and trends, but also insight regarding how institutions function and strategies are developed. It presents an historic background and when necessary, and refers back to outstanding theoreticians of international trade, from Ricardo and Bastiat to Samuelson and Krugman, to refresh with some sharp observations.

Readers will find it fascinating how the author outlines what she considers to be the future of trade, but not in the sense that this future would unfold irrespective of decisions. The future of the international economy will be shaped by policies chosen and requires an adaptation of the existing institutional infrastructure. The explanation of these institutions and policies rests on the unrivalled experience of the author gained during her public service at the European Commission, the World Trade Organisation, the United Nations, as well as the International Trade Centre, topped up by being a Minister of Foreign Affairs, European Union and Cooperation in the Spanish government, and the Dean of the Paris School of International Affairs at Sciences Po (Paris).

19th century progressives pursued the policy of free trade. 21st century progressives must be committed to fair trade, and develop international economic relations simultaneously with the pursuit of social rights and environmental sustainability. Making trade work for social gains, decent work, and for a sustainable environment is possible, as long as it comes with the right incentives but also broader economic policies that stimulate and support investment with the right orientation.

This is indeed a time to think seriously about the multiple benefits of international trade. If the EU is striving for "open strategic autonomy", it must be able to reconcile the keen interest in global economic cooperation with resilience and risk mitigation, especially what concerns avoiding excessive imbalances and dependencies. This book will help readers not only in developing an understanding of such strategic and practical dilemmas but also with arguments for policy debates of the years to come.

Dr László Andor
FEPS Secretary General

Preamble

A path toward making trade work for prosperity, people and planet

We are living in turbulent times: the devastating impact of climate change, the multiplication of conflicts in many parts of the world including the return of war in the European continent, a global pandemic that has worsened the situation for millions around the world, rising geopolitical tensions, persistent gaps relating to income, investments, infrastructure, gender and technology. A new international order is in the making and trade is one of the faultlines.

A vehicle for the reduction of poverty which may lead to rising inequalities. An effective tool for development which creates challenges for the environment. A process which may be used to thrive collectively, or which may be weaponised to weaken others. Acclaimed by some as a source of resilience, rebuffed by others as a root cause for major shocks. Trade has many faces.

Trade, as globalisation, is subject to major economic and societal shifts: the rise of global value chains, the servicification and digitalisation of the economy, regionalisation of trade relations, growing domestic precautionist policies to protect consumers, workers and the environment. Today and tomorrow's trade is far from the tariffs-and-goods-focused topic it once was.

A growing sino-american rivalry is also severely impacting international trade. Concerns around national security, dependencies and technology are redrawing trade maps and could lead to a costly fragmentation of the global trade framework. Navigating the choppy waters of trade is not an easy task, and it is unlikely to become one any time soon.

This easy-to read *Trade Handbook* will help readers break through the complex barriers surrounding trade and help address essential questions of this day and age: Why does open trade still matter? Why is its performance so different across countries? Where is trade headed? How can trade multilateralism be safeguarded? And, most importantly, how can it work for common prosperity, people and planet?

If in the past the focus has been on **making trade possible**, i.e. negotiating trade agreements, it is time governments pay the same attention to **making trade happen**, and most importantly, to **ensure trade works for all**, including for the planet. This is not just the task of Ministries or Departments responsible for trade. It is a whole-of-government and whole-of-society task. It is ultimately about coherence and alignment of domestic and international policies. This is the purpose of the *Trade Handbook*: offer policy-makers concrete proposals towards more coherent policies on and around trade. It places a particular focus on the European Union which is where the coherence agenda has been pushed quite far.

Trade has a clear record of raising living standards and increasing prosperity in advanced and developing economies alike. Comparative advantage, specialisation, economies of scale and economic efficiency allow trading partners to benefit from one another's respective strengths in the production of certain goods and services. The Multilateral Trading System – operated by the World Trade Organization – has been crucial in making trade possible on a global scale. It is the prerequisite for a global trade environment that is more open, transparent, stable and predictable.

Today the WTO is more needed than ever before. But its objective will most probably not be so much to foster convergence of the trade policies of its members, but rather to help manage their coexistence. Avoid trade conflicts from turning into trade wars and ultimately prevent a large-scale fragmentation of the global trading system. For it to happen four areas will require a rethink: the use of state subsidies, rebuilding a binding dispute settlement, the definition of a new framework for "national security" and measures to support the inclusion of the smaller and weaker members in international trade.

The WTO would also need to develop a framework to support the protection of global public goods such as the fight against climate change and the protection of biodiversity, to limit the negative spill-over effects of purely national measures.

But trade relations are neither self-regulating nor self-sustaining. The global trade framework makes it possible for trade to thrive. Making trade actually happen, however, requires local policies and stimuli which must provide a healthy environment for inclusive and green trade to prosper. This means trade intelligence and for-ward-looking strategies, accessible trade finance and aid for trade, a conducive infrastructure environment, and effective enforcement mechanisms.

Notwithstanding the key contribution of open trade to greater de-velopment and poverty reduction worldwide, there have also been many 'losers' from globalisation, trade, technology and economic integration. These are people, sometimes entire regions, who have found themselves on the wrong side of gaping economic inequality, having endured some of the worst effects of import competition and technological evolutions, without benefitting from the opportunities that ensued. Making trade work for all requires concrete policies and investments both at home and internationally to transition toward wider social gains and advancing the environmental agenda. Fair tax policies and greater fiscal integration, skills policies for decent and better jobs, strong social safety nets and advancing green goals in agriculture, energy, transport and competition. In a nutshell, trade requires a robust coherence agenda.

Making trade possible, making it happen and making it work for all within a reformed WTO and a strong domestic and international coherence agenda. A clear agenda. A tall order.

Introduction

Trade covers a unique breadth of areas. It is the common thread running through innovation and entrepreneurship, finance and investment, competition, science and technology, industry, health, development, education and employment. It is indispensable for procuring the goods we consume, for the services we rely on and for the intellectual property which allows us to innovate. Trade regulation is also an incredibly comprehensive topic, comprised of multilateral, plurilateral, regional, preferential and bilateral government relations, with outcomes and ongoing negotiations on tariffs, subsidies, dumping, technical and sanitary regulations, e-commerce, both small and big businesses, fisheries, plastics, among countless other issues. Trade is contingent on domestic policies, which may either act as impediments or, on the contrary, help it thrive. Tax, skills and knowhow, energy and resources, monetary and budget matters, healthcare, personal rights and freedoms, business regulations, infrastructure, legal enforcement and judicial systems – these are all domestic issues which may impact trade activities.

Trade is also a double-edged sword. On the one hand, it may drive rapid job creation, growth, technological advancements, development and unprecedented poverty reduction across the globe. On the other hand, trade has been challenged. It has raised many legitimate concerns on resilience, distribution, inclusion and the environment. It is regularly subject to various narratives which portray its links with non-commercial considerations in many different ways. The resilience of trade in the face of major events has also been put to the test. Globalisation and economic interdependence mean that crises may resonate on a global scale in a much faster and more intense manner. This includes, for example, the economic slowdown resulting from the Covid-19 pandemic. Furthermore, both the trade tensions between the US and China, and the economic sanctions adopted by various governments in the context of the Russian invasion of Ukraine, illustrate the use of trade as a foreign policy weapon. Still, one does not have to look far to see that trade has often been instrumental in cushioning shocks and addressing issues of the global commons, as long as it was coupled with the necessary policies. In many cases, value chains were a source of resilience rather than vulnerability such as during the Covid-19 pandemic, allowing countries to step up their production of essential medical goods as well as vaccines which require hundreds of input materials from multiple countries.

As international trade relations deepen and major geopolitical shifts occur, trade is becoming increasingly complex. The interactions between these numerous factors make navigating the cloudy waters of trade a challenging task. This is where the *Trade Handbook* comes in. Throughout this publication, the *Handbook* seeks to break through the complex array of barriers surrounding trade. It provides readers with a comprehensive view of why open trade matters, where trade is headed, how it is regulated and how it can work for everyone, not just for some or most. The *Handbook* also aims to promote a much needed social and environmental perspective on the topic.

Part I examines the correlation between trade, growth and poverty reduction. Extreme poverty has been sliced in half since 1990[1], a feat which would not have been possible without trade openness. It is therefore important to untangle some of the main theoretical aspects that help explain the positive impact of trade. These include comparative advantage, specialisation, economies of scale and economic efficiency. Still, trade and economic integration have flaws. Shocks to trade such as trade tensions, conflicts, natural disasters or pandemics may impact its resilience and, in turn, global welfare. Trade sustainability is a major challenge of the 21st century which must be addressed imperatively – as does the unfair distribution of the costs and benefits trade may entail. The latter may be reflected in demographics, employment, income, or gender. For instance, wom-

---

1   World Bank and World Trade Organization, *The Role of Trade in Ending Poverty*, 2015, p.14.

en entrepreneurs have traditionally been facing more constraints than men in the global trading system. Going forward, one must note that 20th century global trade was significantly different from today's trade. Being acquainted with major trends is therefore essential to work towards modern policies that are adapted to modern problems. The future of trade lies in global value chains, services, digitalisation and precautionism – and it must become greener and more inclusive. The next generation (NextGen) of trade agreements will help shape this future by going beyond the traditional goods and tariffs policy areas.

Part II outlines some of the main features of the trade opening and regulating agenda which makes trade possible. The road from World War II to the creation of the WTO was paved by trade's potential to foster peace. It was also long and winding. The WTO's creation was nonetheless historic and indispensable to regulate global trade. The Multilateral Trading System (MTS) helps keep the global trade environment more open, transparent, inclusive, stable and predictable. It provides a sea of open trade principles in which lie islands of protective exceptions that governments may rely on to protect key interests. The WTO is there to help enforce existing trade rules and to provide a forum for negotiating new ones. But it has also shown it needed to be improved, not least because of an impaired dispute settlement system and difficulties in delivering timely and meaningful outcomes on topics that matter for today and tomorrow. Hence, enhanced efforts to address existing shortcomings must be coupled with work in less-than-multilateral settings with interested partners. In this context, however, policymakers should bear in mind risks of fragmentation and issues concerning legal architecture that may arise.

Part III highlights that there are no self-sustaining or self-regulating trade relations. Making trade happen requires policy adjustments and stimuli which must provide a healthy environment for inclusive trade to prosper. Like a performance athlete, trade needs a sound mind in a sound body. This means a functioning brain, i.e. one capable of making sound strategies which will enable the trade agenda to meet broader objectives of strategic autonomy, sustainability, inclusion, innovation, development, etc. Trade intelligence, meaning the ability to harness pertinent trade data and knowledge tools, is also crucial to make sound trade and market choices. Keeping the heart of trade pumping means injecting sufficient capital in trade activities, especially for smaller businesses and developing countries. Consequently, trade finance and aid for trade act as lifeblood. In addition, the backbone supporting a trade-conducive environment is its infrastructure: logistics and transport, customs, telecoms and payments. A supportive infrastructure must leverage digitalisation to facilitate trade and increase efficiency. Finally, a system which induces compliance vis-à-vis trade and investment obligations is a must. Effective enforcement mechanisms with muscles and teeth will help ensure the protective environment required for all to engage in and benefit from trade.

Part IV looks at policies to ensure that trade contributes to broader social inclusion, decent work and the advancement of the environmental agenda. Notwithstanding the contributions trade has made around the world for development and poverty reduction, there have been many 'losers' from globalisation, trade and economic integration. These are people who have found themselves on the wrong side of gaping economic inequality, or sometimes entire regions that have endured the negative impact of import competition and technological evolution, without benefitting from the opportunities that ensued. How can trade work for all? Domestic policies must support a transition towards a greener, fairer, more resilient and equitable system. As with any transition, however, significant costs need to be managed. And such a major transition will not come cheap. A fair taxation system is therefore crucial to remedy certain enduring inequalities and to power up the EU's 21st century transitions. This is all-the-more important as many governments worldwide are experiencing reduced public tolerance on the perceived unfair nature of the tax system, notably due to the insufficient contribution of multinational enterprises which reverberates through individuals. Making trade work for all means adopting a progressive lens, where multilateralism, trade and climate diplomacy, NextGen trade agreements, and sustainability policies will all have a role to play. This final part also dives into some of the main elements contained in the EU Green Deal strategy presented in 2019. It concludes with a section on the protection of labour rights on a global scale through international trade agreements and on the role of skills and education policies, which are intrinsically linked to trade, decent work, better jobs, growth and welfare. The objective: leaving no one behind.

Part I: why trade and economic integration matter

Open trade, and the process of integration into cross-border production networks for goods and services, are powerful tools to boost growth, improve people's living standards, and protect social and environmental interests.

The Preamble to the 1994 Marrakesh Agreement establishing the World Trade Organization says it all:

Trade and economic endeavour should be conducted with a view to raising standards of living, ensuring full employment and a large and steadily growing volume of real income and effective demand, and expanding the production of and trade in goods and services, while allowing for the optimal use of the world's resources in accordance with the objective of sustainable development, seeking both to protect and preserve the environment and to enhance the means for doing so in a manner consistent with their respective needs and concerns at different levels of economic development.[1]

The drafters of this text reflected something that today seems obvious: it is almost impossible to talk about trade without factoring in issues such as labour, sustainability and development.

The role played by global trade in the global reduction of poverty must not be minimised. Since 1990, extreme poverty has been halved and developing countries' share of global trade has grown exponentially.[2] There is a clear rationale for open trade, including for triggering sustained economic growth – reducing poverty and improving welfare on a global scale.

---

1   Marrakesh Agreement Establishing the World Trade Organization, 1994.

2   World Bank and WTO, *The Role of Trade in Ending Poverty*, 2015, p. 14.

Given the strong link between trade and development, it is essential to look at the theory behind open trade, in particular the notions of comparative advantage, economies of scale, specialisation and efficiency. These processes create gains and at the same time imply major structural and societal changes. Not everyone has been able to adapt and benefit from them, however. There is an evident and long-standing tension between trade-related benefits and public support for open trade, which makes it essential to consider the different existing narratives on the topic. These narratives depict in different ways the relationship between labour and capital, between trade and non-economic aims including social and environmental considerations. To help us address the existing challenges linked to trade regulation and its integration of such considerations – in particular sustainability, distribution and resilience issues – it is key to look at existing trends. These trends say a lot about how the future of trade will be shaped, and about how future policies will be essential in helping trade work for all. The next generation of trade agreements must broaden their scope and go much deeper than previous generations of trade deals so as to adapt to the evolving aspects of trade.

Setting the scene: the rationale for open trade

At the outset, one should stress the following: *open trade is not a utopian ideology!* Trade openness has a proven record of bringing higher living standards and increased prosperity in advanced and developing economies alike. Although it should be recalled that there are indeed 'losers' in this process, open trade is an engine for global economic growth.[3]

The correlation between trade, growth and poverty reduction

The correlation between trade and growth is clearly visible; and there is no shortage of data to highlight this. From the 1960s to the

---

3   International Monetary Fund, World Bank and World Trade Organization, Making Trade an Engine of Growth for All: The Case for Trade and for Policies to Facilitate Adjustment, 2017.

global financial crisis in 2007, real gross domestic product (GDP) grew at approximately 3% per annum globally, following the trend of trade in goods and services which grew at a real rate of 6%, on average.[4] This expansion occurred at an accelerated pace in the latter part of the 20th century, not least as a result of policy choices (such as an unprecedented set of tariff cuts) and important technological innovations (including telecommunications, containerisation, electrification and improved rail transport) which helped reduce trade costs significantly.[5]

The Commission on Growth and Development – a World Bank panel established in 2006-08 – is still today an important source of pragmatic reflection and analysis on the nexus between trade, growth and poverty reduction. Under the lead of Nobel laureate Michael Spence, the Commission found that one common theme among the greatest development success stories is the full use of the global economy as a driver for growth and structural transformation.[6] Despite significant variance in the pace at which economies opened up, the open global economy provided them with a source of demand far greater than that offered by their home markets. The global economy was also leveraged to allow for the import of knowledge, ideas, technology, and knowhow – sometimes through foreign direct investment. Some other common characteristics of high and sustained growth include "leadership and governance" with "credi-

---

4   IMF, World Bank and WTO, Making Trade an Engine of Growth for All: The Case for Trade and for Policies to Facilitate Adjustment, 2017.

5   World Trade Organization, World Trade Report 2018: The Future of World Trade: How Digital Technologies are Transforming Global Commerce, 2018.

6   Here, the Commission is looking at jurisdictions with at least 7% GDP growth sustained for a period of 25 years or more since 1950, a rate at which economies double every decade. Only 13 had, by that point, accomplished the feat: Botswana, Brazil, China, Hong Kong (China), Indonesia, Japan, Korea, Malaysia, Malta, Oman, Singapore, Taiwan (China), and Thailand.

ble commitment to inclusion", "capable administration" as well as "sustainable public finances".[7]

Extreme poverty has been halved since 1990. Several studies, prepared by the World Bank and the World Trade Organization, point directly to the role of trade openness in global poverty reduction. Open trade helps provide a stable macroeconomic environment which channels ideas and technology for local firms and individuals. It is helping drive innovation – including via technology and knowledge transfer – promoting fair competition and supporting economic growth.[8] A striking case in point is the fact that change in real income of the poorest quintile of the population in developing countries is strongly connected to the change in trade openness over the same period (1993-2008).[9]

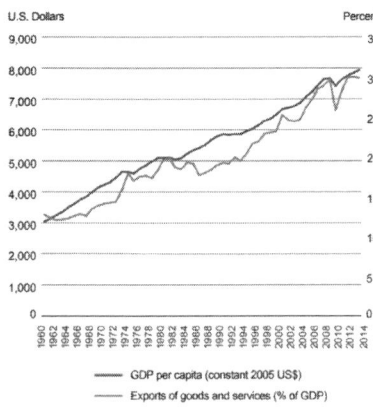

Fig. 1: GDP per capita and world exports.[10]

7   Commission on Growth and Development, The Growth Report: Strategies for Sustained Growth and Inclusive Development, 2008.

8   World Bank and WTO, *The Role of Trade in Ending Poverty*, 2015, p.19.

9   IMF, World Bank and WTO, Making Trade an Engine of Growth for All: The Case for Trade and for Policies to Facilitate Adjustment, 2017, p.45.

10   World Bank and WTO, *The Role of Trade in Ending Poverty*, 2015, p. 14.

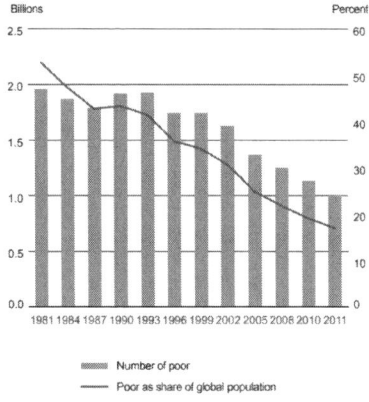

Billions   Percent

Legend:
- Number of poor
- Poor as share of global population

Fig. 2: Billions of extreme poor and share of population.[11]

In the first quarter of the 21st century, however, the world has been hit by major successive crises. These crises have all severely impacted trade and, as a corollary, growth, which further shows that interplay. Following the global financial crisis, and despite a brief rebound in the immediate aftermath, trade has sharply slowed down compared to its past performance. This deceleration was also reflected in lower growth which can – at least in part – be explained by a fall in global value chain (GVC) growth, increased protectionism and thus less trade openness.[12] Many economists had warned against the effects of trade conflicts and the associated tariff escalation to global GDP growth.[13] And indeed, in 2019 – one year and a half after the first series of tariffs imposed by the United States on various trade partners (including China, the EU, Canada and Mexico) economists

---

11   *Ibid.*, p. 14.

12   IMF, World Bank and WTO, Making Trade an Engine of Growth for All: The Case for Trade and for Policies to Facilitate Adjustment, 2017, p.9 and p.43.

13   I. Unibanco, "How a trade war would impact global growth", *World Economic Forum*, 2019, https://www.weforum.org/agenda/2019/01/how-trade-war-would-impact-global-growth-tariff/, accessed 1 September 2022.

observed a 0.7 percentage points drop in global GDP growth (down to 2.8%).

This was later followed by the Covid-19 pandemic. On top of tragic health consequences across the globe, the pandemic caused an unprecedented blow to the world economy. Both merchandise and services trade took a severe hit (-8% and -21% respectively in 2020),[14] and so did global growth, which was down to -3.3% that same year.[15] As discussed in the section on trade and resilience, trade still remained a major driver of economic recovery from the pandemic. On the whole, markets stayed open, and most measures adopted during the pandemic were actually trade facilitating rather than trade restrictive.[16] This allowed supply chains to function, despite certain bottlenecks. Resilient supply chains were of vital importance to the production and supply of vaccines, for example, which require hundreds of inputs from multiple countries.[17]

Nevertheless, as the world continues to cope with, and recover from one tragedy, another one has come along. It goes without saying that the consequences of the war in Ukraine are primarily felt in the catastrophic loss of lives and the associated humanitarian crisis. In addition, this conflict has serious global economic implications. The supply disruptions created by this conflict, as well as the influence of both Russia and Ukraine as major commodity suppliers, are additional shocks to the already existing supply chain challenges and high commodity prices.

Overall, global trade has been instrumental in poverty reduction, and it must continue to play this role even in the midst of successive major global challenges. So far, trade has helped improve wel-

14   WTO, World Trade Statistical Review 2021, 2021, p.7.

15   World Bank, *Data, GDP growth (annual percent)*, https://data.worldbank. org/indicator/NY.GDP.MKTP.KD.ZG, accessed 1 September 2022.

16   WTO, World Trade Report 2021: Economic Resilience and Trade, 2021, p.16.

17   Pfizer, *An Open Letter from Pfizer Chairman and CEO to Colleagues*, 2021, https://www.pfizer.com/news/articles/why_pfizer_opposes_the_trips_ intellectual_property_waiver_for_covid_19_vaccines, accessed 1 September 2022.

fare, driven productivity, improved market conditions, increased the number and quality of jobs in many developing countries, and triggered sustained economic growth. Developing countries' share of world trade grew from 33 to 48% from 2000 to 2015. In the next section, examining the theoretical aspects behind open trade will help explain benefits that may result from integration and the gradual deepening of trade and economic relations.

Theoretical aspects behind open trade

According to a well-known 'trade geek' anecdote, Paul Samuelson (1970 Nobel laureate) was once challenged by the mathematician Stanislaw Ulam to name "one proposition in any of the social sciences which is both true and non-trivial". Although Samuelson could not provide an answer on the spot, he later pointed to the principle of comparative advantage.

> *That it is logically true need not be argued before a mathematician; that it is not trivial is attested by the thousands of important and intelligent men who have never been able to grasp the doctrine for themselves or to believe it after it was explained to them.*[18]

David Ricardo is commonly considered the one who conceptualised comparative advantage,[19] according to which a specialisation of a country's economy would lead to greater gains from trade. Here, it is not the absolute advantage at producing a good or service that matters – it is the relative advantage, that is the ability of a country to produce goods or services at a lower opportunity cost. Opportunity costs represent the potential losses of a country when choosing a course of action, foregoing other alternative options. The country with the greatest comparative advantage is that with the lowest opportunity costs when producing a good or service. For instance, when a country is relatively better at producing wine than cars, it

---

18   P.A. Samuelson, "The Way of an Economist", in P.A. Samuelson, ed., International Economic Relations: Proceedings of the Third Congress of the International Economic Association, 1969, Macmillan: London, p.1-11.

19   D. Ricardo, 1772-1823. *On the Principles of Political Economy and Taxation*, London: John Murray, 1817.

would make sense for it to specialise in wine making – placing more inputs (e.g. resources, labour, equipment) into that sector, and using the earnings from it to import cars instead. This foundational economic insight suggests that nations may gain from engaging in trade relations with others by exporting the goods and services they have a relative advantage in producing.

Trading partners stand to benefit from one another's respective relative advantages in the production of certain goods and services. In turn, this creates the incentive for a more competitive global market and, eventually, more affordable products for consumers. Moreover, even if a country does not benefit from an absolute advantage in the production of any given good or service, it will still stand to gain from specialising. Conversely, should a country have an absolute advantage in the production of all products imaginable, it would still have an interest to trade with other nations as they would continue to have a comparative advantage in the production of some goods or services. They would thus still have the ability to sell them at lower cost than would the country with the absolute advantage.[20]

Specialisation can be further deepened and segmented; take 'trade in tasks', for instance. This concept generally refers to the outsourcing of activities that a company initially provided in house; or 'offshoring' if this implies relocation of the activity abroad to a foreign company. With developments in information technology and communications, firms are able to locate different tasks in different countries. This enables them to make use of a country's comparative advantage at the task level, thus improving efficiency. The diversity of tasks ranges from problem-solving, monitoring and managing resources, maintenance and repair, to document or information processing, conflict resolution and negotiations.[21] At the same time,

---

20   The concept of absolute advantage was developed by Adam Smith, often considered the father of modern economics, in *The Wealth of Nations*, 1776. David Ricardo later built on this work by developing the concept of comparative advantage in his work *On the Principles of Political Economy and Taxation*, 1817.

21   R. Lanz, S. Miroudot and H. K. Nordås, "Trade in Tasks", *OECD Trade Policy Working Papers*, No. 117, OECD Publishing, 2011, p.8 and p.18.

trade-offs need to be made between efficiency and risk. For example, an excessive concentration of a company's major suppliers exposes it to certain risks, including if these suppliers go bankrupt or are subject to natural disasters. Different firms may find different balances optimal.

Countries not only trade to exploit an existing comparative advantage they have, but also to exploit economies of scale. This analysis emerged following the observation that, post-World War II, international trade was happening between similar countries with similar comparative advantages (e.g. between France and Germany, and their car manufacturing industries). Countries with similar products can still scale up their production, leading to both lower prices and more product variety (e.g. different car models) which are highly valued by consumers and may target different market segments. The idea behind this observation is that countries need not be different, or produce dissimilar products, in order to benefit from trade.[22]

Hence, specialisation is an important source of economic growth, but it remains limited to the size of a given market. The rise of global value chains (GVCs) has come to remedy this, as the different stages of the production process are located across different countries. GVCs and the increase in production combined with the lowering of production costs have allowed businesses to reach economies of scale, and to expand to markets that may otherwise not have been available to them. This also entails improved consumer choice with the availability, at affordable prices, almost everywhere, of even high-technology products. This process ultimately aims to create an environment where countries can operate in an economically efficient manner. But, as many things, trade is also subject to various narratives and to various trends that are shaping the global economy and society.

---

22   P. Krugman, "Increasing Returns, Monopolistic Competition, and International Trade", *Journal of International Economics*, Vol. 9, Issue 4, November 1979, p. 469-479.

Trade, integration and related challenges: a question of narrative?

There is a tension between the benefits open trade can bring and public support for it. A 2019 poll organised by the European Commission set out to find what Europeans had to say about international trade and EU trade policy.[23] More than a third of respondents said that they did not believe they benefitted from international trade, invoking reasons such as trade-related harm to the environment, unemployment, decreased quality of certain goods and price surges. However, most respondents (60%) said that they "somewhat benefitted" or "benefitted a lot" from international trade (a significant increase since the previous survey in 2010). The latter respondents welcomed the wider choice available for consumers, job creation, cheaper and better-quality products. Furthermore, a significant share of respondents did not know whether they benefit from international trade (7%) or whether they are better off with the EU defending the trade interests of its member states rather than member states acting on their own (8%), illustrating a clear, yet diminishing, lack of awareness. Europeans' perception of whether trade is beneficial differs considerably across member states. For instance, there is a stark contrast between the 86% of Swedes who replied positively and the 35% of Italians or 45% of Greeks who continue to feel that they do not benefit from international trade. Is it a question of narrative?

Different narratives and viewpoints may be adopted when referring to 'winners' and 'losers' of international trade and, more broadly, of integration.[24] Learning about these different perspectives is essential for policymakers. They set out different views on the relative

---

23 European Commission, *Special Eurobarometer 491: European's Attitudes on Trade and EU Trade Policy*, Summary, May 2019, available at: https://europa.eu/eurobarometer/surveys/detail/2246, accessed on 1 September 2022.

24 A. Roberts and N. Lamp, *Six Faces of Globalization: Who Wins, Who Loses, and Why it Matters*, Harvard University Press, 2021.

power and influence of labour vs. capital, as well as on the relationship between trade and non-economic goals including the achievement of progressive social values. A first narrative may oppose workers in developed countries with those in developing countries. It may describe a zero-sum game where jobs in the former are lost to the latter. For instance, the 'China shock' to western economies describes China's steep export growth, becoming the 'world's factory'. This process also led to shocks to employment within Western economies such as the US and EU. Such a narrative may fuel anti-trade and anti-globalisation sentiments which may in turn influence voters during major elections. Another possible narrative is one which advocates that trade can lead to overall win-win situations, whilst acknowledging that it may create both winners and losers within each economy. One could also look further and focus on the limitations of national economies and on finding ways to address challenges posed by global trade, building on concepts like resilience, distribution and sustainability. Finally, as discussed in the section on trade and sustainability towards the end of this *Handbook*, different narratives exist on growth and the environment. 'Degrowthers', 'agrowthers', 'green growthers', and so on, all have a different outlook and propose different solutions to the question of trade and climate change.

Still, in this wide array of potential and often competing narratives, it must be stressed that sound open trade policies and economic integration are consistent with, and actually can support non-trade objectives – if coupled with the required political will and if the right set of policies and institutions are in place, that is. Calls have been made to better communicate the benefits of open trade to the wider public – such efforts should continue. Popularising and advocating its role in growth, in improving living standards globally, and in addressing contemporary issues is too vital to be left to economists alone. Politicians and civil society have an important role to play.[25]

---

25   For instance, see European Commission, *G20 Leaders' Communique Hangzhou Summit*, Statement, 2016, https://ec.europa.eu/commission/presscorner/detail/en/STATEMENT_16_2967, accessed 1 September 2022.

Against this backdrop, it is paramount to recall the basics; that trade is driven by the concept of comparative advantage. Nations stand to gain from trade specialisation and by focusing on producing certain goods and services. An important element here is the ability of a country to produce a particular good or service at a lower 'opportunity cost' than its trading partners. There is clear evidence supporting the link between open trade and higher productivity, income growth, living standards and thus decreasing poverty. Trade can stimulate growth in a number of ways, including by facilitating the exploitation of economies of scale and knowledge spillovers, enhancing competition and improving institutions. Through lower prices and better access to a wider variety of goods and services, consumers have benefitted from higher purchasing power and more options at hand. Evidence also suggests that the effect of trade on income has remained consistently positive over time. Tech upgrades and innovation are essential avenues to increase productivity. Trade also indirectly encourages domestic institutional reform, improves governance capacities and may contribute to bridging the digital divide.[26]

While the benefits associated with deeper global economic integration and interdependence are clear, concerns may arise. Who is left behind in this process? How can it be made more inclusive and sustainable? Is there a way to alleviate concerns about social disparity? How can trade contribute to the resilience of nations in the face of health, geopolitical or environmental crises? In order to chart a course forward for policies that will make trade work for all, it is essential to examine the flaws and risks associated with open trade, as will be discussed in the next section. In addition to these questions, one should also be aware of new forces that have been increasingly driving trade and also influencing the way trade relations are evolving. These trends include the rise of services, global value chains, digitalisation, inclusiveness, greener economy and behind-the-border measures. Each trend brings opportunities to harness and challenges to address.

---

26   IMF, World Bank and WTO, Making Trade an Engine of Growth for All: The Case for Trade and for Policies to Facilitate Adjustment, 2017, p.19.

Trade and integration: processes with flaws and risks

Even though trade theory clearly predicted that increased trade would create winners as it made societies richer overall, many countries came up short on ensuring that the winners' gains compensated for the losers' losses. Moreover, many assumed that everyone, everywhere would automatically adjust to the major structural and societal changes brought by globalisation, trade and economic integration; but empirical research demonstrates that many did not. However, it is only in recent years that greater regulatory attention was paid to the distributional consequences of trade. Still, the fact remains that domestic trade and economic policies need to implement a range of redistributive measures in an effort to compensate those that otherwise lose out in the process.

Distribution

Distributional consequences can manifest in different ways. They can be reflected in demographics (e.g. local or regional population decline), in employment (e.g. job losses in a given sector, labour reallocations to other sectors) or in compensation (e.g. personal income, government transfer programmes).[27]

The Covid-19 pandemic prompted another example of global disparities in terms of equitable distribution of vaccines and health equipment. In early 2022 – two years after the start of the pandemic – 10.5 billion vaccine doses had been administered worldwide. However, nearly 90% of people in low-income countries had not received a single shot.[28] Trade-related issues (such as export restrictions, trade and supply chain facilitation) as well as intellectual property aspects

---

27 D. Autor, D. Dorn and G.H. Hanson, "On the Persistence of the China Shock", *NBER Working Paper Series*, Working Paper 29401, 2021, https://www.nber.org/system/files/working_papers/w29401/w29401.pdf, accessed 1 September 2022.

28 A. Gonzalez, T*rade Thoughts from Geneva, by Deputy Director-General A. Gonzalez: One year of exporting Covid-19 vaccines: what does the evidence show?*, World Trade Organization, 2022, https://www.wto.org/english/

(mainly linked to patents) can and must play a central role in mitigating the effects of such a vaccine divide.

New forms of trade are likewise affected. The digital divide remains a major concern to developing and least developed countries. Many continue to face constraints compared to more advanced economies (technological and infrastructure incapacity, lack of practical knowhow, technical knowledge, and connectivity). The internet is at the heart of it all; only 40% of people living in developing countries are internet users, compared to more than 80% in developed economies.[29]

Distributional consequences can also be gender-based. Women traditionally face more constraints than men in the global trading system. And some of these constraints are inherently linked to the way cross-border trade in goods and services operates.[30] These obstacles include higher trading costs, in part due to the fact that women are overrepresented in sectors that have high trade barriers whether in the form of tariffs or non-tariff measures (e.g., in agriculture and the textile sector). One can add to that potential discrimination risks at border-crossings as well as a series of behind-the-border constraints (e.g. more limited access to education, technology and trade finance). Such barriers considerably reduce women's share in the gains from trade. For instance, access to basic financial services was 7 percentage points lower for women than men globally (9 percentage points lower in developing countries).[31]

But nothing is inevitable when it comes to distribution, for instance regarding income inequality. The OECD-led process on corporate income taxation holds out the possibility of ending excessive tax competition which has led many governments to become in-

---

blogs_e/ddg_anabel_gonzalez_e/blog_ag_22feb22_e.htm, accessed 1 September 2022.

29   International Telecommunication Union, *Measuring the Information Society Report*, Vol. 1, 2018.

30   World Bank and World Trade Organization, *Women and Trade: The Role of Trade in Promoting Gender Equality*, 2020, p.95.

31   World Bank and WTO, *Women and Trade: The Role of Trade in Promoting Gender Equality*, 2020, p.96.

creasingly reliant on consumption and labour income taxes, prompting feelings of unfairness amongst the population. This initiative will help strengthen governments' ability to generate sources of revenue from the biggest beneficiaries of globalisation. At home, tax policies are a key lever for addressing income inequality and may have a more immediate effect. Nothing is inevitable indeed, as some EU member states have done better than others at curbing inequality. Some (e.g. Ireland and Denmark) have effectively been using their tax and benefit system to reduce high income inequalities, while others (e.g. Cyprus, Bulgaria, Latvia, Lithuania and Estonia) have seen less compelling effects.[32] Hence, some countries' tax and social policies – or lack thereof – have stronger redistributive effects than others. Another central aspect of inequality is unemployment. Part IV touches upon this issue with a focus on skills and education policies as essential tools for long-term social gains and promoting equal opportunities for all.

Resilience

A system's resilience is expressed in its capacity to successfully adapt and respond to challenging adverse events, and to recover from them. Global market integration can be a part of the solution to vulnerabilities, facilitating the mobilisation of various resources (e.g. economic, technological) needed to respond to shocks. Interconnected economies can more easily pool resources and diversify their supply sources, as shown during the Covid-19 pandemic when supply chains adapted. The production of certain vaccines required almost 300 components from close to 20 different countries.[33] This example is striking; it explains why most measures adopted during

32   European Commission, *European Semester Thematic Factsheet: Addressing Inequalities*, 2017, available at: https://ec.europa.eu/info/sites/default/files/file_import/european-semester_thematic-factsheet_addressing-inequalities_en_0.pdf, accessed 1 September 2022.

33   Pfizer, *An Open Letter from Pfizer Chairman and CEO to Colleagues*, 2021, https://www.pfizer.com/news/articles/why_pfizer_opposes_the_trips_intellectual_property_waiver_for_covid_19_vaccines, accessed 1 September 2022.

the pandemic were actually trade facilitating rather than trade restrictive.[34]

However, with today's highly interconnected global economy it may also be easier for shocks like Covid-19 or the food crisis to resonate on a global scale. The trading partners of both Ukraine and Russia are highly vulnerable to shocks caused to the existing integration of the agricultural and energy sectors. Many highly dependent economies, especially in Africa and Asia, see their resilience challenged; but developed economies have undoubtedly suffered the consequences of the crisis too.[35]

Close interconnection and excessive concentration also give certain countries the possibility to 'weaponise' trade, i.e. to use trade as a foreign policy tool, for strategic and political influence. This is not new. Trade restrictions of various sorts and embargoes are centuries-old concepts. More recently, we have seen that trade has been wielded coercively in the context of conflicts, where it has been used as a means to achieve national security objectives. For example, we have also seen how trade and economic measures served as a response to the Russian invasion in Ukraine.

Persisting trade tensions and an escalating geopolitical situation has led some to call for 'friend-shoring',[36] i.e. reshoring either back to domestic production or to allies which are deemed 'reliable' trade partners.

Geopolitics-focused, 'friend-' or 'home-shoring' strategies are not always perfect. First, they may be undermined – and trust may be eroded – when long-lasting reliable trade partners pursue other strategies influenced by their own geopolitical objectives. The 'submarine gate' incident between France, Australia, the United States

---

34 World Trade Organization, *World Trade Report 2021: Economic Resilience and Trade*, 2021, p.16.

35 World Trade Organization, The Crisis in Ukraine: Implications of the War for Global Trade and Development, 2022.

36 P. Coy, "'Onshoring' is so Last Year. The New Lingo is 'Friend-Shoring'", *Bloomberg*, 2021, https://www.bloomberg.com/news/articles/2021-06-24/-onshoring-is-so-last-year-the-new-lingo-is-friend-shoring#x-j4y7vzkg, accessed 1 September 2022.

and the United Kingdom provides such an example.[37] Second, there is an underlying danger that pursuing the legitimate objective of strategic autonomy may eventually precipitate protectionist behaviour. Third, 'concentration at home' cannot fully replace the efficiency and resilience created through diversification of suppliers from strategic partners. The US-wide shortage of baby formula in 2022 provides a recent and striking example of resilience risks posed by a concentration of supply chains.[38] An all-domestic manufacturing of these products made US citizens more vulnerable to day-to-day business hazards such as the shutdown of a major factory. A deeper and more diversified market would have very likely been more resilient.

Others have spoken of resilience, highlighting the need to develop diversified strategic partnerships and mutually beneficial relations whilst protecting them from unfair and abusive practices.[39]

Some strategic industries may indeed have to adapt their business practices or models in the face of geopolitical challenges. For instance, in the energy sector, this means seeking longer-term supply deals from a wider diversity of sources as well as other measures such as strategic stocks that can help navigate these risks.[40] With resilience in mind, the vehicle industry also seems to be increasingly moving towards 'vertical integration' as a path towards strategic autonomy. Cars have become computers on wheels and, accordingly, companies want control over every possible aspect of their business, ranging from raw materials (for electronics, batteries, etc.) to

---

37   In September 2021, Australia walked out of a nuclear submarine deal it had struck with France, in favour of a rival bid from the United States and the United Kingdom (so-called 'AUKUS pact'), as part of building a strategic alliance in the Indo-Pacific. This caused a major diplomatic incident. (*See* BBC News, *AUKUS: Australia to pay €555m settlement to French firm*, 11 June 2022, https://www.bbc.com/news/world-australia-61770012, accessed 1 September 2022.)

38   B. Masters, US Baby Formula Crisis Highlights Risk of Reshoring, Financial Times, 18 May 2022.

39   European Commission, Communication, COM(2020) 456 final, 2020

40   European Commission, Shaping and Securing the EU's Open Strategic Autonomy: By 2040 and beyond, JRC Science for Policy Report, 2021, p.87.

design, to production, to distribution; Tesla's business model has paved the way in that regard.[41] Others may hedge against geopolitical risks by developing specific value chains for specific countries (local for local).

Sustainability

The impact of trade on environmental sustainability is another major challenge faced by trade and market integration. Addressing it is one of the main requisites, if not the main one, to ensure long-term gains for all. Part IV sets out some of the main challenges relating to trade and the environment and lays out different existing narratives.

The nexus between trade, technology and the environment covers a wide range of topics. In 2010, transport – a pivotal sector in trade – already caused more than 20% of global energy-related carbon emissions.[42] These emissions are bound to increase as trade activities do if nothing is done to remedy this. Additional important sustainability topics include trade in plastics, subsidies targeting fossil fuels, those that contribute to overfishing, and the list goes on. These trade-related matters have a proven impact on pollution and the depletion of biodiversity, including in our oceans. The production of many types of renewable energy actually relies on global value chains (GVCs), and thus on the transport sector. They also rely on materials such as rare earths and other minerals, steel, plastic, aluminium and copper which can have a significant environmental cost.[43] Digitalisation is also not without its own environmental costs, from the increase of e-waste (digital hardware) to rising energy consumption (such as that linked to the multiplication of server farms).[44]

---

41   The Economist, *The Great Teslafication*, 18 June 2022, https://www.economist.com/business/2022/06/12/how-supply-chain-turmoil-is-remaking-the-car-industry, accessed 1 September 2022.

42   Intergovernmental Panel on Climate Change, *AR5 Climate Change 2014: Mitigation of Climate Change*, 2014, p.603.

43   International Renewable Energy Agency and World Trade Organization, Trading into a Bright Energy Future: The Case for Open, High-Quality Solar Photovoltaic Markets, 2021.

44   United Nations Environment Programme, *The Growing Footprint of Digitalisation*, Foresight Brief 27, November 2021.

Multilateral cooperation must act as a vehicle for addressing sustainable development challenges which is an issue of the global commons. In this respect, the United Nations and the WTO are uniquely positioned to contribute.

The future of trade...

The Director General of the World Trade Organization (WTO), Dr Ngozi Okonjo-Iweala, noted that the future of trade is exciting as it "is digital, it is green, it is services".[45] Indeed, the future of trade will inevitably be shaped by various forces: digital evolutions, the growing importance of services, and the imperatives of environmental, health and social goals.

20th century trade essentially meant goods crossing borders; 21st century trade is fundamentally more complex.[46] It is an intertwining of trade in goods (especially parts and components), investment (in productions facilities, training, tech), services (telecoms, internet, transport, finance, customs clearance) and intellectual property (the cross-border flow of knowhow). This section examines some of the main trends in international trade to help the reader build a holistic understanding of the current trade environment and make a sound assessment of where it is headed.

The future of trade is resilient global value chains

Strategic autonomy objectives have a geopolitical aspect, including for security, as highlighted in the above section on resilience. But geoeconomics – at the core of which lie global value chains (GVCs) – are also essential for strategic autonomy. The development of complex GVCs is a hallmark of 21st century globalisation which

---

45   World Trade Organization, *National Foreign Trade Council: Strengthening the WTO and the Global Trading System*, Remarks by Director General Okonjo-Iweala, 27 April 2022, https://www.wto.org/english/news_e/spno_e/spno25_e.htm, accessed 1 September 2022.

46   R. Baldwin, "Global Supply Chains: Why they Emerged, Why they Matter, and Where they are Going", in D. K. Elms and P. Low, *Global Value Chains in a Changing World*, WTO Publications, 2013.

has prompted countries to further integrate their economies. This occurred gradually through successive 'unbundling' of production and consumption. In a situation where trade is entirely restricted and trade costs are extremely high, production and consumption are necessarily bundled together, as everything must be made near the consumers.

At the end of the 19th century steam power and the telegraph greatly reduced the impediments to, and the costs of, transport and communications.[47] At the end of the 20th century, the trade openness agenda was underway, and communication and coordination costs plummeted. These advancements, along with the further specialisation of economies, differences in labour costs and economies of scale, have drawn businesses to the internationalisation of their innovation and production chains. In particular, the rise of both GVCs and services is intertwined. Behind the term 'servicification' lies the observation that businesses, including the manufacturing sector, are increasingly dependent on services both for production processes and sales. Global production networks have continued to operate in large part through the deployment of services (transport, distribution, financial and telecoms, to name a few).

GVCs have also been groundbreaking for many developing economies, as they have lowered the threshold for them to participate in international trade. They have thus found a way to boost growth and gain access to larger markets, and that without the need to develop an entire industry from scratch.

GVC growth has plateaued since 2008: the previous offshoring expansion from the G7 counties to a group of emerging economies has slowed down and the overall complexity of supply chins nationally and internationally has fallen.[48] But as described in the World Bank 2020 World Development Report, they still offer economies across

47   World Trade Organization, World Trade Report 2018: The Future of
       World Trade: How Digital Technologies are Transforming Global Com-
       merce, 2018, p.105.

48   Richard Baldwin, CEPR, The Peak Globalisation Myth part 3, How
       Global Supply Chains are Unwinding, 2 Sept 2002

the globe a path towards economic development.[49] And it seems that GVCs will keep their relevance, not least thanks to a growing digitalisation and servicification of the economy, as detailed below. Figure 3 illustrates the numerous service inputs that may come into play throughout the different stages of production processes.

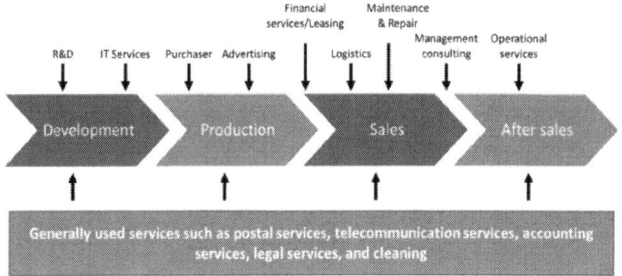

Fig. 3: Stages of production processes and reliance on services. The example of the servicification of Swedish manufacturing.[50]

The policy debate on whether the gains from international specialisation in GVCs outweigh potential risks, such as resilience to shocks, has intensified in the aftermath of the Covid-19 outbreak. The latter brought to light major risks of disruptions in the supply chains of some manufacturing and medical products. It also created tensions in the GVC debate, including supply security and domestic pressures and incentives for re-shoring or friend-shoring. If Covid-19 highlighted weaknesses inherent to GVCs, it also highlighted the strengths of the international production networks which are inherent to the efficiency gains stemming from specialisation and comparative

49   World Bank, *World Development Report 2020: Trading for Development in the Age of Global Value Chains*, 2020, p.66. GVCs offer increased productivity and income growth – more so than what countries achieve through domestic production but also than what they achieve through trade in finished goods.

50   R. Baldwin and T. Ito, "The Smile Curve: Evolving Sources of Value Added in Manufacturing", *Canadian Journal of Economics*, 54(4), 2022, p.1846.

advantage. In the absence of GVCs, the OECD has demonstrated, countries are indeed less exposed to foreign shocks, although what would tend to dominate this scenario is rather a significant loss in efficiency and their ability to cushion shocks through trade.[51] In many cases, GVCs were actually a source of resilience rather than vulnerability during the pandemic, as exemplified by the South Korea's reliance on the value chain to step up its production of medical test kits. Still, in the future more resilient production networks will have to be achieved through better risk management strategies at the firm level, by promoting transparency in the value chain and diversifying suppliers. Governments and international cooperation have a key role to play in supporting firms in each of these aspects, including by sharing information on potential concentration and bottleneck risks and creating a facilitating policy environment for resilient global production networks.

The future of trade is services

In 1970, the advanced industrial economies, i.e. the G7 (United States, Japan, Germany, Britain, France, Italy and Canada), produced over 70% of the world's total manufactured goods. Following a slight decline in the number between the 1970s and 80s, from 1990 onwards it plummeted. In just twenty years (1990-2010), the share of G7 countries in global manufacturing fell from two thirds to less than half. The services transformation of our economies helps explain the fast decrease in manufacturing that occurred in these former industrial giants, and the correlated industrialisation of other nations which, in the process, benefitted from these countries' know-how along with offshored stages of production. For example, when Toyota offshored some parts of its production to China, it also sent its knowhow and technology to ensure the end product would remain consistent.[52]

---

51   Organisation for Economic Cooperation and Development, Global
      Value Chains: Efficiency and Risks in the Context of Covid-19, 2021.

52   R. Baldwin, The Globotics Upheaval: Globalization, Robotics and the
      Future of Work, Oxford University Press: 2020, p.63.

But this is not the end of the story. In these past decades, economies have been experiencing how trade in services can assist them in achieving accelerated growth, enhancing competitiveness and consumer welfare. Today, trade in services has become the backbone of a modern global economy, growing at a much faster rate than trade in goods, as illustrated in Figure 4. It generally accounts for three quarters of GDP in developed economies. In developing countries too, the share of trade in services has grown by more than 10 percentage points since 2005.[53]

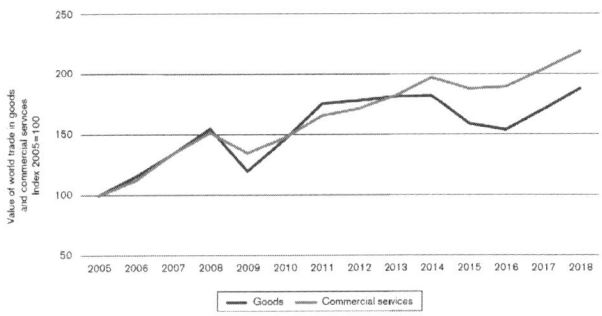

Source: WTO-UNCTAD-ITC estimates.
Note: World trade is calculated as the average of world exports and world imports.

Fig. 4: Growth of world trade in goods and commercial services.[54]

The advent and development of digital technologies (e.g. artificial intelligence, machine translation services, the improvement of digital connectivity worldwide) also raise the question of whether we are entering a new phase of globalisation; a phase where more services are becoming tradable, and where 'telemigration' – people sitting in one country and working in offices in another – will progressively become a new mass phenomenon. One may also consider that this new phase will likely shape the future of trade in a similar way as automation disrupted the manufacturing job market, but perhaps on

---

53   World Trade Organization, *World Trade Report 2019: The Future of Services* Trade, 2019, p.7-11.

54   *Ibid.*, p.14.

an even more significant scale given the accrued weight of the services sector in the global economy.[55]

Services-led development provides another path forward for low- and middle-income countries. Indeed, growing digitalisation and growing servicification are bound to influence GVCs; and as recapped above, GVCs enable the participation of developing countries in international trade. Economists and policymakers are yet to fully grasp how disruptive these new aspects of globalisation will be to the services sector and to professional jobs around the world. Still, thanks to their large workforces, lower labour costs and the diffusion of telecoms firms, many developing countries may exploit a comparative advantage and enhance their integration in global production networks. However, this may take some time to develop as services-related knowledge transfers tend to be more sluggish and harder than manufacturing-related technology transfers.[56]

The future of trade is digital

Digitalisation has played a major role in enabling the growth of the services sector – and thus the GVCs – as well as the integration of micro, small and medium-sized enterprises (MSMEs) in trade. Digital technologies have helped further reduce trade costs by improving customs procedures and communications, simplifying logistics and increasing contract enforcement (e.g. via the blockchain). Nonetheless, while digitalisation and new technologies may be a source of hope and excitement for some, it may also lead to legitimate concerns and anxiety for others, including workers. This is the case, for instance, with the acceleration of advances in artificial intelligence (AI), affecting not only blue collar jobs but also white collars, including in sectors such as education or legal.

Another key topic is e-commerce, which lowers the barriers for smaller traders in smaller economies or distant markets to connect

---

55   R. Baldwin, The Globotics Upheaval: Globalization, Robotics and the Future of Work, Oxford University Press: 2020, p.2.

56   Asian Development Bank and World Trade Organization, *The Global Value Chain Development Report 2021: Beyond Production*, 2021, p.116.

with trading routes.[57] Covid-19 acted as a catalyst for the acceleration of the digitalisation of the economy and consequently the uptake of e-commerce,[58] a trend that is continuing.

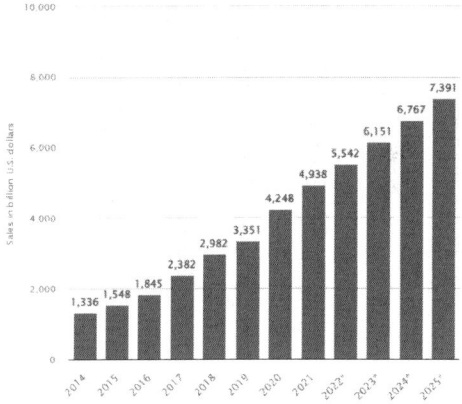

Fig. 5: Growth of e-commerce retail sales worldwide in billion USD, 2014-2025 (including future projections).[59]

The future of trade must be green

Our future economies must be green – or else our future itself will be at risk. Trade can help lower the cost of decarbonising our economies. According to the United Nations' Intergovernmental Panel on Climate Change (IPCC), prices have dropped rapidly over the past years for several key energy system mitigation options, notably solar photovoltaic (PV), wind power, and batteries.[60] It is fair to say that

57   M. Smeets, ed., Adapting to the Digital Trade Era: Challenges and Opportunities, World Trade Organization, 2021.

58   World Trade Organization, World Trade Report 2021: Economic Resilience and Trade, 2021.

59   Statista, *Global retail e-commerce sales (2014-2025)*, available at: https://www.statista.com/statistics/379046/worldwide-retail-e-commerce-sales/, accessed 1 September 2022.

60   Intergovernmental Panel on Climate Change, *Sixth Assessment Report: Mitigation of Climate Change*, 2022, p.6.3., available at: https://report.ipcc.

trade, competition, specialisation and scale were key factors in this. From 2015 to 2020, the prices of electricity from solar PV and wind systems respectively dropped by 56% and 45%. During the same period, battery prices also dropped significantly, by 64%. Renewable energy is now outcompeting fossil-fuels in many regions across the globe.

In addition, lowering trade barriers in the environmental goods and services sector (EGSS), which encompasses products and services aimed at environmental protection and resource management, would make it cheaper to go green.[61] These past years, Europe has seen EGSS consistently outperform the overall economy, as shown in Figure 6.

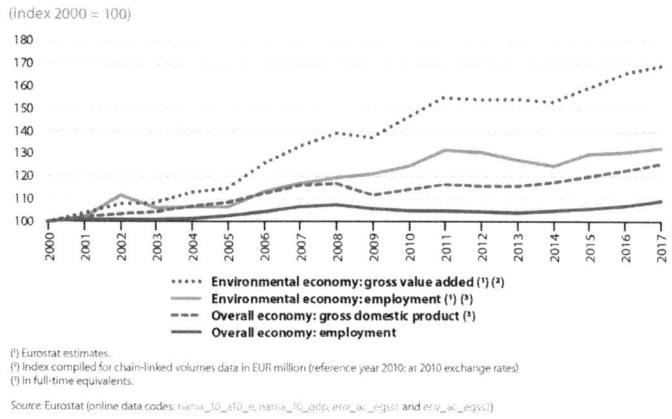

(index 2000 = 100)

····· Environmental economy: gross value added (¹) (²)
— Environmental economy: employment (¹) (³)
- - Overall economy: gross domestic product (³)
— Overall economy: employment

(¹) Eurostat estimates.
(²) Index compiled for chain-linked volumes data in EUR million (reference year 2010: at 2010 exchange rates)
(³) In full-time equivalents.

Source: Eurostat (online data codes: nama_10_a10_e, nama_10_gdp, env_ac_egss1 and env_ac_egss2)

Fig. 6: Key indicators for the environmental economy and the overall economy, EU-27, 2000-2017.[62]

ch/ar6wg3/pdf/IPCC_AR6_WGIII_FinalDraft_FullReport.pdf, accessed 1 September 2022.

61   Eurostat, Energy, Transport and Environment Statistics, European Union, 2020, p.129.

62   Eurostat, Energy, Transport and Environment Statistics, European Union, 2020, p.129.

This is the case notably in terms of job growth and value added (i.e. the difference between the value of inputs used up in the production and the value of the good or service produced, the output).[63]

However, collective political will and adequate policy design matter if trade is really to move towards a greener, more sustainable future. This also links to how digitalisation can be leveraged to facilitate this transition in spite of the increasing awareness with respect to the energetic (and environmental) cost of digital technologies. The latter have the potential to help the greening process by measuring progress in sustainability, facilitating the circular economy, optimising the use of resources and helping reduce greenhouse gas emissions.[64] In that regard, it should be mentioned that non-tariff measures (e.g. quotas, regulations affecting transit, licensing requirements and procedures) can significantly influence the move towards green trade.[65]

The future of trade must be inclusive, fair and ethical

There is a clear interest in including and increasing labour standards in trade agreements and, in general, in creating a more ethical and inclusive business environment. This has led many to believe that the existence and enforcement of minimum standards through labour clauses in trade agreements can actually be beneficial for trade, in that it will help meet an undeniably growing consumer demand

---

63 While Gross Value Added (GVA) is sector-specific, Gross Domestic Product (GDP) is the addition of the GVAs of all sectors of the economy, adding taxes and reducing subsidies.

64 J. Anderson and G. Caimi, "3 ways digital technology can be a sustainability game-changer", *World Economic Forum*, https://www.weforum.org/agenda/2022/01/digital-technology-sustainability-strategy/#:~:-text=Todaypercent2Cpercent20digitalpercent20technologiespercent-t20arepercent20being,alsopercent20enablepercent20innovationper-cent20andpercent20collabouration, accessed 1 September 2022.

65 F. S. Bellelli and A. Xu, *How do environmental policies affect green innovation and trade? Evidence from the WTO Environmental Database (EDB)*, World Trade Organization, Staff Working Paper ERSD-2022-03, 2022, https://www.wto.org/english/res_e/reser_e/ersd202203_e.pdf, accessed 1 September 2022.

for ethically produced goods and services. However, the growing importance of labour clauses in trade agreements has also been criticised by some as potentially leading to disguised trade protectionism. Such clauses have been accused of reducing trade through the withdrawal of trade preferences accorded to developing countries, and some have also held them responsible for eroding their comparative advantage.

It is true that the number of labour clauses has sharply risen since the North American Free Trade Agreement (NAFTA) was enacted in 1994 (later replaced by the US-Mexico-Canada Agreement, USMCA, in 2020). From 1995 until 2014, the ratio of agreements with such clauses has grown from 34% to 84%.[66] Labour clauses in trade agreements aim to condition preferential access to domestic markets for trade partners that comply with workers' rights in the exporting country.

The number and share of regional trade agreements (RTAs) with gender-related provisions has also increased significantly these past years, as illustrated in Figure 7. Gender-related provisions are also becoming more detailed and are touching upon a broader set of topics. For instance, the 2016 trade agreement between Chile and Uruguay – which inspired many subsequent agreements to follow the same route – incorporated detailed provisions on international agreements, domestic policies, cooperation and institutional arrangements (such as the creation of a committee devoted to trade and gender).[67]

---

66   C. Carrère, M. Olarreaga and D. Raess, *Labour Clauses in Trade Agreements: worker protection or protectionism?*, 2017, available at: https://www.wto.org/english/res_e/reser_e/gtdw_e/wkshop17_e/rass_e.pdf, accessed 1 September 2022.

67   J.A. Monteiro, *The Evolution of Gender-Related Provisions in Regional Trade Agreements*, World Trade Organization, Staff Working Paper ERSD-2021-8, 2021, p.8, https://www.wto.org/english/res_e/reser_e/ersd202108_e.pdf, accessed 1 September 2022.

Inclusiveness should go beyond gender, and cover persons with disabilities,[68] youth[69] and other priority groups[70] who face unique challenges which hinder them from thriving in today's economy. The United Nations Sustainable Development Goals (SDGs) commit to the empowerment of such vulnerable groups whilst recognising that international trade is an engine for inclusive economic growth and that it is an important means to achieve the SDGs.[71]

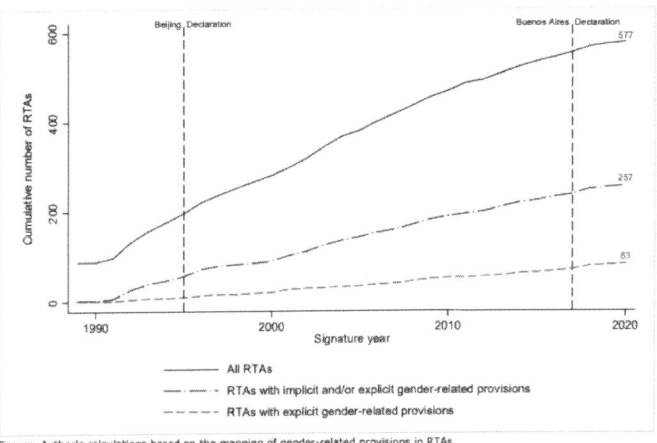

Source: Author's calculations based on the mapping of gender-related provisions in RTAs.
Note: Implicit gender-related provisions refer to provisions addressing human rights, vulnerable groups and the social dimension of sustainable development, including labour discrimination, fair trade and corporate social responsibility without any explicit reference to gender. The GTGA is excluded from the analysis.

Fig. 7: The number of RTAs with gender-related provisions has increased steadily.[72]

68   International Labour Organization, Trade Union Action on Disability and Decent Work: a Global Overview, 2017.

69   International Trade Centre, *Youth and trade*, available at: https://intra-cen.org/our-work/topics/youth-and-trade, accessed 1 September 2022.

70   International Trade Centre, *Priority groups*, available at: https://intra-cen.org/our-work/priority-groups, accessed 1 September 2022.

71   United Nations, *The Sustainable Development Goals Report 2016: Leaving no one behind*, available at: https://unstats.un.org/sdgs/report/2016/leaving-no-one-behind, accessed 1 September 2022.

72   J.A. Monteiro, *The Evolution of Gender-Related Provisions in Regional Trade Agreements*, World Trade Organization, Staff Working Paper ERSD-2021-8, 2021, p.5.

The future of trade is 'precautionism'

The above trends imply that obstacles to open trade have also been evolving. Despite intense trade tensions in the late 2010's, and the omnipresence of tariffs in the news during that period, the general tendency for trade has rather been increasingly shifting towards 'precautionist' measures, a term coined by former WTO Director General Pascal Lamy. The latter focus less on the protection of domestic firms but rather on efforts to protect people from various risks (consumer protection, health, safety, environment, etc.).[73] But as non-tariff measures (NTMs) have proliferated – see Figure 8 – they have loomed increasingly large as potential barriers to entering foreign markets, particularly for micro, small and medium-sized enterprises from developing countries. In WTO parlance, these requirements fall under the rubric of sanitary and phytosanitary (SPS) measures and technical barriers to trade (TBT). Generally, they are 'technical' measures (e.g. regulations, standards, testing, certification) but may also be 'non-technical' (e.g. quotas, quantitative restrictions, and forced logistics or distribution channels).[74]

Looking ahead at Part III of this publication, one major challenge in order for trade to happen is how to ensure that (i) people benefit from safe products and that, along the way, (ii) economic and social opportunities are not sacrificed by keeping trade inclusive, especially allowing for the participation of smaller businesses in developing countries.

---

73 P. Lamy, in "Biennial Conference on Competition, Regulation and Development", organised by the CUTS International, November 2021, available at: https://cuts-ccier.org/precautionism-is-risking-open-trade-more-than-protectionism-pascal-lamy-2/, accessed 1 September 2022.

74 Organisation for Economic Cooperation and Development, *Non-Tariff Measures - Tariffs are the tip of the iceberg: How behind the border issues impact trade*, available at: https://www.oecd.org/trade/topics/non-tariff-measures/, accessed 1 September 2022.

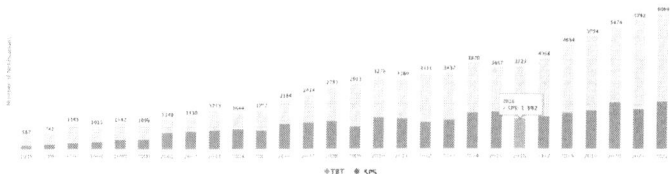

Fig. 8: ePing SPS and TBT Platform – Number of SPS and TBT notifications per year since the creation of the WTO.[75]

NextGen trade agreements and the EU: going beyond trade policy

Facts often – if not always – precede the law. Legal frameworks generally lag behind in terms of regulating new forms of trade and ensuring inclusive gains from emerging opportunities. It seems difficult for regulators to overcome this dictum, especially given today's dynamic environment driven by technology, innovation and constantly adapting trading practices. The next generation (NextGen) of trade agreements will provide a chance to update trade rules and relations, attuning them to the above-mentioned trends. They will contribute to enhancing market access between trading partners, to establishing broader integration in goods and services trade (the output market) and to better managing the interdependence created by GVCs. They will also establish broader integration in the input market (i.e. the 'factor market', including land and resources, labour, entrepreneurship and capital).

Ultimately, NextGen trade agreements will contribute to setting the framework around how economies will integrate, operate and develop. They can also contribute to addressing the distributional,

---

75   World Trade Organization, *ePing – SPS & TBT Platform* (WTO, UN, ITC), available at: https://eping.wto.org/en/FactsAndFigures/Notifications, accessed 1 September 2022.

sustainability and resilience concerns that have been raised. The EU can – and should – remain a leader in that respect.

Deep trade agreements: a tool to adapt to an evolving trade environment

The 'newer' policy areas addressed in existing deep trade agreements (DTAs) are crucial to making trade fit for purpose. DTAs are fundamentally different to previous generations of agreements.[76] Indeed, an average trade agreement in the 1950s covered only eight policy areas. In recent years, this number has more than doubled with, on average, 17 policy areas. There is also evidence that agreements are deepening not only in terms of the number of policy areas they touch upon, but also regarding specific commitments within a given policy area.[77]

A pattern arises in the coverage of different policy areas in trade agreements. Agreements containing few policy provisions tend to focus on traditional trade policy (tariffs and customs). Deeper agreements will generally include trade-related regulatory issues, such as subsidies or technical barriers to trade. Finally, the deepest agreements (those covering more than 20 provisions) will tackle issues such as labour, the environment, intellectual property, services, movement of people, consumer protection, research and technology, as well as financial assistance. One can expect NextGen trade agreements to continue down that road; addressing more policy areas with more commitments, and thus seeing the percentage bars in Figure 9 progressively fill up.

76 P. Lamy, "Foreword", in A. Mattoo, N. Rocha and M. Ruta, *Handbook of Deep Trade Agreements*, World Bank, 2020.

77 A. Mattoo, N. Rocha and M. Ruta, *Handbook of Deep Trade Agreements*, 2020, p.3.

Nº Provisions	Less than 10	Between 10 and 20	More than 20
Tariffs on manufacturing goods	97%	100%	100%
Tariffs on agricultural goods	96%	100%	100%
Export taxes	73%	81%	95%
Customs	67%	95%	100%
Competition policy	58%	73%	88%
State aid	39%	69%	88%
Anti-dumping	35%	88%	98%
Countervailing measures	22%	77%	98%
Statistics	20%	0%	23%
TRIPS	18%	75%	98%
STE	18%	69%	68%
TBT	17%	73%	95%
Movement of capital	15%	68%	93%
GATS	14%	67%	98%
SPS	12%	72%	98%
Public procurement	12%	59%	80%
IPR	6%	56%	73%
Environmental laws	3%	14%	83%
Labor market regulation	3%	13%	75%
Investment	2%	58%	75%
TRIMS	2%	42%	73%
Visa and asylum	2%	37%	57%
Industrial cooperation	2%	5%	33%
Social matters	2%	5%	30%
Agriculture	1%	10%	45%
Energy	1%	8%	40%
Data protection	1%	5%	20%
Anticorruption	1%	5%	18%
SME	1%	4%	25%
Regional cooperation	1%	3%	15%
Taxation	1%	2%	30%
Approximation of legislation	1%	2%	25%
Political dialogue	1%	1%	8%
Research and technology	0%	6%	38%
Public administration	0%	6%	5%
Consumer protection	0%	5%	38%
Mining	0%	5%	13%
Education and training	0%	4%	33%
Information society	0%	4%	15%
Innovation policies	0%	4%	5%
Illegal immigration	0%	3%	23%
Illicit drugs	0%	3%	3%
Economic policy dialogue	0%	2%	43%
Cultural cooperation	0%	2%	38%
Financial assistance	0%	2%	25%
Audiovisual	0%	2%	18%
Terrorism	0%	2%	8%
Money laundering	0%	2%	3%
Health	0%	1%	38%
Human rights	0%	1%	3%
Nuclear safety	0%	0%	15%
Civil protection	0%	0%	5%

Source: Mattoo et al. 2017.

Fig. 9: Share of policy areas for different PTAs.[78]

---

78   A. Mattoo, N. Rocha and M. Ruta, *Handbook of Deep Trade Agreements*, World Bank, 2020, p. 7.

Citius, altius, fortius – communiter: the EU as a leader in driving change through rational deep integration

Citius, altius, fortius – communiter ("faster, higher, stronger – together") is the motto of the Olympic Games, yet it could equally describe the ambition of the European Union in its trade policy.

The EU's DTAs seem inspired by the Union's own domestic experience – be it in the integration of goods, services and ideas, or the protection of core values. In fact, Europe has been a trailblazer in the process of deep integration, making it the region that has the largest share of intra-regional trade today.[79] The 1957 Treaty of Rome establishing the European Economic Community (EEC) – and successive enlargements – already included more than 20 trade-related provisions. Today, the EU27 is also, in itself, the 'deepest' agreement globally, with more than 40 provisions ranging from traditional trade in goods and services to e-commerce to labour to environmental protection.[80]

Moreover, not only do the agreements concluded by the EU go deeper, but they are more numerous than for any other nation. The EU has the world's the largest trade network, with 45 applied trade agreements, totalling 77 partner countries in 2020.[81] Consequently, EU member states are among the most integrated countries in the world. With adequate policies and institutions in place, this approach can be successful at promoting trade, economic integration and growth, whilst also supporting non-trade objectives.

---

79   United Nations Conference on Trade and Development, *UNCTAD e-Handbook of Statistics 2021*, https://hbs.unctad.org/trade-structure-by-partner/#:~:text=Intrapercent2Dregionalpercent20tradepercent20waspercent20most,mostpercent20tradepercent20waspercent-t20extrapercent2Dregional, accessed 1 September 2022

80   A. Mulabdic, A. Osnago and M. Ruta, "Deep integration and UK-EU trade relations", *World Bank*, Policy Research Working Paper 7947, 2017, p.2 and p.14, https://openknowledge.worldbank.org/bitstream/handle/10986/25956/WPS7947.pdf?sequence=1&isAllowed=y, accessed 1 September 2022.

81   European Commission, *EU trade agreements: delivering for Europe's businesses*, 2020, https://ec.europa.eu/commission/presscorner/detail/en/ip_20_2091, accessed 1 September 2022.

For example: protecting forest resources. The scope of provisions that aim at protecting forest resources varies significantly across agreements. Trade agreements may contain general language to promote the conservation and sustainable use of biological diversity as well as sustainable forestry management. They can also go further and provide for specific action, including measures to combat illegal logging and related trade. In general, environmental provisions have proven to be effective in limiting deforestation once agreements enter into force. The inclusion of specific provisions aimed at protecting forests and biodiversity has entirely offset net increases in forest loss that were observed in similar agreements that did not contain such provisions. This effect primarily works by limiting agricultural land expansion in ecologically sensitive regions and is mainly concentrated in tropical developing countries with greater biodiversity. Such provisions seem to furnish a solid institutional framework that allows signatories to commit to policies that encourage "more sustainable patterns of trade integration and economic growth."[82]

Still, going faster, higher and stronger on key issues, including those aimed at addressing environment imperatives, requires appropriate consideration of, and consultation with, other trade partners. It should be noted that the EU's Deforestation Regulation adopted in 2023 was criticized for lacking proper *a priori* consultations with certain South-East Asian countries impacted by its application.[83] As highlighted in Part IV of this *Handbook*, policies must ensure a balance between economic, development and environment objectives. Dialogue among trade partners is therefore key to work towards outcomes that not only seek to remedy environmental pressures, but also stimulate economic opportunities for all and support countries' respective development targets.

---

82   A. M. Fernandes, N. Rocha and M. Ruta, eds., *The Economics of Deep Trade Agreements*, World Bank, 2021, p.131.

83   M. Ruehl, "EU deforestation law triggers ire of its trading partners", *Financial Times*, 2023, https://www.ft.com/content/c2f2eea9-1eb5-478f-ac53-5666776c0a35, accessed 18 June 2023.

Part II: making trade possible – the trade opening and regulating agenda

According to a quote attributed to 19th century French economist, Frédéric Bastiat: "If goods do not cross borders, soldiers will". It is with a similar spirit that the General Agreement on Tariffs and Trade was formed in 1947, in the shadow of World War II, and the political extremism fostered by the Great Depression, which itself was made worse by the protectionist breakdown of global trade.

The Multilateral Trading System (MTS) – a system operated today by the WTO – is an attempt by governments to make the global trade environment more open, transparent, stable and predictable. Its aim is to encourage economic agents to trade and to promote global economic welfare, whilst allowing for the preservation of key economic and non-economic principles, and to enable more equitable trading relations. With stability and predictability, investment is encouraged, jobs are created, and consumers can fully enjoy the benefits of competition – more and better choices as well as lower prices.

The main objective of this framework is therefore to anchor trade relations in a set of agreed rules and principles that would prevent unilateralism. However, the road from WWII to the WTO was not always smooth. It took numerous rounds of negotiations over a period of almost fifty years to get there. Regardless, today the WTO is the framework within which the vast majority of trade is regulated, with 164 members representing 98% of world trade.[1]

---

1   World Trade Organization, *The WTO in Brief*, https://www.wto.org/english/thewto_e/whatis_e/inbrief_e/inbr_e.htm, accessed 1 September 2022.

The MTS, its agreements and principles open up opportunities: for trade to flourish, for more inclusive growth and for greater poverty reduction worldwide. Part II is about the trade opening and regulating agenda which makes trade possible. However, making trade possible does not guarantee that trade will in fact happen nor that it will work for all, leaving no one behind in the process. For a deeper discussion of these aspects, turn to Parts III (making trade happen) and IV (making trade work for all) of the *Handbook*. This second part provides the reader with a historical background of the MTS, outlines its main functions and the core set of principles enshrined in it. Here, the reader will find that, within a sea of open and regulated trade principles, there also exists islands of protective exceptions, various tools at the disposal of governments to protect key interests. This framework is a crucial first step towards making trade possible. But can we effectively address 21st century challenges with 1990's rules springing from a seventy-five-year-old system? Are "downsized" trade regimes and negotiations – e.g. plurilateralism or regionalism – an effective solution to addressing the challenges facing the MTS? And, finally, how can the WTO survive this period of great power competition between the United States and China?

The institutional foundation of the multilateral trading system

A brief history of the multilateral trading system: from WWII to the WTO

The concept of multilateralism contrasts with actions taken by subsets of countries, whether regionally or in other groups. The multilateral trading system (MTS) refers to the system that is today operated by the WTO, and it is somewhat synonymous to the 'world' or 'global' trading system. Indeed, with 164 members, the WTO has a quasi-universal membership which includes the vast majority – if not all – of the main trading nations.

Created in 1995, it is the youngest of the major international economic organisations. But the road to the creation of the WTO was winding and potholed. Indeed, the MTS itself is half a century older, having risen out of the ashes of World War II. A strong desire for world peace, security and stability was the driving force behind the ambition to create a global economic system. The Atlantic Charter, a one-page statement issued in 1941, outlined the main objectives and common principles of crucial importance to the United States and the United Kingdom for the post-WWII era. It already underscored the key role to be played by trade and economic cooperation as a stepping-stone for peace.[2] The Atlantic Charter was a first step in what would then become remarkable achievements in global economic rulemaking and cooperation.

---

2   For instance, Clause 4 of the 1941 Atlantic Charter provides that states "will endeavour, with due respect for their existing obligations, to further the enjoyment by all States, great or small, victor or vanquished, of access on equal terms, to the trade and to the raw materials of the world which are needed for their economic prosperity". Clause 5 provides the following: "They desire to bring about the fullest collaboration between all nations in the economic field with the object of securing, for all, improved labour standards, economic advancement and social security".

The Bretton Woods Institutions were founded in 1944, namely the International Monetary Fund (IMF) and the International Bank for Reconstruction and Development – soon called the World Bank – with the aims of promoting international economic cooperation and of helping a devastated world economy recover from the war. The original Bretton Woods Agreement also included plans for an International Trade Organisation (ITO). However, the ITO did not see the light of day, despite extensive efforts to bring it into being. The 1948 Havana Charter, the outcome of multilateral negotiations aiming to create the ITO, was never ratified by the Congress of the United States, due to domestic opposition to its rules. By 1950, the Truman administration abandoned its efforts to obtain Congress' support for the creation of the ITO.[3]

Still, the work of diplomats and negotiators was not in vain. The General Agreement on Tariffs and Trade lived on. It was initially designed as a provisional agreement to regulate international trade relations before the ITO came into effect, and it eventually gave birth to an unofficial, de facto international organisation.[4] For 47 years, this structure, known informally as GATT, provided the rules governing most of global trade in goods, including during periods of historic highs in economic growth. Until the mid-90s, the GATT evolved through successive rounds of negotiations. The first rounds mainly focused on tariff reductions but progressively included other areas such as trade rules (e.g. anti-dumping and NTMs). The 1986-94 round – the Uruguay Round – was the longest, most difficult, and the last of the GATT rounds of negotiation. It led to what is considered the most important reform of the global trade framework since 1947. Nearly half a century after the failed attempt to create an ITO, the

---

3   R. Toye, "The International Trade Organization", in A. Narlikar, M. Daunton and R.M. Stern, eds., *The Oxford Handbook on the World Trade Organization*, online edn, Oxford Academic, 2012, p.85-101, https://doi.org/10.1093/oxfordhb/9780199586103.013.0005, accessed 1 September 2022.

4   World Trade Organization, *Understanding the WTO: Basics – What is the World Trade Organization*, https://www.wto.org/english/thewto_e/whatis_e/tif_e/fact1_e.htm, accessed 1 September 2022.

Uruguay Round package was signed in Marrakesh in 1994, leading to the creation of the WTO.

Functions of the WTO

Article III of the 1994 Marrakesh Agreement Establishing the World Trade Organization clearly outlines the main functions of the institution. These are: (i) facilitating the implementation of existing agreements and rules; (ii) providing members with a forum for negotiations; (iii) settling trade disputes among members; (iv) reviewing members' policies; and (v) cooperating with other organisations with a view to achieving greater coherence in global economic policymaking. In addition, one could emphasise that at the core of the WTO's functions lie two additional elements: (vi) supporting developing and least-developed countries in trade; and (vii) acting as a major provider of knowledge and research on international trade issues.

Facilitating the implementation of existing agreements and rules

First, the WTO facilitates the implementation, administration and operation of the various agreements under its purview. These agreements are at the heart of the system; they have been negotiated, signed and bind the bulk of the world's trading nations to keep their trade policies within the agreed limits. They spell out main guiding principles for open trade, they detail members' commitments regarding tariff and non-tariff measures, and they describe relevant exceptions. The coverage goes much beyond trade in goods, keeping the GATT in a revised form alongside new rules for services (General Agreement on Trade in Services; GATS) and intellectual property (Agreement on Trade-Related Aspects of Intellectual Property; TRIPS). For goods and services, there are additional agreements and annexes dealing with special requirements, specific sectors or topics.

The WTO's institutional structure also reflects this, with the existence of councils, committees and other bodies that are in charge of work in these respective areas (e.g. agriculture, rules of origin, subsidies, dumping, market access, financial services).

A forum for negotiations

Second, the WTO provides a forum for negotiations among its members. The organisation was born as a result of negotiations and, still today, negotiations constitute a core pillar of the WTO's day-to-day work. The MTS is not static; ongoing negotiations aim at improving existing agreements and at creating new ones too. In that respect, the top-most decision-making body of the WTO, the Ministerial Conference, is a key driver of results and of impetus for the organisation's work programme.[5] In 2001, the Fourth Ministerial Conference, held in the capital of Qatar, Doha, launched a new round of negotiations on various topics including potential new rules like fisheries subsidies, agriculture, development and services. The objectives of these negotiations were not only aimed at opening trade relations among members. Much of this work was also intrinsically linked to non-trade objectives, such as development and environmental sustainability.[6] More recently, as described below, negotiations are ongoing

---

5   The Ministerial Conference meets, in principle, every two years. In intervals between the Ministerial Conference, the General Council carries out the functions of the WTO as the highest decision-making body, in Geneva.

6   For example, the Agreement on Fisheries Subsidies concluded at the Twelfth Ministerial Conference in Geneva (2022) aims to deliver on UN SDG 14.6 by prohibiting subsidies for vessels and operators engaged in illegal, unreported, or unregulated fishing and by establishing new rules on subsidies for the fishing of stocks that are already over-exploited. The Agreement also contains certain flexibilities for developing

among subsets of members, under a plurilateral – or "less-than-multilateral" – setting.

Settling trade disputes

Third, the WTO provides a process for its members to settle their trade disputes. Dispute resolution has become an emblematic – and somewhat controversial – aspect of the WTO's work. A dispute generally arises when a member believes that another member is violating a WTO Agreement. Since 1995, more than six hundred disputes have been brought to the WTO's dispute settlement system, objectively making it one of the most prolific international dispute settlement mechanisms. It has greatly contributed to the enforcement of global trade rules these past decades, and to having a more secure and predictable global trading system. Once a complaint has been filed, a dispute can be settled in two ways. The parties may find a mutually agreeable solution, in particular through bilateral consultations. Otherwise, the dispute may be subject to adjudication. Should that be the case, a panel of trade experts is established. The report of the panel is then adopted by the WTO's Dispute Settlement Body, unless the full membership rejects it (including the 'winning' party – this is the 'negative consensus' rule). Parties may also decide to appeal the findings of a panel to the Appellate Body (a second tier in the dispute settlement process), on the basis of legal matters. At any point in time during the process, the priority always remains to settle disputes through consultations and a mutually acceptable solution, to the extent possible.

Since November 2020, the Appellate Body (AB) has been unable to review appeals due to the lack of consensus among WTO members

---

WTO members (e.g. technical assistance, transitional periods before implementation).

on the appointment of new AB members. This follows a series of debates and concerns raised mainly by the United States on the dispute settlement process, including findings by the AB relating to subsidy disciplines and trade remedies (anti-dumping measures and countervailing duties). Other concerns, also raised by the United States, relate to transitional rules for outgoing AB members, their term-length and compensation, the lack of observance of a 90-day deadline to issue appellate reports, the scope of the appeals and potential 'overreach' by the AB and other issues. In 2020, the EU alongside a subset of other WTO members created a stopgap attempt to overcome the AB situation, by agreeing to participate in a Multi-Party Interim Appeal Arbitration Arrangement (MPIA).[7] The participating members have indicated their intention to resort to arbitration under Article 25 of the Dispute Settlement Understanding (DSU). This interim appeal arbitration procedure is in place as long as the AB is not in capacity to hear appeals of panel reports in disputes arising among the participants. The rationale of the MPIA is therefore to preserve the core features of the WTO dispute settlement system until a permanent solution is found for the AB impasse. Whilst it is not a vehicle for, or an attempt at, reform, it does aim to enhance the efficiency of the appeal procedure. Arbitrators have been appointed in the context of the MPIA, with the aim to uphold the WTO appellate review rules in future disputes between its participants. There are close to 50 WTO members participating in the MPIA and any WTO member may join it after having notified the WTO's Dispute Settlement Body. Parties to several ongoing disputes have notified their commitment to using the MPIA to resolve their dispute, should either party appeal the relevant WTO panel report.[8]

WTO members need to collectively deliver on their commitment adopted at the WTO's Twelfth Ministerial Conference held in June 2022:

---

7   The MPIA was announced on 30 April 2020, in WTO document JOB/DSB/1/Add.12.

8   Geneva Trade Platform, *Multi-Party Interim Appeal Arbitration Arrangement (MPIA)*, https://wtoplurilaterals.info/plural_initiative/the-mpia/, accessed 1 September 2022.

We acknowledge the challenges and concerns with respect to the dispute settlement system including those related to the AB, recognise the importance and urgency of addressing those challenges and concerns, and commit to conduct discussions with the view to having a fully and well-functioning dispute settlement system accessible to all Members by 2024.[9]

Reviewing members' policies

Fourth, surveillance of members' domestic trade policies is a fundamental part of WTO activities. This is accomplished through the Trade Policy Review Mechanism (TPRM). Reviews for each member are conducted through peer-group assessments (i.e. by the rest of the WTO membership) in the Trade Policy Review Body (TPRB), on the basis of reports prepared by the WTO Secretariat and a policy statement delivered by the member under review. All members eventually undergo this process, albeit at different intervals, depending on their trade share. The larger the share, the more frequently will a member undergo surveillance (either every three, five or seven years). Although it does not contain a binding component, one should not underestimate the importance of the TPRM. As a result of the repetition on a regular basis of rather 'humble modalities' such as observation and scrutiny by other members, Governments may gradually become 'trained' and more compliant with respect to global trade rules. This is the dichotomy between 'disciplinary' power and 'triumphant' power which Michel Foucault referred to in Discipline and Punish (1975). The former can induce compliance just as well – if not better sometimes – than the latter.

---

9   Twelfth Session of the WTO Ministerial Conference, "Outcome Document" – WT/MIN(22)/W/16/Rev.1 (2022), paragraph 4.

The WTO's monitoring role is all the more important in turbulent times. In 2009, the Director-General proposed using an obscure provision in the TPRM to start monitoring and reporting on trade protectionist measures adopted by its members as a result of the economic and financial crisis – thus effectively enlarging the scope of its monitoring function. Initially intended for G20 members the mechanism was extended to cover the entire membership. The likelihood that certain measures taken following the financial crisis may have harmful effects on international trade was recognised by international leaders who pledged to "refrain from raising new barriers to investment or to trade in goods and services" and to "notify promptly the WTO of any such measures" so it can monitor and report publicly on these matters.[10] WTO monitoring proved essential during the Covid-19 pandemic too. The organisation's "Covid-19 and world trade" webpage provided information on relevant measures implemented by members and observers, be it on trade in goods, services or intellectual property. This included restrictive measures but also trade facilitating and support measures which were implemented in response to the pandemic and communicated to the WTO Secretariat, in an attempt to increase transparency.[11]

Cooperating with other international organisations
Fifth, with a view to achieving greater "coherence in global economic policymaking", the WTO also aims to cooperate, where appropriate,

---

10   G20, *G20 Action Plan for Recovery and Reform, London Summit – Leaders' Statement*, 2 April 2009, https://www.oecd.org/g20/summits/london/ G20-Action-Plan-Recovery-Reform.pdf, accessed 1 September 2022.

11   World Trade Organization, *Covid-19 and world trade*, https://www.wto. org/english/tratop_e/covid19_e/covid19_e.htm, accessed 1 September 2022. This WTO web portal provides trade-related information including notifications by WTO members, the impact of the pandemic on exports and imports and how the MTS has responded to the pandemic.

with other international organisations. The Marrakesh Agreement sets out a clear mandate in that respect with the Bretton Woods institutions (the World Bank and the IMF).

But the pursuit of coherence goes beyond those institutions. The Preamble to the TRIPS Agreement (on Trade-Related Aspects of Intellectual Property) calls for "a mutually supportive relationship between the WTO and the World Intellectual Property Organization" (WIPO), as well as "other relevant international organizations". Co-operation can be seen in a broad sense here, including participating as an observer in other organisations' meetings, providing coordinated technical assistance and supporting capacity building efforts for developing and least developed countries, or consulting on or discussing specific issues as necessary. In 2021, the Directors General of the World Health Organization, WIPO and the WTO agreed on an intensified cooperation in support of global access to medical technologies to address the Covid-19 pandemic. In 2022, following the food crisis stemming from the war in Ukraine, the WTO, the IMF, the World Bank and the World Food Programme jointly called for urgent and coordinated support by the international community and proposed actions to help vulnerable countries.

The expanding scope of trade policy, as seen in Part I, has somewhat exacerbated the problems of coherence in global governance. While trade in the vast majority of goods initially fell squarely within the ambit of the GATT and WTO, today's trade affects and is increasingly reliant on other areas, including some that also fall under the purview of other international organisations and agreements. The above-mentioned example of trade and health during the pandemic is striking in that regard.

The fact that the WTO benefits from a unique dispute settlement system unlike any other international organisation – albeit weakened by the AB paralysis – explains to a certain extent the 'forum shopping' that may occur. For instance, many developing countries wished to see intellectual property (IP) delt with in WIPO rather than GATT/WTO.[12] Cooperation in that field was therefore essential given the ever-growing link between trade and IP. Differences in members' protection and enforcement standards for IP rights increasingly became a source of tension in international economic relations. This required a specific bridge to be built between the two issues to avoid tensions and incoherence regarding what should fall under each organisation's respective purview. Hence, the WTO was put specifically in charge of the 'trade-related aspects' of IP, including on how the principles of the MTS apply to the topic and settling trade disputes that may arise in relation to the TRIPS Agreement. The complementary relations between the two organisations were even further strengthened by the 1995 WIPO-WTO Cooperation Agreement.[13]

Many countries were equally insistent that labour rights be handled by the ILO rather than the WTO, despite the evident link between trade and labour. These were mostly developing countries that feared labour rights provisions in trade deals may erode their competitive advantage.[14] However, unlike with WIPO, the bridge between the ILO and WTO did not prove to be a sturdy one. This is in contrast with the initial ambition of the 1948 Havana Charter – outcome of the multilateral negotiations aimed at creating the ITO – which specifically refers to labour standards:

1. The Members recognize that measures relating to employment must take fully into account the rights of workers under inter-governmental declarations, conventions and agreements. They recognize that all countries have a common interest in the achievement and mainte-

---

12   C. VanGrasstek, The History and Future of the World Trade Organization, WTO, 2013, p.14.

13   Agreement Between the World Intellectual Property Organization and the World Trade Organization, 1995, available at https://www.wto.org/english/tratop_e/trips_e/wtowip_e.htm, accessed on 1 September 2022.

14   Z. Ionel, "Labour Rights in EU Trade Agreements: Towards Stronger Enforcement", *European Parliament Research Service*, January 2022, https://www.europarl.europa.eu/RegData/etudes/BRIE/2022/698800/EPRS_BRI(2022)698800_EN.pdf, accessed 1 September 2022.

nance of fair labour standards related to productivity, and thus in the improvement of wages and working conditions as productivity may permit. The Members recognize that unfair labour conditions, particularly in production for export, create difficulties in international trade, and, accordingly, each Member shall take whatever action may be appropriate and feasible to eliminate such conditions within its territory.

2. Members which are also members of the International Labour Organisation shall cooperate with that organization in giving effect to this undertaking.

Article 7 of the Final Act of the United Nations Conference on Trade and Employment, Havana Charter for an International Trade Organisation, April 1948

As previously mentioned, due to opposition in the US Senate, the ITO never came into existence. Meanwhile, the 1947 GATT which lived on, and which was initially to fall under the umbrella of the ITO, did not cover labour standards. Compared to the ITO's ambitious mandate, none of the WTO Agreements resulting from the Uruguay Round address labour issues, with the exception of GATT Article XX.(e) and its mention of 'products of prison labour'. Attempts have been made to increase the synergies between the work of the ILO – the first and oldest UN agency dating all the way back to 1919 – and the WTO, still a relatively young organisation.

In the 1996 Singapore WTO Ministerial Declaration, also reaffirmed in the 2001 Doha Declaration, members renewed their "commitment to the observance of internationally recognised core labour standards", recognised the ILO as "the competent body to set and deal with these standards", and rejected "the use of labour standards for protectionist purposes". In the 2008 ILO Declaration on Social Justice for a Fair Globalization, employees, employers and governments took a step further and agreed that "the violation of fundamental principles and rights at work cannot be invoked or otherwise used as a legitimate comparative advantage and that labour standards should not be used for protectionist trade purposes" and that, "as trade and financial market policy both affect employment, it is the ILO's role to evaluate those employment effects to achieve its aim of placing employment at the heart of economic policies".

Given the importance of decent work for all, and despite these unresolved tensions between the WTO and ILO on trade and labour issues, the EU has been moving the ball forward. It has in fact gone much beyond the WTO in this regard, including through its own Generalised Scheme of Preferences which clearly supports sustainable development as a whole, since it conditions preferential trade relations to partners that respect human and labour rights as well as environmental protection. Part IV of this *Handbook* focuses more extensively on labour policies and EU-led efforts to address the imperative of ensuring decent work on a global scale.

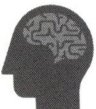

A knowledge and research hub on international trade

The WTO serves as a knowledge and research hub on issues relating to international trade. This is one area where the organisation's Secretariat can take some initiative without consistently needing its members' approval. This role is carried out by the WTO Secretariat through publications, databases, technical assistance and capacity building missions, workshops, seminars, conferences as well as online and offline forums which involve academics, researchers, diplomats, business representatives, NGOs and other various actors. Such events are not limited to Geneva and its surroundings, they span across the world.

The World Trade Report is the WTO's flagship publication. It is an annual publication that aims to deepen its readers' understanding of trends in trade, a wide array of trade policy issues and the MTS. It has covered various topics in the past two decades, including economic resilience and trade, government policies to promote innovation in the digital age, the future of trading services, the impact of technology on trade and jobs, small and medium enterprises, and trade in natural resources, to name a few.

The WTO also produces joint reports and analyses with other international institutions – further expanding on the above-mentioned cooperation function. A recent example is the 2022 joint WTO-World Bank policy note on "The Role of Trade in Developing Countries' Road to Recovery",[15] which discusses how international trade can support the recovery from the Covid-19 pandemic as well as potential future global shocks. This *Handbook* also refers to other joint work which served as essential resource materials, including with the World Bank (e.g. on trade and gender, and on the role of trade in ending poverty), the OECD (e.g. on aid for trade), the ILO (e.g. on investing in skills for inclusive trade) as well as the International Finance Corporation (e.g. on trade finance), among others.

Several databases have been set up and are regularly maintained by the WTO Secretariat – they are a key provider of statistics and information on different trade-related issues under the purview of the organisation.[16] For example, there are databases on disputes, regional trade agreements, intellectual property, services commitments, trade facilitation commitments, non-tariff measures, tariffs and imports. Most recently, in 2021, the Secretariat issued the WTO Trade Cost Index which, for the first time, allows users to monitor the evolution of global trade costs by economy and sector, to have a better understanding of the main components of trade costs (such as tariffs, non-tariff measures and infrastructure), and to determine who faces the largest trade costs (e.g. in terms of gender, income and skill set).

Cooperation with academic institutions is yet another way for the WTO to act as both a wellspring and a beneficiary of trade-related knowledge. Launched in 2010, the WTO Chairs Programme aims to promote, foster and disseminate research among academics on

---

15   World Bank and World Trade Organization, The Role of Trade in Developing Countries' Road to Recovery: Joint Policy Note, 2022.

16   World Trade Organization, *WTO Data – Information on trade and trade policy measures,* https://data.wto.org/en, accessed 1 September 2022.

issues relating to the trading system, to provide teaching support for the preparation of trade policy courses, and to respond to the needs of policymakers in developing countries and LDCs. It targets selected universities from developing and least developed countries.

The WTO's Trade Dialogues initiative and its Public Forum – the organisation's largest annual outreach event – provide unique platforms for heads of states and governments, parliamentarians, civil society, business groups and the academic world to come together and discuss an incredibly rich array of trade topics. More specifically with respect to parliaments, the latter play a crucial – yet often underestimated – role in the MTS. Deals struck following intergovernmental negotiations at the WTO will most likely be subject to subsequent approval from legislators. As such, the WTO seeks to foster dialogue with its members' parliaments to improve their understanding of the institution and its work.

Supporting developing and least developed countries

More than two-thirds of WTO members are developing and least developed countries. The organisation exists to support them and to ensure that they can effectively participate in, and benefit from, own international trade. Economic and developmental asymmetries persist; the WTO acknowledges and addresses this through its special and differential treatment (SDT) principle, which aims to provide adequate flexibility and rights adapted to their development needs. An entire section is dedicated to SDT below.

In addition, the role played by the WTO in supporting developing and least developed countries is in large part linked to the above section on its function of true knowledge and research hub. The Secretariat has developed a range of technical assistance and training tools to help participants improve their understanding of WTO-related issues. These include e-learning platforms, face-to-face and online training as well as learning by doing (via internship programmes). The organisation's technical assistance activities aim to help build members' capacity so that they can more effectively participate in international trade. The Secretariat undertook more than two hundred technical assistance activities in 2021 to help government officials better understand WTO rules and the MTS, attracting close to 12,000 participants. Most were delivered to African audiences (18%) followed by the Asia-Pacific region (15%).[17]

The WTO is not an aid and development agency per se – its core mandate is to set global trade rules. Nonetheless, the organisation acts as a catalyst, ensuring that existing development assistance mechanisms work better together and take into account members' respective trade needs. The section on Aid for Trade in Part III sheds more light on how such mechanisms may act as the lifeblood of trade by helping developing and, in particular, least developed countries build the trade capacity and infrastructure they need to effectively participate in and benefit from global trade.

17   World Trade Organization, *Annual Report 2022*, WTO, p.162., https:// www.wto.org/english/res_e/booksp_e/anrep_e/ar22_e.pdf,accessed 1 September 2022.

Principles of the multilateral trading system

One could break down and simplify the main principles of the MTS in the following manner. The MTS is composed of a sea of principles and rules guiding the trade opening and regulating agenda. Within that sea, however, lie islands of protective exceptions to the trade opening agenda, each with different aims. Figure 10 below is a visual representation of the principles of the MTS.

Fig. 10: The sea of open and regulated trade and its islands of protective exceptions.

A sea of open and regulated trade

Non-discrimination

Non-discrimination (ND) is a foundational pillar of the MTS. There are two basic ND principles.

According to the most-favoured-nation (MFN) principle, a member is not allowed to discriminate between and among trading partners. This means that, for any favourable treatment it decides to grant to a certain member (e.g. lower tariffs on certain goods), it shall grant the same treatment to its other trading partners. An important concept here (and throughout many other WTO rules) is that of 'like products'. This treatment shall be the same for like products, regardless of the trading partner they came from.

The second key ND principle is 'national treatment', which entails that a member is not allowed to discriminate between domestic products or services and products or services supplied by foreign entities. Here, the concept of 'like product' is also essential. For instance, should the national treatment obligation apply, when imported products from a foreign supplier enter the domestic market, they should not be subject to less favourable treatment (e.g. higher tariffs or more burdensome regulations) compared to 'like domestic product'.

The national treatment obligation has a general application to all measures affecting trade in goods, but is applied differently in the context of trade in services, where it is subject to certain caveats. It would only apply to specific services sectors where a member has explicitly consented to grant national treatment in their respective schedule of commitments. This links to another foundational aspect of the MTS, market access, which is discussed further below.

There are exceptions and mechanisms that allow departures from non-discrimination principles, including special and differential treatment for developing and least developed countries (discussed below) as well as regional trade agreements (RTAs). For the sake of clarity, in WTO parlance, RTAs are understood as a generic term encompassing reciprocal agreements of a various kinds, without necessarily being related to a specific region (e.g. the EU-Canada Comprehensive Economic and Trade Agreement may be referred to as an RTA).

RTAs, by their very nature, are discriminatory given that their participants accord each other more favourable market access conditions. However, they are permitted to do so, and this is considered legitimate in WTO rules, as long as they solely aim at further facilitating trade between RTA parties – i.e. 'WTO-plus' – without raising additional trade barriers for non-participants.

Three sets of WTO rules govern the formation and operation of RTAs:

- Customs unions and free-trade areas covering trade in goods are governed by GATT Article XXIV.
- Relevant arrangements for trade in goods specifically between developing country members are governed by the 'Enabling Clause' – which is discussed in the SDT section below.
- WTO+ agreements covering trade in services are governed by GATS Article V on economic integration.

Market access

Market access is an umbrella term which covers a number of measures that may be used to restrict imports or access to domestic markets. Such measures can be tariffs and other charges, as well as non-tariff barriers to trade. Tariffs (or customs duties) are not prohibited. In fact, they are often considered a legitimate trade policy tool. However, in keeping with the view to further open up trade, WTO members are encouraged (e.g. GATT Article XXVIII) to negotiate mutually beneficial tariff reductions. Tariff levels are inscribed in members' respective Goods Schedules. For each product, the schedule provides a tariff binding, i.e. the duty level that a member commits to respect. The member shall not apply tariffs on that product at a higher level than what it had agreed ("bound to") in its schedule. It should be emphasised that tariff bindings serve as 'ceilings'; members cannot be more 'protective' than the rate set out in their respective schedule. However, if they so wish, they can be more generous. Other non-tariff obstacles to trade also affect market access. This may include the lack of transparency regarding the applicable trade laws, regulations, and procedures; the unfair and arbitrary application of trade measures; technical barriers to trade; sanitary and phytosanitary measures; customs formalities and procedures; government procurement laws and practices; and the lack of effective protection of intellectual property rights.

Members' respective schedules are legal instruments that define the treatment that they must provide to their trade relations with other members, thus ensuring more transparency, security, and predictability.[18] Schedules are the result of negotiations among members, and each member must have one schedule for goods and one for services (see Figures 11 and 12 for a visual illustration). There is an internationally agreed product nomenclature developed by the World Customs Organization (WCO) called Harmonized System (HS).[19]

Finally, the study of market access within the sea of open trade would not be complete without a reference to the general elimination of quantitative restrictions (QRs).[20] The scope of this provision

---

18   World Trade Organization, *Backbone of the multilateral trading system: WTO goods schedules*, https://www.wto.org/english/news_e/news17_e/mark_27jul17_e.pdf, accessed 1 September 2022.

19   World Customs Organization, *What is the Harmonized System (HS)?*, http://www.wcoomd.org/en/topics/nomenclature/overview/what-is-the-harmonized-system.aspx, accessed 1 September 2022.

20   General Agreement on Tariffs and Trade, 1994, Article XI.

includes all prohibitions or restrictions other than tariffs or other taxes applied or maintained by a WTO member on the importation or exportation of goods (e.g. quotas, import or export licensing procedures, or other such measures). QRs may be allowed under specific circumstances that fall under the 'islands of protective exceptions' (e.g. balance of payments, or general and security exceptions), which will be discussed below.

Tariff item no. (HS 2012)	Ex	Description of products	Base rate of duty		Bound rate of duty	
			Ad val. (%)	Other	Ad val. (%)	Other
1		2	3.A	3.B	4.A	4.B
6505.00.20		--- Knitted, crocheted or woven, for use in the manufacture of hats			0	
6505.00.3		--- Felt hats and other felt headgear, made from the hat bodies, hoods or plateaux of heading 65.01, whether or not lined or trimmed:				
6505.00.31		---- Of fur-felt or wool-felt, for use in the manufacture of hats			0	
6505.00.39		---- Other			12.8	
6505.00.40		--- Other hats, hoods, caps, bonnets or berets			12.8	
6505.00.90		--- Other			15.7	
6811		Articles of asbestos-cement, of cellulose fibre-cement or the like.				
6811.40.00		- Containing asbestos			5.3	
6811.8		- Not containing asbestos:				
6811.81.00		- - Corrugated sheets			5.3	
6811.82.00		- - Other sheets, panels, tiles and similar articles			5.3	

Fig. 11: Excerpt taken from Canada's goods schedule.[21]

21   Excerpt from WTO document WT/LET/1469.

Modes of supply: (1) Cross-border supply (2) Consumption abroad (3) Commercial presence (4) Presence of natural persons			
Sector or subsector	Limitations on market access	Limitations on national treatment	Additional commitments
2.C TELECOMMUNICATIONS SERVICES Telecommunications services supplied by a facilities based public telecommunications network (wire-based and radioelectric) through any existing technological medium, included in subparagraphs (a), (b), (c), (f), (g) and (o). Radio broadcasting, cable television, satellite transmissions of DTH and DBS services and of audio digital services are excluded.	(1) None, except the following: International traffic must be routed through the facilities of an enterprise that has a concession granted by the Ministry of Communications and Transport (SCT). (2) None (3) A concession' from the SCT is required. Only enterprises established in conformity with Mexican law may obtain such a concession. Concessions for spectrum frequency bands for specific uses will be granted by public invitation to tender. Foreign governments may not participate in an enterprise set up in accordance with Mexican law nor obtain any authorization to provide telecommunications services.	(1) None (2) None (3) None	Mexico undertakes the obligations contained in the reference paper attached hereto.

Fig. 12: Excerpt taken from Mexico's services schedule.[22]

Special and differential treatment

The 1994 Marrakesh Agreement establishing the WTO explicitly recognises the need for "positive efforts to ensure that developing countries, and especially the least-developed among them, secure a share in the growth in international trade commensurate with the needs of their economic development". More than two-thirds of WTO members are developing countries and LDCs. The WTO Agreements recognise the particular situation of these countries and the link between trade and development by providing special and differential treatment (SDT) in their favour. SDT is considered an essential tool which recognises the economic and developmental asymmetries among countries and sets out to provide adequate flexibility or rights adapted to the needs of developing countries and

---

22   Excerpt from WTO document GATS/SC/56/Suppl.2.

LDCs. The aim of such measures is to enable these members to fully benefit from trade openness and to better integrate into the MTS. SDT provisions are spread across WTO Agreements and other legal instruments, such as Decisions adopted by the WTO Ministerial Conference or General Council. They include:

- Longer periods to implement WTO obligations (transitional time periods)
- Measures to increase trading opportunities
- Provisions calling upon WTO members to safeguard the interests of developing countries
- Provisions offering flexibility of commitments, action and use of policy instruments
- Provisions to support developing countries implement WTO Agreements and thus better participate in international trade, e.g. through capacity building programmes such as Aid for Trade and WTO trade-related technical assistance (TRTA)
- Provisions specifically in favour of LDCs

The 'Enabling Clause'[23] is the legal basis in the WTO for its Generalized System of Preferences (GSP), under which developed countries can provide non-reciprocal preferential treatment to products originating in developing countries (e.g. lower or no tariffs). SDT operates as an exception to the MFN principle, due to the inability of these countries to commit to all of the WTO obligations at their current stage of economic development. Some have referred to it as "an acceptance of deviation from the general rule of quid pro quo or reciprocity for the developing countries".[24] But the end goal of SDT

---

23   The 'Enabling Clause' is the name given to the "Decision on Differential and More Favourable Treatment, Reciprocity and Fuller Participation of Developing Countries". It was adopted in 1979, still under the GATT, with the objective to facilitate developed countries' ability to offer differential and more favourable treatment to developing and least-developed countries.

24   This wording was reflected in a 2001 communication delivered to the WTO General Council by Cuba, India, Pakistan, et. al., entitled *Preparations for the Fourth Session of the Ministerial Conference, Proposal for a*

continues to be further enabling participation in open trade, notwithstanding other exceptions discussed below which have a protective dimension.

Below are some noteworthy SDT examples:

- Article 65.2 TRIPS: developing countries were allowed to delay for a further period of four years the date of application of the provisions of the TRIPS Agreement, other than Articles 3, 4 and 5. Extensive use of this transition period was made until it expired in 2000.
- Article IV.1 GATS: "The increasing participation of developing country members in world trade shall be facilitated through negotiated specific commitments," including opening "market access in sectors and services modes of supply of export interest to them."
- Article 12.3 of the TBT Agreement: in the preparation and application of technical regulations, standards and conformity assessment procedures, members must take account of the special development, financial and trade needs of developing country members.
- Article 6.2 of the Agreement on Agriculture: it gives developing countries the flexibility to maintain certain subsidies in favour of resource-poor farmers.
- Waivers are also a key tool for developing members and especially LDCs. They are a permission granted by the membership to allow a member (or group of members) not to comply with normal commitments. Waivers are time-bound, and any extension has to be justified and agreed.[25]

Framework Agreement on Special and Differential Treatment. See para. 6 of WTO document WT/GC/W/442.

25   E.g., on 21 June 2021, WTO members agreed to extend the TRIPS transition period for LDCs until 1 July 2034 (also known as the 'TRIPS LDC waiver'). It is provided in Article 66.1 of the TRIPS Agreement, and since its inception, LDCs have benefitted from an extended transition period to apply provisions of the TRIPS Agreement, in recognition of their special need and constraints, and their need for more flexibility in order to create "a viable technological base". See World Trade Organ-

Transparency and notifications

Transparency is a cross-cutting principle in the MTS, and it is also a key principle in this sea of open trade. Compliance by members to new regulations put in place by other trading partners induces costs. It is essential for traders to obtain the necessary information, in a timely manner, regarding any new foreign regulations and requirements that affect their trade relations. The Covid-19 pandemic shed more light on the importance of transparency. With timely and accurate information, governments are better equipped to effectively address the health crisis through sound policy choices, including on trade-related aspects of a response to the pandemic. Transparency is ubiquitous in WTO Agreements and discussions. Members can fulfil this obligation through notification requirements which are also spread throughout the texts.[26] Below are some illustrative examples:

- GATT Article X requires the prompt publication of "laws, regulations, judicial decisions and administrative rulings of general application". It also requires that they be administered in a "uniform, impartial and reasonable manner".

- The TBT (Article 10) and the SPS (Article 7) Agreements also contain language requesting the publication, at an early stage, of information on new regulations and that other members be notified via the WTO Secretariat.

---

ization, WTO *members agree to extend TRIPS transition period for LDCs until 1 July 2034*, https://www.wto.org/english/news_e/news21_e/trip_30jun21_e.htm, accessed 1 September 2022.

26   M. Jansen, "Defining the Borders of the WTO Agenda", in A. Narlikar, M. Daunton and R.M. Stern, eds., *The Oxford Handbook on the World Trade Organization*, online edn, Oxford Academic, 2012, p.161-183, https://academic.oup.com/edited-volume/28190/chapter/213121453, accessed 1 September 2022.

Expanding open trade

The general objective of the MTS continues to be to further open up trade to the benefit of all, be it by (i) continuing trade negotiations in the WTO, (ii) by concluding trade agreements that attempt to go beyond the baseline set at the WTO in terms of trade opening, and (iii) by working towards having universal membership in the MTS. However, the gradual expansion of open trade is a multi-speed process.

Negotiations

Negotiations are ongoing at the WTO in different fora. Following the Uruguay Round which led to the creation of the organisation, a new round was mandated at the Fourth Ministerial Conference held in Doha in 2001. It was launched in turbulent times for the WTO and the world, not long after the 9/11 terror attacks. Development was considered the raison d'être of the Doha Round,[27] hence its alias 'Doha Development Agenda'. The breadth and depth of this Doha mandate give a sense of the great ambition that trade ministers achieved convergence on in 2001, for a stronger and more relevant MTS. But this ambition has since subsided, as several issues have been dropped altogether from the negotiation table. For instance, out of the four so-called 'Singapore issues' – government procurement, trade and investment, trade and competition policy, and trade facilitation – only the latter has been subject to active negotiations and eventually an Agreement.

Apart from multilateral negotiations, subsets of members have also launched negotiations in smaller groups, on a plurilateral basis. Most of these initiatives were launched on the sidelines of the

---

27   World Trade Organization, *Lamy says the Round's development potential must be preserved*, 2005, https://www.wto.org/english/news_e/news05_e/stat_lamy_28nov05_e.htm, accessed 1 September 2022.

Eleventh Ministerial Conference in Buenos Aires (2017), given the resistance of some members to move forward on negotiations that were not initially mandated by previous Ministerial Conferences, especially in Doha. They include negotiations on e-commerce, services domestic regulation, investment facilitation for development, small and medium enterprises, as well as environment-related issues (on sustainability and on plastics). The aim behind these plurilaterals is to update the WTO rulebook, so as to make it fit for purpose and address contemporary issues. More information on plurilateral efforts to open and regulate trade is provided below.

WTO members are clearly making an effort – either multilaterally or in smaller groups – to try to improve and expand trade openness and regulation.

Regional Trade Agreements

Regional trade agreements (RTAs)[28] also go further in the process of opening trade; their proliferation was analysed in Part I. No need to recall that non-discrimination (ND) among trading partners is one of the core principles of the WTO. RTAs are reciprocal preferential trade agreements between two or more partners; they constitute one of the derogations to the non-discrimination principle. Under WTO law, they are authorised but subject to a set of rules, and with the understanding that they would be further opening up – rather than restricting – trade amongst the parties to the agreement. For instance, Article XXIV:5 provides that:

> [T]he provisions of this Agreement shall not prevent, as between the territories of [members], the formation of a customs union or of a free-trade area or the adoption of an interim agreement necessary for the formation of a customs union or of a free-trade area.

---

28   The term RTA continues to be used in WTO language, regardless of the fact that such agreements are increasingly inter-regional (e.g. EU-South Kora Free Trade Agreement, India-MERCOSUR Preferential Trade Agreement, etc.) and not only intra-regional (MERCOSUR or ASEAN, for example).

WTO accession

The WTO accession process can be considered as a pathway towards economic growth and development, and fundamental for national, regional and international stability.[29] With each new member added to the WTO family, the organisation is one step closer to achieving universal membership. Out of the 164 members of the WTO (as of September 2022), 123 were 'original members' in the sense that they had already accepted the terms contained in the multilateral trade agreements when the organisation was first established in 1995. The WTO has come a long way from the 23 founding countries of the first GATT which entered into force in 1948. WTO accession therefore plays a large part in extending the benefits of trade and of participating in the MTS to more people around the world.

There are currently 25 Observer Governments and – except the Holy See – they must start their accession negotiations within five years of benefitting from the observer status. Accession entails negotiations. Any member-to-be will not only have to ratify all existing WTO Agreements, but they will also need to negotiate with all other members who express an interest in the accession process. Through an Accession Working Party they will discuss whether their domestic laws, regulations and practices are WTO-consistent – and if not, what should be done to remedy that – and what market access commitments the applicant will have to uphold vis à vis other members.

---

29   The "Trade for Peace" programme grew out of the launch of the G7+ WTO Accessions Group and was launched in December 2017 at the 11th WTO Ministerial Conference in Buenos Aires. The Group consists of nine LDCs (some recently acceded and others still acceding) and aims to facilitate the integration of fragile and conflict-affected economies into the multilateral trading system. It endeavors to assist countries in transitioning from fragility or conflict towards increased stability and economic well-being, including through: (i) political engagement and partnerships, (ii) outreach and public dialogue, (iii) research, and (iv) training and capacity building.

Islands of protective exceptions

Protection of key non-economic interests

Trade policy is instrumental to creating the adequate economic environment to promote, protect and fulfil broader societal, environmental and security objectives. This can be true in the context of facilitating trade, for instance regarding the transfer of essential medical supplies during a pandemic. But this can also be true in the context of measures that go against open trade principles. Indeed, members may need to adopt measures that constitute barriers to trade, be it inadvertently or deliberately.[30] The WTO recognises this need and provides specific rules balancing open trade and the pursuit of other legitimate interests.

General exceptions

First, there are general exceptions provided for in Article XX of the GATT which sets out a number of specific situations where WTO members may be exempted from open trade rules in that Agreement. Similar to the GATT for trade in goods, the GATS also provides a set of general exceptions in Article XIV to be applied in services trade, under similar conditions.[31] Among other issues, they mainly relate to:

- the protection of public morals
- the protection of human, animal or plant life or health

---

30   P. Van den Bossche, W. Zdouc, *The Law and Policy of the World Trade Organization: Text, Cases, and Materials*, Fifth Edition, Cambridge University Press: 2022. See Chapter 8 on General and Security Exceptions.

31   P. Van den Bossche, W. Zdouc, *The Law and Policy of the World Trade Organization: Text, Cases, and Materials*, Fifth Edition, Cambridge University Press: 2022. See Chapter 8 on General and Security Exceptions, in particular the section on General Exceptions under the GATS.

- securing compliance with laws and regulations that are not themselves inconsistent with GATT or GATS provisions, including in the context of customs enforcement, monopolies, patents, trademarks and copyrights, and the prevention of fraudulent or deceptive practices, safety, protection of individuals' privacy and confidentiality
- products of prison labour
- the protection national treasures of artistic, historic or archaeological value
- the conservation of exhaustible natural resources

For the adopted measure(s) to be considered compatible with WTO law, they must fall within the list of specific instances provided in the relevant GATT or GATS article, and they also have to be applied in a manner that would not constitute "arbitrary or unjustifiable discrimination between countries where the same conditions prevail", nor a "disguised restriction on international trade".

Two exceptions are particularly relevant, and are frequently invoked by respondents in the settlement of disputes at the WTO: the one on the protection of exhaustible natural resources, and the one on the protection of human, animal or plant life or health. More than three quarters of all quantitative restrictions notified to the WTO up to May 2019 relied on GATT Article XX. Half of them relied on the "protection of human, animal or plant life or health".[32]

The WTO Appellate Body clarified that, for any provisional justification under one of the Article XX paragraphs to be valid: (i) the measure at issue must "address the particular interest specified in that paragraph", and (ii) there must be "a sufficient nexus between the measure and the interest protected". The exceptions set out in Article XX provide different thresholds that ought to be met regard-

---

32   P. Van den Bossche, W. Zdouc, *The Law and Policy of the World Trade Organization: Text, Cases, and Materials*, Fifth Edition, Cambridge University Press: 2022. See Chapter 8 on General and Security Exceptions, in particular the section on the Reliance on Article XX.

ing the nexus criteria between the challenged measure and the relevant interest pursued.[33]

Security exceptions

Second, and in addition to the general exceptions detailed above, members can make use of security exceptions provided for in Articles XX and XIVbis of GATT and GATS respectively. The language in both provisions is nearly identical. There are various reasons why security interests may overshadow open trade and its benefits. For example, it may be to preserve domestic industries of a particular strategic importance, by limiting the export of arms or other military products, or to protect other strategic domestic production capacities. As of 1948, this exception was invoked on very few occasions and never subject to a legal dispute. Such caution remained in the first two decades of the WTO's existence, with members favouring out-of-court settlements of disputes on such matters. Recent years have seen some WTO members step away from a longstanding self-restraint vis-à-vis the use of these national security exceptions as justification for trade-restrictive measures. 2016 marked a turning point after which seven national security cases were filed in just four years.[34] In 2016, Ukraine requested consultations with Russia regarding alleged restrictions on traffic in transit through various countries.[35] In 2018, Qatar requested consultations with Saudi Arabia concerning the latter's alleged failure to provide adequate protection of IP rights held by, or applied for, entities

---

33   DS400 and DS401, European Communities – Measures Prohibiting the Importation and Marketing of Seal Products. For more information, it may be useful to turn to P. Van den Bossche, W. Zdouc, *The Law and Policy of the World Trade Organization: Text, Cases, and Materials*, Fifth Edition, Cambridge University Press: 2022. See Chapter 8 on General and Security Exceptions.

34   P. Van den Bossche and S. Akpofure, "The Use and Abuse of the National Security Exception under Article XXI(b)(iii) of the GATT 1994", *World Trade Institute*, Working Paper No. 03/2020, 2020, https://www.wti.org/media/filer_public/50/57/5057fb22-f949-4920-8bd1-e8a-d352d22b2/wti_working_paper_03_2020.pdf, accessed 1 September 2022.

35   DS512: Russia – Measures Concerning Traffic in Transit.

based in Qatar; Saudi Arabia had invoked the national security exception under the TRIPS Agreement.[36] That same year, the US president at the time – Donald J. Trump – imposed additional duties on steel and aluminium imports on grounds of national security, a measure which was contested by no less than seven complainants (China, India, the European Union, Norway, Russia, Turkey and Switzerland).[37]

This potentially continuing proliferation of security exceptions raises legitimate concerns. Has a Pandora's box been opened, thanks to which members may now have relatively free reign to escape their obligations under the MTS? The role of the WTO and its dispute settlement has been challenged in the context of the use of security exceptions as some members argued that a dispute settlement panel had no jurisdiction when GATT Article XXI has been invoked.[38] The extent of the role that the WTO can play in containing the abuse of such national security exceptions is subject to ongoing debate. The Appellate Body paralysis, however, will not be helping the WTO's case in that respect. In an era of strategic rivalry between the United States and China, where national security is invoked to restrict trade and apply discriminatory trade measures, it will be necessary to redefine the perimeter of the security exception to ensure it does not become the joker that can be invoked whenever respecting WTO rules is simply not convenient.

Protection against 'unfair trade practices'

In the MTS, there are also rules to protect against so-called 'unfair trade practices'. WTO members regularly refer to 'fairness' as an

---

36   DS567: Saudi Arabia – Measures concerning the Protection of Intellectual Property Rights.

37   *See* DS544, 547, 548, 552, 554, 556 and 564: United States – Certain Measures on Steel and Aluminium Products.

38   *See* DS512: Russia – Measures Concerning Traffic in Transit.

overarching principle for international trade relations. However, one should bear in mind that WTO law does not provide general rules that would apply to all forms of unfair practices. The fact is that there is no clear consensus on what the term 'unfair' can exactly encompass. Still, two specific trade practices are commonly referred to as being unfair, although differences persist on this point, both in mentalities and in domestic economic systems. These are dumping and subsidisation.

Dumping

Dumping occurs when the selling price of a product is higher in the home market of the producer compared to its selling price on a foreign importing market. In other words, it refers to exporting a good at a lower price than the price charged for it at home. It is in principle authorised under WTO rules, unless the importing country can prove it has been adversely impacted by the predatory pricing. There may be consequences caused by the artificial depression of the price of the exported product. It may also sometimes be supported by subsidies for the exporting business. Consequently, these elements may affect the importing nation's economy by putting at risk local producers, by driving them out of business and ultimately by leading to job losses and higher unemployment rates, thus killing competition over time.[39] WTO law does not regulate the actions of companies engaged in dumping activities. Its focus is rather on how governments can or cannot respond to dumping. Article VI of the GATT provides the right for the importing member to apply anti-dumping measures when such dumped imports result in an injury to its domestic industry. The Anti-Dumping Agreement[40] provides further elaboration on the basic principles set forth in Article VI itself.

39 *For instance, see* European Commission, *Trade defence*, https://policy. trade.ec.europa.eu/enforcement-and-protection/trade-defence_en, accessed 1 September 2022.

40 Officially known as the Agreement on Implementation of Article VI of GATT 1994.

Subsidies

Rules on subsidies are perhaps an even more sensitive topic in WTO law. They are key policy tools often used by governments to pursue and promote legitimate and essential objectives, whether of an economic or social aspect. Still, their potential adverse effect on other trade partners entails that they may be considered 'unfair trade practices'. Subsidies imply some kind of financial assistance from a government or a public body within the territory of a member which confers a benefit to the entity that receives it.

Some subsidies, such as export and import substitution subsidies, are prohibited under WTO law. Other subsidies are not prohibited per se but are 'actionable', meaning that they can be challenged if they cause adverse effects. When an 'actionable subsidy' is found to 'injure' the domestic industry of another member, or if it causes 'serious prejudice' to its interests (e.g. undercutting the price of a 'like product'), then the subsidising member should take steps to withdraw the subsidy or remove its adverse effects. Any type of subsidy (be it domestic or export, prohibited or actionable) that injures another member's domestic industry enables it to impose countervailing duties to offset the subsidisation and its negative effects. In WTO law, the concept of specificity is also a condition which ought to be met in order to activate this defense mechanism, i.e. it applies to a subsidy given only to an enterprise, an industry, a group of enterprises, or a group of industries in the subsidising country. The Agreement on Subsidies and Countervailing Measures disciplines the use of subsidies and regulates the defense actions members may adopt to offset their effects. The massive expansion of national subsidy schemes aimed at supporting technological developments and the fight against climate change necessitates a redefinition of WTO disciplines concerning industrial subsidies to prevent a race to the bottom with significant negative spillover effects on third countries.

Protection of key economic interests

Governments also have tools at their disposal specifically to protect key economic interests. The following exceptions are distinct from general and security exceptions in the sense that they focus on pecuniary or broader economic matters. They are also distinct from unfair trade practices as the latter are remedies against a prejudicial practice in order to 'level the playing field', whereas the following exceptions are pure escape clauses (see Figure 13 at the end of the section).

Safeguards

Members can respond to sudden and sharp increases in imports of a given product that causes or threatens to cause a serious injury to their domestic industry. If such a situation occurs, members may adopt Safeguard measures, which entail a temporary restriction (e.g. quotas or tariffs) over the imports of the product at issue. When a trade agreement is concluded, not all future events can be predicted, including those that lead to an unexpected increase in foreign competitive pressure on the domestic industry. This can be a real problem if imports boom, domestic production lags and the labour market does not have sufficient time to adapt. In addition, rising unemployment would become a serious threat.

Balance of payments

Members can adopt measures to protect their balance of payments (BoP). A BoP crisis occurs when a government runs out of foreign exchange reserves; it cannot finance its current account deficit. At a lower stage, this can reflect in foreign creditors' doubts regarding the likelihood of full and timely repayment. This will often lead to a rise in risk premia. But, when creditor confidence is rock-bottom, risk premia can skyrocket, or financing can even be halted. No access to foreign funds means that it is urgent for the government to restore a 'balance' between exports and imports, or between government income and spending.[41] BoP measures are time-bound, they should not exceed what is necessary to address the threat or decline – or to achieve a reasonable rate of increase – in its monetary reserves. They must also avoid unnecessary damage to the commercial and economic interests of other members.[42]

Prudential carveout for financial services

In the area of services, the Annex to the GATS on Financial Services provides a 'prudential carve-out' (PCO) for the financial sector. Notwithstanding the provisions in the GATS, the PCO allows members to remain free to adopt prudential measures to:

- protect "investors, depositors, policy holders or persons with whom a financial duty is owed by a financial service supplier"; or
- ensure the "integrity and stability of the financial system".

Most trade agreements with financial services section include a provision aiming to preserve some policy space for signatories wishing to step in and alter their existing domestic rules on financial services for 'prudential reasons'.

41   S. Cecchetti and K. Schoenholtz, "Sudden stops: A primer on balance-of-payments crises", Vox EU, 2018, https://cepr.org/voxeu/blogs-and-reviews/sudden-stops-primer-balance-payments-crises, accessed 1 September 2022.

42   *See* GATT Articles XII and XVIII:B.

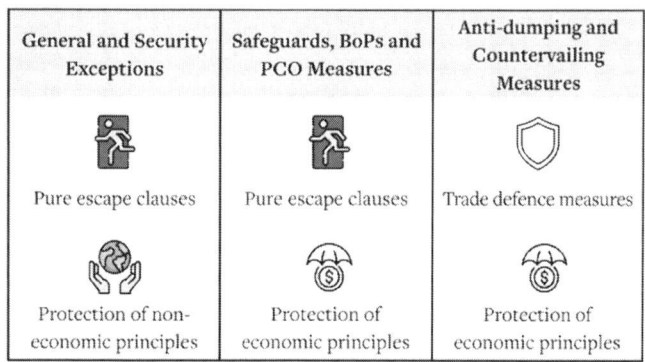

General and Security Exceptions	Safeguards, BoPs and PCO Measures	Anti-dumping and Countervailing Measures
Pure escape clauses	Pure escape clauses	Trade defence measures
Protection of non-economic principles	Protection of economic principles	Protection of economic principles

Fig.13: Recap of the islands of protective exceptions: what form of exception and what aim?

Operating under the multilateral trading system: adapt and overcome

As discussed above, the WTO's legal framework allows a departure from multilateralism, provided that these 'less-than-multilateral' agreements imply further integration and open trade. Bilateral or regional trade agreements are not new; but they have been on the rise these past years as illustrated in Part I. Each agreement can be considered as a 'miniature trade regime' that ties countries in various ways. It has also been suggested that a world map depicting the numerous trade relations would resemble a 'spaghetti bowl'.[43]

On top of that, the existence of several challenges to the way the MTS operates has led to an increase in the recourse by governments to 'downsized', plurilateral fora to regulate their trade relations. Sometimes, such initiatives also intend to cover newer topics that are not part of the multilateral discussions, but which are relevant to address 21st century challenges.

---

43   J. Bhagwati, "US Trade Policy: The infatuation with free trade agreements", *Columbia University*, Discussion Paper Series, No. 726, 1995, p.4.

The multiplication of 'downsized' trade regimes entails that global trade and integration have a variable geometry and that they are a multi-speed process. However, there may also be challenges and risks associated with these proposed approaches, not the least of which are fragmentation and a confusing legal architecture. Finally, there are issues of the global commons such as climate change that cannot be fully addressed if not all governments are directing their efforts towards the same goals. International trade and climate diplomacy, as well as relevant commitments, are vehicles for making greener trade possible on a global scale. The WTO has a crucial role to play in this respect.

'Downsized' trade regimes: a response to the challenges affecting multilateralism?

Discussions on WTO reform tend to be broad in scope and some premises date back to the early days of the organisation. But work towards reform has gained momentum from 2018 onwards, as the global trading system and the WTO were faced with a number of unprecedented challenges that were straining the system.

Some of these were unilateral trade actions and counter measures amidst escalating trade tensions; increasing protectionist sentiments, including a new high in import-restrictive measures; the growing importance of politics in decision-making, including the 'weaponisation' of trade; disfunctions in the WTO's dispute settlement system, in particular the Appellate Body; the pace of technological development; and the perception that the benefits of economic growth were not being distributed equitably.

To respond to these challenges several members started to call for collective action including the need to reform the WTO. In 2022, at the Twelfth WTO Ministerial Conference in Geneva, members committed to "work towards necessary reform" of the organisation, and "to having a fully and well-functioning dispute settlement system accessible to all members by 2024".[44]

---

44   WTO document WT/MIN(22)/24 – WT/L/1135, Paragraphs 3 and 4.

However, while there is a desire to improve the functioning of the organisation, members do not hold a uniform view of what reform should encompass. Some seem eager to take action while others are responding slowly. Many members have also pointed out that the efforts need to be pragmatic, realistic and inclusive and reflect the views and perspectives of all. General concerns were raised, including on the following:

- On negotiations, and the challenges members face in initiating and concluding negotiations both on longstanding and newer issues
- On the need to strengthen the institutional aspects of the WTO, such as the work of the regular bodies, as well as transparency and notification requirements
- On potential further improvements to be made to the SDT system
- On WTO dispute settlement, and the question of whether and how to effectively restore a functioning Appellate Body
- Part of the concerns raised also relate to the role of state intervention in the economy, in particular regarding China.[45]

With respect to negotiations, there were various reasons why the WTO found itself in this predicament. The trade policy landscape has become more complex over the years, which has raised new challenges. The agenda has become increasingly complex too, as the number of subjects, governments, and trade-offs expanded. Under the Uruguay Round, which concluded in 1994, all issues were considered part of a 'single undertaking'; meaning that "nothing is agreed until everything is agreed". All of this has led to slower progress in the negotiations or even outright blockages, even for the 'easier' areas. The geopolitical context has also not helped as trade concessions have been perceived as a zero-sum game. A large membership and

---

45   P. C. Mavroidis and A. Sapir, "All the Tea in China: Solving the 'China Problem' at the WTO", *Global Policy*, Volume 12, Supplement 3, April 2021, p.41-48, https://onlinelibrary.wiley.com/doi/epdf/10.1111/1758-5899.12925, accessed 1 September 2022.

the practice of consensus for decision-making had certainly made the negotiating function much more difficult.

Difficult, but not impossible. Recent developments have shown that the WTO negotiating system can adapt to new challenges. At Ministerial Conferences, notably in Geneva (2022), Nairobi (2015) and Bali (2013), 'packages' of decisions and declarations were adopted. Achievements like the Trade Facilitation Agreement (TFA), and the Decision on Eliminating Agricultural Export Subsidies, the Agreement on Fisheries Subsidies and the Ministerial Declaration on the WTO Response to the Covid-19 Pandemic and Preparedness for Future Pandemics, among others, offer important lessons for negotiations in other areas.

Despite the stalemates existing across the MTS, plans to overcome blockages and to move ahead with openness and integration remain strong in international trade governance. Several developments are worth noting:

1. New practices are emerging with respect to the implementation of certain multilateral trade agreements. This includes individualised commitments which are explicitly linked to members' respective resource capacities. The Trade Facilitation Agreement is a striking example where members can determine their own individual implementation schedules. Developed and some developing members have committed to implement the Agreement upon its entry into force, in 2017. Other developing and least developed countries have committed to a different schedule for implementation, and their notification requirements thus correspond to the relevant category they fit into (e.g. "members who need additional time" or "members who need additional time and capacity building").

2. Governments are also moving forward outside the MTS via FTAs (whether bilateral or regional). The latter continue to enhance trade openness, albeit at a scaled-down level. As detailed in Part I, the rise of regional trade agreements has fundamentally changed global trade.

3. Finally, there are developments in the context of the MTS, but with engagement from a more limited number of members in

a 'plurilateral' (i.e. less-than-multilateral) setting.[46] Since 2017, groups of members have launched a series of plurilateral negotiations with the ambition to address modern challenges that other members were not yet ready to start multilateral work on. The above-mentioned Multi-Party Interim Appeal Arbitration Arrangement also constitutes a plurilateral stop-gap solution to a multilateral issue: the absence of a functioning Appellate Body to hear WTO disputes.

Fragmentation challenges

An increasing number of 'blocks' (whether regional or inter-regional strategic trade alliances), coupled with the steady and continuous rise in FTAs, may further split an already fragmented trade environment. This poses serious questions as to how global economic welfare and the coherence of international trade rules will be affected. Geopolitical fragmentation and a proliferation of sources of international trade law can cause economic harm by producing trade diversion from efficient producers to less efficient producers, and potentially heightening the transaction costs facing all economic actors, from states to businesses. In 2022, IMF Managing Director Dr Kristalina Georgieva stressed that this trend of fragmentation is a strong one.[47] She warned against the risk of reconfigured supply chains as well as higher barriers to trade and investment. It would impact productivity and growth, in particular that of developing nations, who would find it much harder to sell to developed countries, gain know-how and build wealth. It would also fuel inflation, which would not spare anyone, even in developed countries. According to

---

46 As discussed in the above section on the functions of the WTO, since 2017, groups of members have launched a series of plurilateral negotiations with the ambition to address modern challenges that other members were not yet ready to pursue in a multilateral context.

47 K. Georgieva, G. Gopinath and C. Pazarbasioglu, "Why we must resist geoeconomic fragmentation – and how", *International Monetary Fund*, Blog, 2022, https://blogs.imf.org/2022/05/22/why-we-must-resist-geoeconomic-fragmentation-and-how/, accessed 1 September 2022.

IMF research, technological fragmentation, or decoupling, can lead to losses of 5% of GDP for many countries.[48]

According to Arancha Gonzalez, currently dean of the Paris School of International Affairs (Sciences Po), previously Spanish Minister of Foreign Affairs: "now is not the moment to divest from the WTO – quite the opposite". One should ask whether further fragmenting the trade system and chaotically retreating from globalisation would actually benefit non-trade objectives in the long run.[49] For instance, would it enable or rather hinder long-term achievements in the area of environmental protection? Would trade 'disintegration' not prove considerably less efficient than 'better trade integration' which nurtures resilience to shocks for nations around the world and builds a more inclusive and sustainable global economy?

In fact, some of the biggest losers of this fragmented, polycentric and complex regulatory environment will be developing countries – which may struggle to offset a diminishing demand from more advanced economies – as well as MSMEs.

A typical example, in line with today's growing digital economy, where small businesses would be the most impacted is the existing e-commerce governance framework. MSMEs lack the capacity of their bigger counterparts – both financial and legal – in order to fulfil a myriad of regulations. Over time, and overall, the e-commerce governance network illustrated in Figure 14 has become less fragmented. But it is still dominated by a handful of central actors, each with varying domestic regulations (for consumer protection, data flows, protection of source code, etc.).

By nature, the digital economy supposedly knows no borders. But there is an irony here: the digital economy is in some ways more fragmented than the physical one. China is currently the US' largest goods trading partner with over USD 650 billion in total (two-

48   D. A. Cerdeiro, R. Mano, J. Eugster, D. V Muir and S. J Peiris, "Sizing Up the Effects of Technological Decoupling", *International Monetary Fund*, Working Paper WP/21/69, 2021.

49   A. Gonzalez Laya, "Global Insecurity is No Reason to Divest from the WTO", *Financial Times*, 2022, https://www.ft.com/content/bb1fab70-02e0-4392-8fa5-e88c03398d44, accessed 1 September 2022.

way) goods trade in 2021 - a near record high.[50] At the same time, the 'splinternet' is also a reality. Many internet services – mostly US-based – continue to be totally or partially blocked in mainland China due to its 'Great Firewall',[51] including Google, YouTube, Wikipedia, Facebook and WhatsApp, to name a few. In the US, regulators have been casting a suspicious look at Chinese-owned TikTok, citing security concerns about consumer data.[52] The current rise of geopolitical tensions will not be helpful in reducing fragmentation. On the contrary, it may even lead to a new 'digital iron curtain'. Businesses have been reconsidering their ties and cutting their services in Russia, whilst the latter has also blocked access to several Western websites. Fragmenting regulatory frameworks may affect the benefits of trade, and here more specifically of digital trade and innovations.[53] The WTO has an important role to play in establishing an international regulatory framework and in facilitating coherence between domestic frameworks. RTAs also play a big part in moving towards less fragmentation, and may be seen as complementary to multilateralism by leading to more, not less, global integration.[54] Additionally, the plurilateral negotiations taking place at the WTO on new e-commerce rules (the Joint Statement Initiative on Electronic Commerce) are an attempt to reduce this fragmentation. A significant subset of WTO members is participating in these negotiations, which accounts for over 90% of global trade.[55] The co-conven-

50   United States Census Bureau, *Trade in Goods with China*, https://www.census.gov/foreign-trade/balance/c5700.html, accessed 1 September 2022.

51   S. Venkataramakrishnan, "National security concerns pile pressure on 'splinternet' cracks", *Financial Times*, 2021, https://www.ft.com/content/e4b87d3d-d2f4-4ba2-9602-6fd330bac6f6, accessed 1 September 2022.

52   D. McCabe, "How Frustration Over TikTok Has Mounted in Washington", *The New York Times*, 2022, https://www.nytimes.com/2022/08/14/technology/tiktok-china-washington.html, accessed 1 September 2022.

53   World Trade Organization, World Trade Report 2020: Government Policies to Promote Innovation in the Digital Age, 2020, p.152.

54   A. Mattoo, N. Rocha and M. Ruta, *Handbook of Deep Trade Agreements*, World Bank, 2020.

55   As of February 2023, there are 89 WTO members participating in the e-commerce Joint Statement Initiative.

ers of this initiative (Japan, Singapore and Australia) have reiterated their objective to substantially conclude the negotiations at the end of 2023. Concrete outcomes can already be seen, with convergence reached on more than ten topics, ranging from consumer protection, e-contracts and paperless trading, to cybersecurity, spam and open government data.

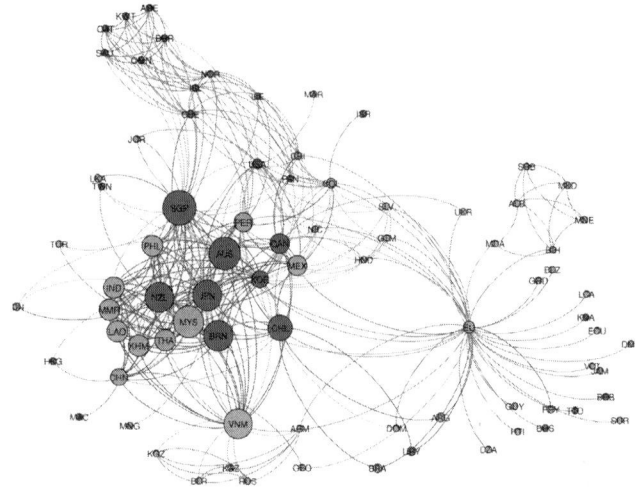

Fig. 14: Example of the fragmentation of the e-commerce governance network (2020).[56]

Legal architecture

As plurilateral negotiations within the WTO are advancing and producing results, the participants of these initiatives are now considering next steps and grappling with architectural issues and legal avenues for possible outcomes. Plurilaterals are not a new thing. They constitute a legal and legitimate way to move the ball forward on is-

---

56   The University of Adelaide, *Institute for International Trade: The Topology of E-commerce Governance*, https://iit.adelaide.edu.au/news/list/2021/09/16/the-topology-of-e-commerce-governance, accessed 1 September 2022.

sues which are considered important for a group of members. Since the creation of the WTO, members have used various legal avenues to apply changes to WTO law, in particular to adopt new commitments and/or to expand on existing WTO rules. Some of these legal avenues have resulted in changes for all members, whereas others have involved changes to commitments only for a subset of members.

Annex 4 to the Marrakesh Agreement is dedicated to Plurilateral Trade Agreements that create rights and obligations only for participating members. There are currently two agreements falling under this category: the Agreement on Government Procurement and the Agreement on Trade in Civil Aircraft. Both were integrated into the WTO framework at the time of creation of the organisation.

In addition, there are other plurilateral agreements which are commitments reflected in participants' schedules and shared with the entire membership on an MFN basis; these are somewhat scattered throughout the WTO framework. For instance, for plurilateral agreements in the area of goods, one could mention the 1996 Information Technology Agreement and its 2015 expansion both aimed at eliminating tariffs on a selection of IT products. In the area of services, one could look at the Reference Paper on Basic Telecommunications which implied the modification of participants' services schedules.

In a 2021 communication brought up on the agenda of the WTO General Council, certain members have raised concerns as to the legal status of joint initiatives and their negotiated outcomes.[57] These concerns – which have been rejected by other members – include the need to maintain a consensus-based mode of decision-making.

Out of the various plurilateral negotiations launched in 2017, some have already produced outcomes via different legal approaches. For instance, in December 2020 the Informal Working Group on MSMEs adopted a package of six declarations and recommendations which was sponsored by close to a hundred WTO members. These are supposedly non-binding outcomes, which have however already

---

57   WTO document WT/GC/W/819, and subsequent revisions.

produced concrete results.[58] In 2021, the negotiations in the Joint Initiative on Services Domestic Regulation were concluded with the overall aim to increase transparency, predictability and efficiency on authorisation procedures for service providers wishing to do business abroad. In line with the Declaration on the Conclusion of Negotiations on Services Domestic Regulation of 2 December 2021,[59] at the end of 2022, a group of WTO Members representing more than 90% of world services trade launched the certification process to make their new commitments on services domestic regulation legally binding as part of their respective schedules of specific commitments. However, in February 2023, two Members notified their objections seeking further clarification as to the implications of the proposed modification to schedules.

Now that other plurilateral initiatives such as the Joint Statement Initiative on E-commerce are advancing towards concrete outcomes too, the legal architecture question is increasingly being raised. This is particularly relevant given the objective, set out by the participants, to achieve a high-standard outcome, building on existing WTO Agreements, with the participation of as many WTO members as possible.

International trade and climate diplomacy: making greener trade possible on a global scale

Multilateral cooperation must act as the world's vehicle for addressing a challenge of a global magnitude such as climate change, an issue of the global commons.[60] Downsized initiatives alone will be

---

58   *See* WTO document INF/MSME/4. One of the recommendations calls on WTO members to provide information on MSME policies during their Trade Policy Reviews to enhance transparency and serve as a source of good practice. Several members have already adopted this practice in their policy reviews. For instance, *see* World Trade Organization, *Working group on small business welcomes three more members*, 2022, https://www.wto.org/english/news_e/news22_e/msmes_08feb22_e.htm, accessed 1 September 2022.

59   *See* WTO document WT/L/1129.

60   United Nations Framework Convention on Climate Change, *Multilateralism Key to Achieving Climate Goals*, 2022, https://unfccc.int/news/multi-

insufficient. Multilateralism will be key to facilitate discussions and linkages between governments and to catalyse the development of rules, guidelines and practices to support these objectives. In this endeavour, the Former UN Climate Change Executive Secretary, Patricia Espinosa, has stressed the need to embrace 'inclusive multilateralism', which means going beyond traditional multilateralism by bringing more groups and diversity to the table, including non-state actors such as youth, women, indigenous groups and others.

A large part of the multilateral work on environment has to do with the United Nations Framework Convention on Climate Change (UNFCC) and its highest-level decision-making body, the Conference of the Parties (COP). The latter aims to review the implementation of various instruments by members, such as the 1992 UNFCC, i.e. the parent treaty, as well as the 1997 Kyoto Protocol and the 2015 Paris Climate Agreement. The COP may also adopt decisions or guidelines to further develop or implement these instruments. The Paris Climate Agreement was adopted at the COP 21, and it is the first multilaterally binding treaty which brings nations from across the globe (194 signatories as of July 2022) together to undertake ambitious efforts to combat climate change. It sets the goal to limit temperature rises to below 2°C with the target of 1.5°C by 2050.

The World Trade Organization is uniquely positioned to contribute to the achievement of greener trade on a global scale, and thus to the objectives set out in the Paris Climate Agreement. This means promoting the design and implementation of measures in a manner which ensures that trade and climate policies are mutually supportive, encouraging the protection of the environment without leading to discrimination and disguised protectionism.

Work in the WTO has contributed to some trade and environment topics moving to active negotiations, as key components of the Doha Round launched in 2001. One noteworthy outcome is the 2022 Agreement on Fisheries Subsidies, through which Members seek to eliminate certain subsidies that contribute to overfishing, those contributing to illegal, unreported and unregulated fishing (IUU),

lateralism-key-to-achieving-climate-goals, accessed 1 September 2022.

and those for the unregulated high seas, can help protect fish stock. This agreement was historic for several reasons. It is the first SDG target to be met (target 14.6), the first one met through a multilateral agreement, the first WTO agreement with an environmental focus and the first broad, binding, multilateral agreement on ocean sustainability. The agreement is also an example of how special and differential treatment is a crucial aspect of generating global consensus on trade and environment issues, which links back to the triple-win objective. It imposes multiple new obligations on members and, as such, some flexibility in the implementation of the agreement was required. It thus contains a two-year 'peace clause' for WTO disputes relating to subsidies granted by developing and least developed members for illegal, unreported and unregulated (IUU) fishing and for fishing overfished stocks. It also requires members to "exercise due restraint" when raising concerns involving an LDC member and to take into account its specific situation when considering the solutions at hand. The agreement also establishes a voluntary Fisheries Funding Mechanism to complement existing assistance under the OECD ODA. It will assist members in implementing the agreement via technical assistance and capacity building, help integrate fisheries sustainability elements into fisheries subsidies policies and practices, strengthen sustainable fisheries management systems and also help members comply with transparency and notification requirements. Total support to the fisheries sector in developing and least developed countries remains significantly less than the estimated USD 22 billion per year in harmful fisheries subsidies worldwide according to a 2022 WTO report.[61] Increased financial support and coordination of existing and future related funding mechanisms will be essential to improve the effectiveness of the implementation of the Fisheries Subsidies Agreement, with the aim of making trade policy work for the health of our oceans. The Agreement has not yet come into force at the time of writing this *Handbook*. For that, two-

---

61   World Trade Organization, Implementing the WTO Agreement on Fisheries Subsidies: Challenges and Opportunities for Developing and Least-Developed Country members, 2022, p.21.

thirds of WTO members must formally accept the Protocol of the Agreement on Fisheries Subsidies.[62]

The WTO Committee on Trade and Environment (CTE) provides a forum for members to consider the nexus between trade and the environment. Although the CTE has not recommended changes to the rules of the multilateral trading system, as per its mandate,[63] its work has been focusing on many important issues, including:

1. the relevance of taxes and charges for environmental purposes

2. requirements for environmental purposes relating to products, such as standards and technical regulations, packaging, labelling and recycling requirements

3. the transparency of environmental trade measures

4. the link between trade openness and the environment, for instance how environment measures may impact market access especially in relation to developing and least developed countries

5. the export of domestically prohibited goods, particularly hazardous waste

As part of the Doha mandate, the CTE may also meet in special sessions (CTE-SS) to negotiate specific issues related to trade and the environment. There are three important topics on the CTE-SS mandate which call for renewed multilateral engagement.

The first issue relates to the relationship between the WTO rules and multilateral environmental agreements (MEAs), in particular those containing 'specific trade obligations' (STOs). Post-Doha discussions have led to delegations offering different views on the interpretation of this latter term, and on potential outcomes for the

---

62   The formal acceptance entails the deposition of an "instrument of acceptance" with the WTO, which is usually issued and signed by the head of state, the head of government, the minister of foreign affairs, or another official who has been granted the "full powers" to do so. As of 16 June 2023, ten WTO members had deposited their instrument of acceptance, and six have also donated to the Fisheries Funding Mechanism.

63   Marrakesh Ministerial Decision on Trade and Environment, 1994. Available at: https://www.wto.org/english/docs_e/legal_e/56-dtenv_e. htm, accessed 1 September 2022.

negotiations. A compromise approach was found to avoid a prescriptive definition of STOs in MEAs,[64] and the WTO Secretariat also prepared a non-exhaustive, indicative list of about fifteen MEAs which include provisions to control trade for environment protection purposes.[65]

The second issue is linked to the previous one and relates to the collaboration between the WTO and MEA Secretariats. Information exchange is crucial if the international community is to address climate change and promote development whilst maintaining open trade policies in a coherent, efficient and inclusive manner. This collaboration may happen at the level of the heads of relevant institutions, as well as via observership status granted among international organisations.

The third and final issue under the CTE-SS' purview relates to the elimination of trade barriers (tariffs and NTBs) on environmental goods and services, so as to create a mutually beneficial situation for trade, the environment and development (a triple-win). The work in the area of market access is informed and complemented by other work including that relating to identifying STOs in MEAs. Lack of progress on the latter may also impede advancements on this third front. Hence, elusive as this area of work has been, it should remain of great interest to all actors. Indeed, for the eco-industry it is important to adopt a holistic approach as both environmental goods and services are intertwined. For example, renewable energy production services will necessarily rely on related environmental goods (e.g. photosensitive semiconductor devices, including photovoltaic cells). In the vast majority of cases, environmental goods help equip renewable energy production, environmental monitoring analysis, management of solid and hazardous waste and recycling

---

64   M. A. J. Teehankee, Trade and Environment Governance at the World Trade Organization Committee on Trade and Environment, Wolters Kluwer: Global Trade Law Series, vol. 53, 2020, p.189.

65   World Trade Organization, *WTO Matrix on Trade-Related Measures Pursuant to Selected Multilateral Environmental Agreements (MEAs)*, https://www.wto.org/english/tratop_e/envir_e/envir_matrix_e.htm, accessed 1 September 2022.

systems, air pollution control, wastewater management and potable water treatment.[66]

But as technology is moving fast, multilateral negotiations or discussions would need to adopt a forwardlooking and flexible approach to facilitating market access for environmental goods. New products may be appearing whilst others my become obsolete. This could also represent an opportunity to expand the coverage to increasingly adopt a 'green GVCs approach' to environmental goods. Such an approach would not only cover final goods, but also intermediate products and components that play a crucial role in the environmental goods' global value chains (GVCs). As explained in Part I, GVCs offer weaker economies and MSMEs a path towards economic development via specialisation. A green GVCs approach would allow many developing countries to participate in and benefit from the chain of production of environmental goods. This approach would also be important to build and maintain resilient green GVCs. For example, solar photovoltaic (PV) energy is an important pillar of energy transition globally. However, the solar PV supply chain may be subject to vulnerabilities and risks at various stages in the manufacturing process – be it to produce polysilicon, ingots, wafers, cells and modules – to the distribution stage. Certain policy actions may help ensure solar PV security of supply, including diversifying raw material supplies and manufacturing, facilitating investment in solar PV manufacturing through financial and tax incentives so as to 'de-risk' the PV investment, as well as fostering innovation to further improve solar PV efficiency and strengthening recycling capabilities.[67]

In recent years, WTO members have showed a renewed interest in addressing trade and the environment in a plurilateral context at

---

66   C. Kuriyama, "A Review of the APEC List of Environmental Goods", *Asia-Pacific Economic Cooperation*, Policy Brief No. 41, 2021, https://www. apec.org/docs/default-source/Publications/2021/10/A-Review-of-the-APEC-List-of-Environmental-Goods/221_PSU_Review-of-APEC-List-of-Environmental-Goods.pdf, accessed 1 September 2022.

67   International Energy Agency, *Special Report on Solar PV Global Supply Chains*, 2022, https://www.iea.org/events/special-report-on-solar-pv-global-supply-chains, accessed 1 September 2022.

the WTO. Four initiatives are worth mentioning; the EU has been an active player in all of them.

1. In 2014, 46 WTO members launched negotiations on an Environmental Goods Agreement (EGA). This followed the conclusion of the 2012 Asia-Pacific Economic Cooperation (APEC) agreement that opened trade via tariff reductions for more than 50 environmental goods, mainly targeting products aimed at air filtering and minimising air pollution.[68] However, the EGA negotiations collapsed in 2016 and have not been revived since.

2. In 2020, a group of WTO members launched a Structured Discussion on Trade and Environmental Sustainability (TESSD).[69] As of May 2023, 74 members are participating in this initiative intended to complement the work of the CTE by intensifying experience sharing, promoting transparency, strengthening coherence, identifying areas for future work on trade and sustainability within the WTO and working on possible actions and deliverables, among others.

3. Another initiative was also launched in 2020 by a group of WTO members, this time constituting an Informal Dialogue on Plastics Pollution and Sustainable Plastics Trade (IDP). As of May 2023, 76 members are participating in this initiative aimed at identifying opportunities for enhanced cooperation regarding WTO rules and mechanisms to contribute to domestic, regional and global efforts to reduce plastics pollution and to support efforts in other relevant fora. It is therefore intended to be part of the broader WTO green agenda.

4. Finally, a group of WTO members has also been active in the context of Fossil Fuel Subsidy Reform (FFSR). To date, as per the statement circulated in December 2021, 45 members have joined this initiative aimed at encouraging the rationalisation and phasing out of inefficient fossil fuel subsidies that incite wasteful consumption, whilst also bearing in mind the needs of

---

68   Asia-Pacific Economic Cooperation, Leaders' Declaration, 2012. *See* Annex C – APEC List of Environmental Goods.

69   WTO document WT/CTE/W/249

developing and least developed members. The overall goal is to increase dialogue, information sharing and gradually build momentum and support.

At a joint event held in December 2021, the three active initiatives (TESSD, IDP and FFSR) each shared their respective ministerial statements. This provided a good opportunity for all plurilaterally-driven environment-related initiatives in the WTO to showcase their work to the world together; such joint events and efforts may help increase the outreach and visibility of these initiatives.

The TESSD Ministerial Statement[70] sets out future work for the initiative in areas such as trade and climate change, circular economy, subsidies as well as capacity building and technical assistance for sustainable trade. Other important areas of work set out relate to trade in environmental goods and services and sustainable supply chains.

The EU should remain a central player in these three initiatives: TESSD, IDP and FFSR. Efforts should be made to work with a view to reach out and progressively integrate more members in the discussions. Also, EU trade-related policies that matter for the environment ought to be explained, discussed and defended within the broader multilateral context, including in the CTE. Indeed, the EU should continue to provide regular updates to members on the ongoing implementation of the European Green Deal and of specific policies such as its Carbon Border Adjustment Mechanism (CBAM), which will both be discussed further in Part IV.

The EU can also take inspiration from other governments who have been, or are still working on agreements specifically on the issue of trade and environmental sustainability. For instance, it is worth considering how to leverage the ongoing work on an "Agreement on Climate Change, Trade and Sustainability", the ACCTS, undertaken by New Zealand, Costa Rica, Fiji, Iceland, Norway and Switzerland. The initiative aims to lower barriers to environmentally friendly goods and services, to address fossil fuel subsidies and to establish guidelines for high-integrity ecolabels. The parties have

---

70   WTO document WT/MIN(21)/6 and subsequent revisions.

stressed their commitment to reach an agreement as swiftly as possible and remain open to welcoming other governments that are ready to meet the future agreement's obligations.

Finally, the reader will learn in Part III that sustainability ranks high in Aid for Trade (A4T) priorities; more than 50% of the financing commitments are climate-related, especially targeting renewable energy infrastructure. A4T can truly add value given the role played by trade in the transfer of technology, skills and know-how – vital ingredients for an inclusive transition. There is a need to continue greening A4T, so that everyone, everywhere can launch their transition process towards a greener economy adapted to countries' respective circumstances.

The crucial role of the EU within the global trade framework

Going forward, the role of the EU will be key to balance, on the one hand, the importance of preserving and strengthening the MTS and, on the other hand, the need to advance in a timely manner on rule-making that matters for 21st century issues. The 'scaled-down' advancement of the open trade regulating agenda – be it through agreements outside the WTO or plurilateral outcomes within the WTO framework – can bring important benefits. Both kinds of agreement can pave the way regarding certain imminent and fundamental issues where not all governments are yet ready to move forward. They can serve as a learning platform both for developing countries (to learn potential best practices in upcoming policy areas) and developed countries (to gain knowledge on the many challenges less advanced economies face when trading internationally). They can establish valuable and forward-looking precedents for action on an international scale, and bolster countries' determination to commit to necessary reforms at the multilateral level.

But an open, transparent, inclusive, equitable, stable global trading system rests on a strong WTO at its heart. There are unparalleled benefits to a well-functioning MTS. It has a core set of rules, applicable to a near-universal membership. It has a strong and credible enforcement mechanism. It has the ability to monitor and surveil governments' trade policies on a transparent and regular basis, which contributes to further disciplining members to the values and principles of the MTS. It is the only forum responsible for global trade where governments cooperate, exchange information and negotiate. It has the ability to address issues that are inherently global, and that require a global response for the global commons (e.g. digitalisation, Covid-19 intellectual property and trade aspects, the depletion of global fish stocks due to harmful subsidies).

Can a system with 1990s rules and practices effectively address 21st century challenges such as harnessing the benefits linked to the digitalisation of the economy? Since 1998, WTO members have consistently agreed not to impose customs duties on electronic transmissions (i.e. the 'moratorium'). This moratorium is currently the only multilateral rule governing global digital trade, which seems largely unfit for today's digital era.

Traditionally, customs duties apply to goods that are physically delivered to customers and, as previously covered, WTO members have listed their tariff commitments in their respective schedules. In the case of the moratorium, however, products that are transmitted electronically are duty-free. Figure 15 provides an example with an e-book compared to its non-digital counterpart, a traditional physical book.

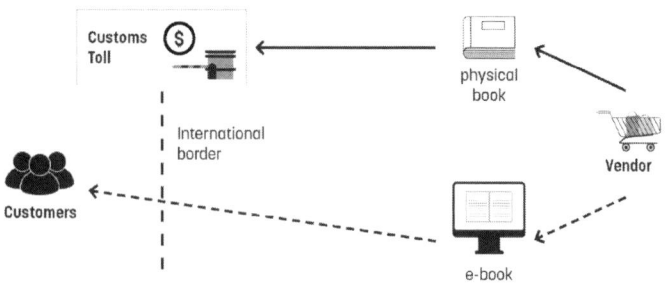

Fig. 15: Application of the WTO moratorium on customs duties on electronic transmissions – example of the e-book.

What was initially considered a temporary moratorium has in fact regularly been extended, often after long negotiations and last-minute trade-offs, generally at WTO Ministerial Conferences. Beyond this, there is an urgent need for the MTS to be relevant in the current digital age. As agreed on the sidelines of the Eleventh Ministerial Conference in Buenos Aires (2017), the EU and a significant subset of other members have thus been advancing on this issue through plurilateral negotiations under the Joint Statement Initiative on e-commerce. One article under negotiation in this potential future agreement relates to the non-imposition of customs duties on electronic transmissions among participants. This is yet another example of how less-than-multilateral fora can be used as a platform to help the global trade system maintain its relevance.

The European Union is a key proponent for WTO reform, to make it fit for purpose in this day and age.[71] The EU believes that the WTO's negotiation pillar – its ability to deliver new rules and further open up trade – should be more effective. New rules should also be on the multilateral agenda, to counter newer and unaddressed forms of unfair competition distortions, such as industrial subsidies and the regulation of state-owned enterprises. The "future of trade" series in Part I also reflects major areas where rules should be further improved, including the rise of services, the digital transformation of the economy and the urgent need to address environment concerns.

Making trade inclusive, fair and equitable for all should also be part of the global trade agenda, and especially in light of the UN SDGs. The WTO has a role to play in helping to achieve gender equality on a global scale. In this context, the EU should continue to pursue a leading role in raising awareness and ensuring that a gender per-

---

71   European Commission, Annex to the Communication from the Commission to the European Parliament, the Council, the European Economic and Social Committee and the Committee of the Regions, Trade Policy Review – An Open, Sustainable and Assertive Trade Policy, 2021, https://trade.ec.europa.eu/doclib/docs/2021/february/tradoc_159439.pdf, accessed 1 September 2022.

spective becomes a conventional part of global trade policymaking.[72] The EU should also be a champion of decent work in every possible forum, by fostering analyses, exchanges of experience and cooperation on how trade can contribute to social development and on how labour protection can incentivise healthy and sustainable growth and development.

Greening trade should be a cross-cutting principle that is considered across the board, throughout WTO work, in regional agreements and plurilateral negotiations. In this light, strengthening the WTO's institutional framework is crucial, as a universal issue like trade and environment can only be fully tackled on a universal scale. As a first step in that direction, the EU should continue its endeavour in plurilateral work on trade and environmental sustainability, fossil fuel subsidies and plastics trade, whilst reaching out to all WTO members to join these discussions. One should bear in mind however that the framework discussed throughout Part II – which needs to be further strengthened and improved to meet modern challenges – is not a guarantee for more, better or sustainable trade. Although it contributes to making greener trade possible on a global scale, this does not automatically transmit change into domestic systems. For that, additional efforts and concrete policies are required in order to make something 'possible' actually happen, and work for all at the same time to ensure long-run social gains. This is what Parts III and IV will focus on.

Trade and labour is another area where there are unresolved tensions in the multilateral arena. The above section on cooperation between the WTO and other organisations stressed that the absence of a clear delineation in the scope of WTO and ILO matters required the EU to continue its efforts to improve working conditions worldwide. Its Generalized System of Preferences is already conditioned to trading partners that uphold relevant labour standards, and the

---

72   Including through initiatives such as the 2017 Buenos Aires Declaration on Trade and Women's Economic Empowerment, and work in the WTO's Informal Working Group on Trade and Gender, which is a "less-than-multilateral" initiative.

EU is a global leader in the domestic implementation of active labour market policies to support workers in Europe. Part IV further expands on the EU's role in this respect.

A priority for the EU – one that the MTS will depend on in order to remain significant and well-equipped – is an institutionally and operationally strengthened WTO. Most importantly, the EU strongly desires a return to a fully functioning two-tier dispute settlement system. Still, with a view to remaining agile in resolving trade concerns, improving work in regular WTO bodies may help facilitate the resolution of conflicts-to-be; thus avoiding escalation to dispute settlement. This also means working towards reinforcing not only the negotiating and dispute settlement functions of the WTO, but also its monitoring activities. In this regard, there is a need to improve transparency and compliance with respect to notification obligations.

The potential of the WTO Secretariat and its Director-General should be fully utilised by WTO members, whilst being respectful of the member-driven nature of the organisation and the overarching objective to facilitate open trade. Let us not forget that, as civil servants of the WTO, Secretariat staff are also employed to uphold to the best of their ability the objectives contained in the Preamble to the Marrakesh Agreement, including raising standards of living, ensuring full employment, inclusive development, protecting and preserving the environment. Overall, the future influence the EU will have on the global trade framework will depend on several – perhaps conflicting – forces. One could argue that the EU economy is, itself, comparable to a 'downsized' global economy, with EU member states reflecting a certain heterogeneity. The EU can come up with tools to address problems it has encountered faster than the MTS could, as it has reached an advanced level of internal openness. It should thus continue to create innovative and efficient answers that can eventually be transposable to MTS challenges.

Part III: making trade happen – mens sana in corpore sano

Making trade possible opens opportunities but does not necessarily guarantee that trade will automatically happen. Additional policy efforts are needed to achieve this goal.

In Satire X, the 2nd century latin author Juvenal refers to the notion of "a sound mind in a sound body" (*mens sana in corpore sano*). There are no self-regulating or self-sustaining trade relations, but in order to prompt and channel trade, Juvenal's philosophy may be applied in this context. To make trade happen, policies need to be intentional. Trade needs to operate within a healthy body of policy adjustments and stimuli, if it is to have a welfare enhancing impact, both locally and globally. Part III of this *Handbook* focuses on several vital pillars for inclusive trade to flourish.

First, trade needs a sound 'brain': There is a far greater potential for policy choices to be sound if they are guided by accessible and pertinent trade knowledge and data. This includes the development of thorough strategies which will help exporters focus on sectors, markets and products in which they have a comparative advantage and make the most of new opportunities. Who and what should they be focusing on?

Second, trade finance and aid for trade are the lifeblood which keep the heart of trade pumping, especially for small companies in the EU and beyond. A healthy trade environment is one where companies, big or small, in developed and developing economies alike, can have timely and adequate access to the resources they need in order to operate in the global market.

Third, supportive infrastructure acts as the backbone of trade. Key quality infrastructure is crucial for creating a trade-conducive environment for all actors, including for MSMEs and developing countries. In this regard, digitalisation should be leveraged to improve infrastructure for logistics and transport, communications, digital payments, as well as streamlined customs.

Fourth, and final, to make trade happen, teeth and muscles are required to effectively enforce trade rules. This means having an arsenal of policy tools to ensure a protective environment for smaller business, innovation, EU values, as well as efficient dispute settlement.

For each of these issues emanate questions, and from these questions there are a series of choices to be made. In this context, how can the EU ensure that its internal policy architecture works to support trade-focused external policy? How can the conditions for a Europe that is trade facilitating and welfare enhancing be created? What legal routes, partners and strategies should be favoured? How can trade policies reflect EU core values? How can these policies remain future-proof, forward-looking, inclusive and promote resilience at the same time?

The framework covered in Part III constitutes a vital step towards making trade happen. But for trade to actually work for all, leaving no-one behind in the process and ensuring long-run social gains, additional efforts will be required. These are discussed in Part IV of the *Handbook*.

Trade needs a sound 'brain': promoting trade intelligence

Intelligence in international trade policy is relevant for governments in terms of what strategies and tools can be used both within an economy and regarding its relations with others. Access to trade and market intelligence is critical for successful economic and business decision-making and to reap the benefits resulting from trade. Particular attention should also be placed on transparency which underpins decision-making.

Harnessing available tools for sound trade and market choices

What are the available tools to assist in making optimal trade and market choices? One way to help optimise such choices is to simplify market research for companies, by integrating trade and business information into a one-stop shop. This is especially relevant for Micro, Small and Medium-sized Enterprises (MSMEs), as this segment of the business community is often confronted with capacity challenges when venturing into cross-border trade. They may lack the skills and resources to generate, acquire or process trade-related information, which clearly places them at a disadvantage and prevents them from exploring trade opportunities.

The EU and other governments all have a strong interest in making trade work for small business; they represent 95% of companies across the globe and account for around two thirds of the world's total employment, in developed and developing countries alike.[1] MSMEs that export tend to experience enhanced productivity, growth and recruitment rates through economies of scale. Increased geographic diversification of export markets is also more likely to lead to better performance for smaller business. The prospect of increased revenue resulting from facilitated exports may also incentivise innovation.

But for all of these opportunities to be seized by MSMEs, and for the challenges they face to be addressed, timely and accurate trade and market intelligence is invaluable. The EU should further promote the following tools and databases that are at the disposal of their business and policymakers. Moreover, these platforms are often available in English, but not everyone in the Union may grasp relevant information due to language barriers. Hence, efforts should be made to facilitate access to key information in the relevant language of the business or policymaker.

There are several international agencies out there that help stimulate trade by providing information, connections and technical advice. The Global Trade Helpdesk[2] is led jointly by the International

---

1   World Trade Organization, *Coordinated global response key to MSMEs' post-pandemic economic recovery — DDG Zhang*, 2021, https://www.wto.org/english/news_e/news21_e/msmes_22oct21_e.htm, accessed 1 September 2022.

2   Global Trade Helpdesk, https://globaltradehelpdesk.org/en, accessed 1 September 2022.

Trade Centre (ITC), the UN Conference on Trade and Development (UNCTAD) and the World Trade Organization (WTO). It allows firms to compare demand for their products across markets, explore market access conditions (tariffs, non-tariff measures and sustainability standards), access details about buyers, navigate procedures to exporting products, and identifying business partners and relevant contacts.

In 2021, WTO's Informal Working Group on MSMEs, one of the several ongoing plurilateral initiatives in the organisation, has launched a Trade4MSMEs online platform[3] in collaboration with the Global Trade Helpdesk, with the aim of facilitating the engagement of smaller companies in the trading system. How so? By providing information not only for companies but also for policymakers and researchers. Various trade guides are available to inform the latter on why trade matters for MSMEs, what are the key issues they face when trying to trade internationally, what are existing data sources and organisations available for MSME trade support.

The World Intellectual Property Organization (WIPO) and the International Chamber of Commerce (ICC) provide business with a WIPO IP Diagnostics tool, which helps firms undertake basic diagnostic of the intellectual property situation of their business.[4] Eventually, this may help them navigate through IP regulation and thus better manage their intangible assets.

Finally, governments should place emphasis on transparency and access as vital ingredients in informed decision-making, both for business and governments. Clear communication with trading partners as well as timely and accurate information create a better decision-making environment in times of crises, both for preparedness and responsiveness. But this largely depends on investments made in transparency instruments during quieter times. The Covid-19 pandemic was a time of regulatory uncertainty for business as new rules were frequently adopted in part to respond to domestic needs

---

3   Trade4MSMEs, https://trade4msmes.org/, accessed 1 September 2022.

4   World Intellectual Property Organization, *WIPO IP Diagnostics*, https://www.wipo.int/ipdiagnostics/en/index.html, accessed 1 September 2022.

to combat the virus and its effects. It also created new obstacles for companies which had to meet new requirements to access foreign markets or import from them. This was clearly depicted in the resilience challenges section of this *Handbook*, especially regarding bottlenecks for vaccine production inputs, where more transparency and communication was needed. Another area where transparency will be ever-more important in the coming years is environment, social and governance (ESG) standards. The EU is already a leader in the adoption of ESG standards, but it is equally important to ensure that suppliers and MSMEs in other developing countries are able to understand and meet such standards and EU consumers' expectations. Therefore, there is great merit in investing in means to further standardise, compile, monitor and clearly communicate relevant information at various levels (national, regional and global). This may also reinforce the efficiency of, and in turn confidence in, the rules-based trading system.

Strategising trade and investments: which sectors and partners for NextGen EU?

Once the data and transparency tools are in place, one is better equipped to strategise an optimal course of action. Indeed, intelligence also requires a debate on which sectors and partners should be prioritised going forward. At the outset, it is important to have an idea of where the EU stands on the trade and investment scale. In the trade arena, Europe is the largest exporter of manufactured goods and services. It is also the biggest export market for more than 80 countries (four times more than the US, as a matter of comparison).[5] For trade in goods, the EU's top ten trading partners – excluding intra-EU trade – are China (16.2% of total EU trade in goods); the US (14.7%); the UK (10%); Switzerland (6.5%); Russia (5%), although the war in Ukraine will certainly have an impact; Turkey (3.7%); Norway (3.1%); Japan (2.9%); South Korea (2.5%); and India (2.1%). As

---

5   European Commission, *EU position in World Trade*, https://policy.trade.
ec.europa.eu/eu-trade-relationships-country-and-region/eu-position-
world-trade_en, accessed 1 September 2022.

regards trade in services, the US is the EU's main trading partner (24.9% of all EU trade in services), followed by the UK (19.3%); Switzerland (9.1%); China (4.4%) and Singapore (2.8%).[6] The EU is also ranked as the global leader for both inbound and outbound foreign direct investments, as per the illustration below (Figure 16).

Country	Inward stock	Outward stock
EU	34.2%	45.4%
US	30%	28.4%
China	6.5%	8.5%
Canada	3.5%	5.8%
Japan	0.9%	7.3%

Source: European Parliament DG EXPO calculations based on European Commission figures

Fig. 16: Share of global foreign direct investment (FDI) in 2018 (%).[7]

Several major investment and trade strategies have been announced in recent years. Although they are inherently linked to the infrastructure-related efforts discussed in the following section, the intention here is to illustrate the strategic aspect of these initiatives, as an inherent element of trade intelligence. Echoing Part I, trade, integration and investment are processes which may also be used as foreign policy tools. Three main players stand out in this global investment and trade strategy arena: China, the United States and Europe. Are their respective initiatives complementary or in competition? Most likely, a bit of both. There is an enormous demand in low- and middle-income countries across the world for investments which foster growth and improve living standards locally. Such initiatives are welcomed by them, oftentimes regardless of their source. Figure 17 (pp. 126-127) contains a non-exhaustive set of initiatives launched by the three major players.

---

6   European Commission, *EU 27 Trade in Goods and Services by Partner* (2021), Eurostat, https://trade.ec.europa.eu/doclib/docs/2006/september/tradoc_122530.pdf, accessed 1 September 2022.

7   M. Damen, "The European Union and its trade partners", *European Parliament*, Fact Sheets on the European Union, 2021, https://www.europarl.europa.eu/factsheets/en/sheet/160/the-european-union-and-its-trade-partners, accessed 1 September 2022.

There are ways for NextGen EU to remain a global investment leader even in the current complex and highly competitive environment, whilst reinforcing its strategic autonomy objectives. Four areas are essential:

1. Supporting the African Continental Free Trade Area (AfCFTA) established in 2018 to promote intra-African trade amongst its more than 50 signatories. There are important challenges and opportunities linked to the operationalisation of intra-African trade relations, and consequently there are many prospects for strengthening EU-Africa cooperation in the area of Aid for Trade such as private sector development, trade facilitation, potential EU investment commitments, adjustment policies, etc. Who knows, such efforts may eventually even lay the foundation for a future 'intercontinental FTA'.

2. What markets will drive tomorrow's economy? Part I already hinted at essential (sometimes untapped) sectors for forward-looking EU trade and investment policies: the booming services sector, the quest for resilient supply chains, the environment imperative and the steady rise of trade in environmental goods and services, digitalisation and the need to address the existing digital divide, the need for inclusive approaches to trade and investment, etc. More generally, there are three main themes that could be seen as sources of positive market disruptors in the coming years.[8] First, topics relating to safeguarding planetary boundaries (e.g. electric vehicles, hydrogen, recycling, water, reforestation and greenhouse gas allowances). Second, means to empower and protect people (e.g. data, digital issues, skills capital, medicine and care). And third, advancing knowledge (research, space, satellites, artificial intelligence, genetics, etc.).

3. Tomorrow's international relations and economic flows will be shaped by trade and investment policy choices made today. Europe has a role to play in promoting development through these initiatives, to generate sustainable growth and create jobs

---

8   World Economic Forum, *Markets of Tomorrow: Pathways to a New Economy*, Insight Report, 2020, p.6.

China's Belt and Road Initiative (BRI)

The BRI (or 'New Silk Road') is China's ambitious project for infrastructure development and supply chain connectivity, reflected in a land-based belt and a maritime route.It was launched in **2013** with an investment target of **over USD 1 trillion by 2027.**

It is driven by China's determination to enhance its economic and political influence over the next decades, notably by grooming foreign markets for Chinese exports. Since 2013, the focus has mainly been on laying the foundation for the BRI through air and maritime transport links as well as telecom infrastructure, energy production, and is increasingly moving towards services (investments in ICT, education, tourism infrastructure).

All EU member states have joined the China-led Asian Infrastructure Investment Bank (AAIB), which is designed to lend financial support to BRI-related projects. Several initiatives supported by the AIIB are co-financed by the EIB and the EBRD.[a]

a   N. Casarini, "Defend, Engage, Maximise: A Progressive Agenda for EU-China Relations", Foundation for European Progressive Studies, FEPS Policy Paper, 2019, p.13.

b   Organisation for Economic Cooperation and Development, The Blue Dot Network: A Proposal for a Global Certification Framework for Quality Infrastructure, 2022, https://www.oecd.org/daf/blue-dot-network-proposal-certification.pdf, accessed 1 September 2022.

c   White House, Fact Sheet: President Biden and G7 Leaders Launch Build Back Better World (B3W) Partnership, https://www.whitehouse.gov/briefing-room/statements-releases/2021/06/12/fact-sheet-president-biden-and-g7-leaders-launch-build-back-better-world-b3w-partnership/, accessed 1 September 2022.

d   European Commission, EU Gateway | Business Avenues supports European companies in Asia, https://fpi.ec.europa.eu/stories/eu-gateway-business-avenues-supports-european-companies-asia_en#:~:text=The%20Programme%20helped%20thousands%20of,%2C%20logistics%2C%20and%20customised%20services, accessed 1 September 2022. The initiative helped leverage trade connections with Asian markets, and led to the subsequent conclusion of several bilateral trade agreements (e.g. EU-South Korea Trade Agreement in 2011, EU EU-Japan Economic Partnership Agreement (EPA) in 2019, EU-Singapore FTA in 2019, EU-Vietnam FTA in 2020...).

e   Team Europe consists of the EU institutions, including the European Investment Bank (EIB), member states and their implementing organisations and development financing institutions and the European Bank for Reconstruction and Development (EBRD).

US driven strategies	EU driven strategies
The 'Blue Dot Network' In 2019, the **US**, alongside **Japan and Australia**, announced their own global infrastructure initiative: the **Blue Dot Network**. At their request, the OECD committed to supporting this initiative in 2021. In 2022, the OECD even proposed a prototype to operationalise infrastructure projects under the Blue Dot Network initiative.[b] Its overall objective is to reduce the infrastructure gap mostly through private sector investments, whilst also aiming to improve domestic policies and promoting transparent, sustainable and responsible investment. Build Back a Better World (B3W) The **B3W**[c] initiative was proposed by the US and agreed at a **Group of Seven** (G7) summit held in June **2021**. The B3W builds off the progress and the principles of the Blue Dot Network.	The EU Gateway with Asia Through the **EU Gateway Programme**, the Union aimed to deepen economic interaction and cooperation between Europe and Japan. After its first achievements, the Programme expanded into other partners in Asia, including South Korea, Singapore, Indonesia, Malaysia, Thailand, Vietnam, the Philippines, and China. It supported European companies in developing and consolidating their businesses in the region. Since 2016, the initiative was rebranded "EU Gateway | Business Avenues".[d] The EU Global Gateway The EU's Global Gateway strategy was launched to foster and strengthen connections across the world on various issues (digital, energy, transport, health, research, education). Team Europe[e] aims to mobilise up to **EUR 300 billion of investments between 2021 and 2027**. The Global Gateway places emphasis on the EU's interests and values: rule of law, human rights and international norms and standards. It is about (i) smart, clean and secure investments in quality infrastructure, and (ii) connecting goods, people and services around the world in a sustainable way.

Joint Efforts: The Partnership for Global Infrastructure and Investment (PGII)

At the **June 2022 G7 summit**, G7 member countries jointly announced the launch of the PGII or ('PGII Bank') initiative. The EU Global Gateway is roofed by the PGII which aims to raise a total of **USD 600 billion by 2027** via public and private financing, with a focus on delivering climate and energy security, digital connectivity, health security, gender equality and equity, and hard infrastructure (e.g. for low-carbon transportation).

Fig. 17: China, the US and the EU: trade and investment strategies.

within the EU and outside by increasing investment opportunities. Over and above that, the EU – as highlighted by the trade and investment numbers above – has the weight to shape a global future based on fair rules. NextGen EU initiatives may also be instrumental in promoting openness, inclusiveness, the rule of law, democracy, and other values that are dear to Europeans.

4. Domestically, it is of strategic interest for the EU to make full use of public-private partnership (PPP) instruments, in particular given its ambitious climate and energy goals. For instance, via joint undertakings (JUs)[9] the Union can pool European resources to address major challenges and support EU competitiveness to deliver high-quality jobs to its citizens.

The lifeblood of trade: inclusive trade finance and Aid for Trade

Inclusive access to trade finance

Trade finance corresponds to the available financial tools and products that are used by businesses to facilitate their participation in international trade and to make transactions possible and easier, both for importers and exporters. This is a common practice which is not necessarily correlated to a business' lack of funds or liquidity. Indeed, up to 80% of trade is financed by credit or credit insurance, often of a short-term nature,[10] which may be used to protect business against

---

9   Article 187 of the Treaty on the Functioning of the European Union (TFEU) specifies that the EU may set up joint undertakings (JUs) or any other structure necessary for the efficient execution of EU research, technological development and demonstration programmes. For instance, the Clean Sky 2 joint undertaking develops innovative technologies to reduce aircraft CO2 emissions and noise levels by 2050, with the participation of MSMEs, research centres, universities and industry actors (over 600 entities in 24 countries). *See* Clean Aviation, *Clean Sky 2*, available at: https://www.cleansky.eu/, accessed 1 September 2022.

10   International Finance Corporation and World Trade Organization, Trade Finance and the Compliance Challenge: A Showcase of International Cooperation, 2019, p.7.

inherent risks linked to international trade (e.g. political instability, currency fluctuations, a party's creditworthiness). Dependence of cross-border trade on short-term financing may also be explained by the fact that exporters wish to receive payment upon shipment, whilst importers expect to pay when the goods are received. Trade finance fills this gap and covers the risk of non-payment, although it remains minimal (on average 0.2% globally).[11]

Adequate provision of trade finance is key for businesses who seek to benefit from trade opportunities, including those resulting from shifting patterns of production brought about by factors such as trade tensions and geopolitical uncertainties, growing demand for certain products, the digitalisation of the economy, and the effects of Covid-19, among others. However, the availability of trade finance is unequal across regions and business actors.

A gap exists within EU member states, as exporting MSMEs have shown that they were more prone to trade finance gaps, including in periods of financial crisis.[12] There is also a gap amongst EU member states, with some requiring increased support. This was the idea behind the European Investment Bank's Trade Finance Facility initiative in order to support the trade and export finance services provided by participating Greek banks to local companies across the country. In early 2022, a further expansion of this initiative launched in 2013 was announced, with a partnership now totaling well above EUR 1 billion for trade finance since its inception.[13] Greece is currently the only country in Europe benefitting from this initiative, but

11   M. Auboin and V. Gonzalez Behar, "Why exporters need to mind the trade finance gap", *World Economic Forum*, 2020, https://www.weforum. org/agenda/2020/02/exporters-mind-trade-finance-gap/, accessed 1 September 2022.

12   World Trade Organization, Trade finance and SMEs: Bridging the Gaps in Provision, 2016, p.17.

13   European Investment Bank, Greece: EIB and Citi to release EUR 350 million to Greek export and import companies through Trade Finance Facilitation initiative, 2022, https://www.eib.org/en/press/all/2022-084-eib-and-citi-to-release-eur-350-million-to-greek-export-and-import-companies-through-trade-finance-facilitation-initiative, accessed 1 September 2022.

one could easily envision that other EU member states would also welcome similar support, especially in Central and Eastern Europe, where numerous international banks have been shrinking their networks of correspondent banking relationships.[14]

Zooming into trade finance from a progressive viewpoint requires a gender lens. This is pertinent to highlight existing trends and challenges pertaining to trade and gender. A 2019 ITC business survey provides that women-led businesses benefit much less from funding by commercial banks (36%) than men-led businesses do (54%), as illustrated in Figure 18. Instead, they seem much more reliant on EU funding to expand their export/import operations.

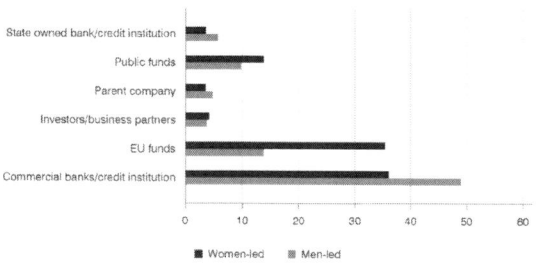

Source: ITC business survey, 2019.

Fig. 18: Sources of funding, by gender in the EU, ITC business survey (2019).[15]

A 2020 discussion paper by the European Commission also collected some striking data from diverse sources regarding the gender gap for trade finance in the EU.[16] For example, only 16% of venture capital firms invest in Dutch mixed- and female-founded start-ups. Such startups receive only 3.5% of total start-up funding. In France,

14   M. Auboin and V. Gonzalez Behar, "Why exporters need to mind the trade finance gap", *World Economic Forum*, 2020, https://www.weforum.org/agenda/2020/02/exporters-mind-trade-finance-gap/, accessed 1 September 2022.

15   International Trade Centre, From Europe to the World: Understanding Challenges for European Businesswomen, 2019, p.30.

16   A. Skonieczna and L. Castellano, "Gender Smart Financing, Investing In and With Women: Opportunities for Europe", *European Commission*, Discussion Paper 129, 2020, p.5.

women-founded start-ups account for only 5% of all funded start-ups; they have 30% less chance of being financed by investors than men-founded start-ups.

Hence, there is room for European commercial banks and venture capitalists to step up their participation and engagement in the financing of companies owned by women, at the same time reducing some of the financial weight carried by the EU. There is also an increased need to build confidence for women seeking external financing, as they tend to be less likely than men to apply for such business loans; perhaps due to fear of rejection and previous bad experiences?[17]

Whilst trade opportunities are increasing in many developing and least-developed countries, they remain the most affected by the trade finance gap. In this regard, several elements are worth mentioning.

Developing and reforming the local financial sector may been seen as a way forward. Indeed, developing economies would typically benefit from the increased presence of global banks and other financial actors who would transfer pertinent knowledge and capital. But since the 2008 global financial crisis, banks have been reluctant to invest in many developing counties, thus harming the prospects for the supply of trade finance in the very locations where the potential for trade, growth and development is the greatest – particularly in Asia and Africa.[18] Banks had already been downsizing their trade finance activities after the financial crises of the 1990s in Asia and Latin America, i.e. the 'de-risking' phenomenon, which was even more prevalent post-2008. All in all, in 2016 the unmet demand for trade finance was at USD 120 and 700 billion in Africa and developing Asia, respectively.[19]

Bank-intermediated trade finance is also a highly concentrated sector. In that regard, MSMEs face the greatest stumbling blocks in affordable and accessible financing. Despite extremely low default

---

17   *Ibid.*, p.7.
18   World Trade Organization, Trade finance and SMEs: Bridging the Gaps in Provision, 2016, p.9.
19   *Ibid.*, p.6.

rates on MSME loans, lenders prefer to finance long-standing and bigger customers. Around three-quarters of all rejected trade finance requests are that of MSMEs, and they account for less than 15% of banks' total trade finance portfolio; similar numbers can be found in Asia too.[20]

An additional element to factor in is that operating in developing countries has often been considered as a higher regulatory risk for business. This is particularly true since the adoption of new standards: know your customer (KYC), anti-money-laundering (AML) and countering the financing of terrorism (CFT). Such regulations have become more rigorous across the financial industry and are driving their business decisions. Such processes allow financial institutions to review and confirm the identity of their clients' business partners, ensuring that those entities or individuals are not involved in illegal activity (e.g. money laundering, terrorist financing or corruption). However, such measures aimed at preventing financing crime may unintentionally undermine MSME financing, especially in developing countries.

Bridging existing trade finance gaps, would help unravel the yet untapped potential of numerous traders, big or small, on both a local and on a global scale. In this light, there is a growing need to support existing capacity building and training efforts that have been undertaken by various international and regional financial institutions (e.g. the International Finance Corporation, the EBRD, the World Bank, the IMF, regional development banks). Such efforts could further focus on tailored, country- or region-specific training, including on compliance with KYC, AML and CFT standards, enabling interactions between businesses (big or small), private financial institutions and regulators. This would also allow for a tailored assessment of risks, which may vary depending on the region (e.g. in the Caribbean Island states, the focus may be more on mitigating risks linked to offshore banking activities).

---

20   International Finance Corporation and World Trade Organization, *Trade Finance and the Compliance Challenge: A Showcase of International Cooperation*, 2019, p.7 and p.15.

Enhancing Aid for Trade for development

Developing countries, and especially the LDCs, often require technical and financial assistance to be able to take advantage of the opportunities that trade might bring about. It is with this in mind that the Aid for Trade (A4T) initiative was launched in 2005 at the Sixth WTO Ministerial Conference.[21] A4T is part of the Official Development Assistance (ODA), which is the key measure – consisting of grants and 'soft loans' – used in practically all aid targets and assessments of aid performance. In fact, the ODA was adopted in the 1960s, by the OECD's Development Assistance Committee (DAC), as the 'gold standard' of foreign aid.

In particular, A4T seeks to mobilise resources – often in the form of grants, loans, technical assistance and training – to address the trade-related constraints identified by receiving governments. It also encourages them and donors to recognise the role that trade can play in development. Such initiatives may (i) enable countries to use trade more effectively to promote growth, development and poverty reduction, and to better integrate the multilateral trading system; (ii) help build their supply-side capacity and trade-related infrastructure in order to facilitate their access to markets and export activities; and (iii) help them adjust to trade reform and openness domestically, by adapting their trade policy and regulations.

The role of the Enhanced Integrated Framework (EIF) in increasing A4T must also be mentioned. The EIF is the only multilateral partnership specifically dedicated to assisting LDCs in using trade as an engine for growth, sustainable development and poverty reduction. It assists LDCs in mainstreaming trade into their national development strategies and provides them with a platform to lever more A4T resources. Donors can sign up to the EIF and use it as a vehicle to increase their A4T support to LDCs. As of July 2022, the

---

21 Ministerial Declaration of the Sixth Session of the Ministerial Conference of the World Trade Organization, "Hong Kong Ministerial Declaration", WTO document WT/MIN(05)/DEC, 2005, Paragraph 57.

EIF programme is supported by 24 country donors through contributions to its Trust Fund.[22]

The WTO, the OECD, the World Bank, the IMF, the ITC, regional development banks, UN agencies, donors – at the international and national level – as well as relevant ministries (trade, agriculture, development and finance) may all choose to play an active role in such initiatives. Ultimately, given the demand-driven nature of A4T, the implementation and operationalisation of A4T programmes are in the hands of developing countries and their development partners. In this context, interactions and coordination with development partners are key to identify and monitor the implementation of A4T projects and to hold stakeholders accountable for policy implementation.

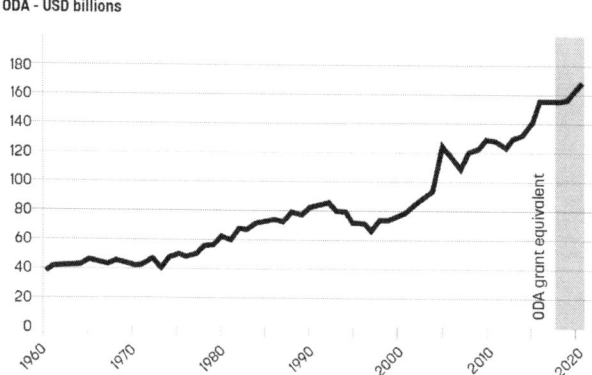

Fig. 19: Total ODA in USD billions from all DAC countries (1960-2021).[23]

22   Enhanced Integrated Framework, *Funding Partners*, available at: https://enhancedif.org/donors, accessed 1 September 2022.

23   Organisation for Economic Cooperation and Development, *Official Development Assistance* (ODA), available at: https://www.oecd.org/dac/financing-sustainable-development/development-finance-standards/official-development-assistance.htm, accessed 1 September 2022. ODA on flows and grant equivalent measures by members of OECD Development Assistance Committee. Constant 2020 USD. Preliminary data for 2021.

In 2021, ODA from official funders rose to USD 178.9 billion, an all-time high, as illustrated in Figure 19. In 2021, the EU and its member states remained the world's leading provider of ODA, followed by the US. In a resilience-driven context, A4T initiatives are essential to help the EU's partners throughout the globe to recover from shocks like Covid-19 and to grow, particularly by helping MSMEs and local authorities implement trade agreements. Moreover, in light of modern imperatives, this support may help develop more inclusive, rule of law oriented and climate conscious economic programmes for the benefit of all and promote the EU's values-based trade agenda.

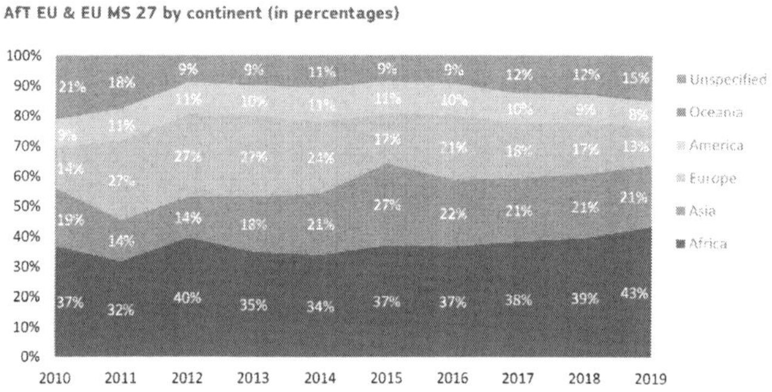

AfT EU & EU MS 27 by continent (in percentages)

Fig. 20: EU & 27 EU member states' Aid for Trade action by geographical coverage (%).[24]

In the past decade, as illustrated above (see Figure 20), EU A4T action generally targeted Africa (around 43% in 2019), followed by Asia, Europe (EU neighborhood and accession countries) and America. This remains coherent with the strong interest the EU has in supporting the African Continental Free Trade Area to operationalise intra-African trade relations and enlarge the prospects for a future EU-Africa cooperation.

---

24   European Commission, *EU Aid for Trade: Progress Report 2021*, 2021, p.123.

A4T must also be seen with a progressive lens. Well-targeted A4T may support women's economic empowerment and gender equality. Some A4T programmes help increase access to finance for women-led businesses, enabling them to export and supporting sectors that were hard hit during the pandemic. Others are also relevant to train women in how to better leverage digital tools for their business. In 2020, more than 40% of A4T spending commitments had a gender focus. Sustainability also ranks high in A4T priorities, as more than half of the financing commitments were climate-related, especially targeting renewable energy infrastructure.

Continuous dialogue amongst stakeholders is paramount to continue to identify and rectify capacity constraints and gaps. In addition, some stakeholders may not be aware of relevant opportunities due to a lack of access to information. The EU and lead trade agencies should continue to identify and reach out to those groups and help build their capacity where appropriate to engage and build trust in the process. Concrete political gains may derive from the EU remaining a leader in supporting A4T, not least a chance to promote EU values and to influence the course of policies implemented abroad, including through greater economic empowerment for women, inclusive economic development and enhanced ESG standards. However, an institution cannot tackle today's complex challenges alone. The EU, other governments, international institutions, the private sector, chambers of commerce, sectoral associations and more generally civil society all have a role to play. Their collective ability and will to work in a cohesive, solution-oriented manner will condition whether A4T programmes can be successful in making trade happen.

The backbone of trade: supportive and conducive infrastructure

The section on trade intelligence shed light on the importance of having coherent and forward-looking trade strategies towards other countries. But domestic policy coherence is also crucial to successfully follow through on these strategies and objectives, and to enable open and regulated trade to flourish for the broader benefits of society. Coherence here refers to situations in which domestic policies and institutions are acting jointly to create a conducive framework for open trade. The absence or inadequacy of policies on may risk undermining the efforts made to reach an open, efficient and inclusive trading environment. In this section, the *Handbook* identifies several broad infrastructure policy areas, particularly those intrinsically linked to trade performance (transport, telecoms, digital, financial, and more generally business infrastructure and related services). In this regard, an emphasis should be placed on leveraging digitalisation with the establishment and maintenance of appropriate tech infrastructure.

But before diving into specifics, however, a side note on industrial entrepreneurship policies is required, given their cross-cutting relevance.

Industrial entrepreneurship policies

Traditional, 'old school' industrial policies generally targeted specific industries (e.g. coal or steel) with the aim of providing the required supporting investments and infrastructure. In post-World War II Europe, such measures contributed to the reconstruction of the old continent and its economy. Today's highly interconnected technology-driven global business environment requires new, more holistic approaches to achieve a thriving economy.

In fact, as the economy evolved, so has the term 'industry' in common parlance. Initially, one could be quite certain that the term was associated with production and manufacturing activities, craft and manual labour.[25] As described in Part I, however, the 'servicification' of trade requires the recognition that such industries both depend on and create services, as exemplified in the section on global value chains (GVCs). The term 'industry' has now become significantly broader, to a point that services also fall under its ambit (e.g. the 'banking industry'). Industrial policies should therefore be revamped to reflect these industrial (r)evolutions.

For the purpose of this *Handbook*, what some authors refer to as 'new industrial policies' will be understood as 'industrial entrepreneurship policies' (IEPs). This aims to better showcase the fact that a conducive, facilitating policy and infrastructure environment is required for entrepreneurs to be increasingly willing to bear the risks (and thus potentially enjoy the rewards) of seizing new business opportunities. IEPs can be considered as a 'package' of interactive strategies and measures aimed at fostering innovation, incentivising business and job creation and, in that regard, identifying what elements might inhibit open trade from realising its full potential, including enhanced welfare.

IEPs must promote and support the synergies between production and associated services, whether the latter are to be outsourced or whether these services are to be provided by the same entity. Additionally, IEPs require a regulatory framework that reduces red tape, guarantees contractual performance and strengthens legal security.

This will ensure a smooth business environment for traders to operate in, and especially to foster R&D and innovation by providing ideal conditions for the development of new projects. Indeed, R&D expenditure is higher in countries with a more favourable environment for entrepreneurs.

Competition policy is also of vital importance. The EU must leverage the size and integration of its single market and its global reach to forge global high-quality standards in alignment with Europe's values, and strengthen its strategic autonomy objective and industrial competitiveness. European industry has set off on a path

---

25   Oxford English Dictionary, *Industry*, https://www.oed.com/view/Entry/94859?redirectedFrom=industry#eid, accessed 1 September 2022.

of transition towards more sustainability and digitalisation. These objectives have to be upheld in a constantly evolving and uncertain world: rising trade and geopolitical tensions, increased protectionist sentiment, market distortions, continuous innovation and a challenged rules-based system. In this context, being competitive holds true both within the EU and vis à vis foreign competitors. IEPs need to provide the necessary conditions for entrepreneurs to turn their ideas into actions, and their actions into material benefits for society. The EU's competition rules should allow for the necessary public and private investments to be made, while at the same time ensuring a competition landscape, including by addressing undesirable business practices (e.g. cartels[26] and price fixing[27]).

Ensuring that smart EU intellectual property policies (on brands, designs, source code and algorithms, patents, etc.) are in place will also help uphold and strengthen European tech sovereignty and innovation, allowing for job-led growth and increased competitiveness.

As touched upon in Part IV, skills policies for training people in view of today's and tomorrow's professions are also closely linked to IEPs, to promoting innovation and maintaining a competitive edge. The EU and its member states should continue to seek to improve the training of their workforce, to invest in higher education and encourage synergies between business (people with specialised knowledge) and academia.

Key infrastructure for a trade-conducive environment

This section highlights several infrastructure areas which are central to enable entrepreneurs to do business, and for governments to regulate trade. First, it is possible to reduce the costs relating to logis-

---

26   Article 101 of the Treaty on the Functioning of the European Union prohibits cartels and other agreements that may disrupt open competition in the European Economic Area's internal market. A cartel in a competition setting is group of independent companies which agree to fix prices, to limit their production or to share markets or customers between them.

27   Price fixing is one component of cartels, it is an anticompetitive agreement between competitors to fix prices.

tics and transport, and to improve existing infrastructure. Second, in the context of telecom infrastructure and services, there should be increased focus on inclusiveness by bridging the digital divide as well as on resilience in the face of cybersecurity threats. Third, having the required infrastructure in place to tap into the benefits of digital payments systems is paramount for inclusive and affordable access to financial services. Fourth, members should seek to have well-oiled customs infrastructure and processes, and a fuller implementation of trade facilitation standards. A common, overarching theme throughout this section is the importance for governments and businesses to leverage digital tools to improve each of these infrastructure areas.

Logistics and transport

Different transport costs across countries may be a source of absolute and comparative advantage, including between different modes of transport. Thus, transport costs have a direct effect on the price, volume and composition of trade. For example, a country with relatively lower air freight costs – which are often at least ten times higher than sea transport[28] – may have a comparative advantage in time-sensitive goods (e.g. perishable seafood or agricultural products, fashion clothing, electronics, pharmaceuticals, emergency shipments such as medical equipment during the Covid-19 pandemic).

Tariffs are traditionally placed at the centre of trade negotiations. However, higher transport costs also impede the realisation of gains from trade openness. Typically, economists tend to say that trade is oftentimes more affected by the cost of transport which generally outweighs that of tariffs.[29] The Covid-19 pandemic has significantly

---

28 World Bank, Air Freight: A Market Study with Implications for Land-locked Countries, Transport Papers TP-26, 2009.

29 World Bank, Global Economic Prospects and the Developing Countries 2002: Making Trade Work for the Poor, 2001.

disrupted global production and distribution networks, leading to shipment delays and rising shipping costs. This, in turn, fuels the inflationary landscape domestically.[30]

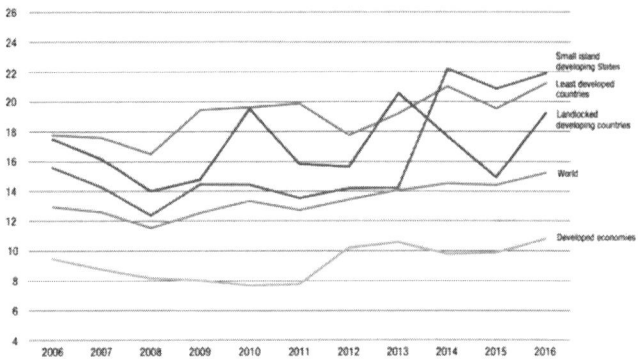

Fig. 21: Transport and insurance costs of international trade across all transport modes and commodities. Percentage share of value of imports, 2006–2016.[31]

As such, reliable, resilient, efficient and cheaper transport infrastructure and services are critical to trade and development. Transport costs may differ depending on the level of development of a country, the availability and quality of transport-related infrastructure and connectivity between transport networks, its geography (scale, distance and location) and the commodities it imports/exports, among others. In particular, as shown in Figure 21, these costs are often more difficult to bear for small island developing states, landlocked developing countries (LLDCs) and LDCs who, on average, have to spend more on international goods transport and its insurance.

30   Y. Carrière-Swallow, P. Deb, D. Furceri, D. Jiménez and J. D. Ostry, "Shipping Costs and Inflation", *International Monetary Fund*, Working Paper WP/22/61, 2022.

31   United Nations Conference on Trade and Development, *Why and how to measure international transport costs*, Transport and Trade Facilitation Newsletter N°89, First Quarter 2021, 2020, https://unctad.org/news/why-and-how-measure-international-transport-costs, accessed 1 September 2022.

There are other ways through which digital infrastructure can help across the board reduce the costs associated with transport and logistics. Shipment logistics may be improved by vehicle telematics, e.g. GPS systems, onboard vehicle diagnostics, 'black box' technologies to record and transmit vehicle data. This can be used in real time to inform on speed, location, maintenance and repair requirements. Such tools are useful to improve the crew's safety and may also improve transport efficiency and performance, thus reducing costs.[32] Finally, the quest for greater transport and logistics efficiency should be seen in light of the environment imperative and greenhouse gas (GHG) reduction targets, an issue covered more extensively in Part IV.

Information and communications technology

Information and communications technology (ICT) infrastructure refers to the equipment (hardware), software, and related services required to operate systems and networks for communications services. It also aims to support the Internet of Things, i.e. the connection of devices within everyday objects via the internet, enabling them to share data.[33] In turn, such infrastructure also supports both offline and digital trade, digital content and applications.

Part I stressed that trade is affected by distributional inequality, including due to the digital divide, which remains a major concern to developing and least developed countries. ICT infrastructure incapacity, lack of tech knowhow, knowledge, and connectivity hinder

---

32   World Trade Organization, World Trade Report 2018: The Future of World Trade: How Digital Technologies are Transforming Global Commerce, 2018, p.66.

33   Oxford Learner's Dictionaries, *internet of things*, https://www.oxford-learnersdictionaries.com/definition/english/internet-of-things, accessed 1 September 2022.

their fuller participation in international trade. In fact, they lag behind in all ICT indicators of development – as illustrated in Figure 22 below – especially in access to broadband internet and mobile access. As a result, traders and consumers in these countries less likely to use the internet for business.

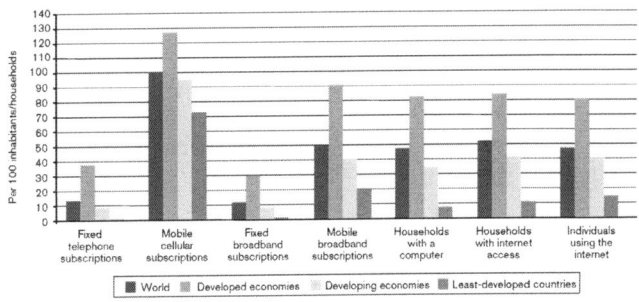

Sources: UNCTAD (2017b), based on ITU data.

Fig. 22: Estimated penetration of ICTs by level of development, 2016.[34]

For example, there is a potential to further connect the EU and Africa. There is a strong incentive to define the contours of future initiatives to build African nations' capacity in the ICT area, in consultation with both European and local authorities, businesses and consumer agencies. The African Union and the European Union have jointly launched the EU-AU Digital Economy Task Force in 2018,[35] with the aim to identify and suggest concrete policy recommendations and actions to address existing barriers and to increase cooperation in the digital field. Covid-19 has heightened the urgency for investments in secure and affordable digital infrastructure in Af-

---

34   World Trade Organization, World Trade Report 2018: The Future of World Trade: How Digital Technologies are Transforming Global Commerce, 2018.

35   African Union, *African Union and European Union step up digital cooperation for Sustainable Development in Africa following EU-AU Summit*, 2022, https://au.int/en/pressreleases/20220323/african-union-and-european-union-step-digital-cooperation-sustainable, accessed 1 September 2022.

rica to build on its innovation and entrepreneurship potential. EU funding and delivery of technical assistance on improving access to infrastructure networks in the field of ICT is also essential in that respect. This is the idea behind the 2019-22 'Technical Assistance to the African Union – Infrastructure Support Mechanism'.[36]

Another very important aspect to consider are the trade-related characteristics of cybersecurity threats. Information technology and related services often rely on a complex and interconnected cyber supply chain ecosystem to operate. This cyber supply chain is often composed of multiple levels of outsourcing, various entities, technologies and practices which interact to design, produce, distribute, maintain and manage ICT products. And global trade networks are vulnerable to attacks particularly along this cyber supply chain. Their inability to anticipate and effectively respond to cybersecurity threats may undermine consumer and business trust when engaging in digital trade. The 2019 EU Cybersecurity Act[37] introduced an EU cybersecurity certification framework for ICT products, services and processes. Such certification schemes may enhance trust on an EU-wide scale. However, digital trade and thus cyber-risks know no borders. Protecting confidence in a digitally connected world should therefore necessarily involve international and multi-stakeholder collaboration, to work towards a common global approach.

Moreover, in some cases, governments may determine that the best policy response to this vulnerability is to prevent certain companies or governments from participating in the supply of key technologies. But collaboration is essential to prevent governments from adopting disguised trade-restrictive approaches in the context of cybersecurity, using it as a 'catch-all' exception to justify the protection

---

36   Infrastructure Support Mechanism (ISM) Africa, *About us*, https://www.ism-africa.eu/about-us/, accessed 1 September 2022.

37   Regulation (EU) 2019/881 of the European Parliament and of the Council of 17 April 2019 on ENISA (the European Union Agency for Cybersecurity) and on information and communications technology cybersecurity certification and repealing Regulation (EU) No 526/2013 (Cybersecurity Act).

of domestic industry from competitors, potentially violating obligations under the WTO and other trade agreements.[38]

Digital payments and other financial infrastructure and services
The distance to the nearest financial institution, the lack of relevant documentation or simply the lack of money are some of the main reasons why 1.4 billion adults are still 'unbanked'. Enabling ICT infrastructure is part of the solution. But going further, leveraging digital payments systems is paramount in order to democratise the use of financial services, to make them more accessible and inclusive.

Wages, sale in agricultural goods and even government transfers are received in cash for many hundreds of millions of people around the globe. In addition, they have no safe way to save or invest their money, and they oftentimes rely on informal lenders or their personal network for credit.

By promoting the digitalisation of payments and creating enabling infrastructure, one can expect an increase in adults' account ownership globally. Many entities will be able to pay their staff and suppliers electronically, thus potentially broadening governments' respective tax base by helping reduce tax avoidance. The World Bank's Global Findex 2021 data showed that many account owners in developing economies opened their first accounts for the purpose of receiving money from the government. Not only did this help the households directly, but it also served as a stepping stone towards more inclusive and efficient digital payment systems.[39]

---

38   J. P. Meltzer and C. F. Kerry, "Cybersecurity and digital trade: Getting it right", *Brookings*, 2019, https://www.brookings.edu/research/cybersecurity-and-digital-trade-getting-it-right/, accessed 1 September 2022.

39   A. Demirgüç-Kunt, L. Klapper, D. Singer and S. Ansar, "The Global Findex Database 2021: Financial Inclusion, Digital Payments, and Resilience in the Age of Covid-19", *World Bank*, 2022.

The policy environment for digital payments should also aim for holistic coverage, which should seek to include the following:

1. *Protecting consumers,* their safety and their privacy so as to foster secure, reliable and fair practices by financial and tech companies.

2. Emphasising the need for *more inclusive access to digital payments.* The gender gap in access to finance has narrowed globally. But women and poorer populations still tend to lack a mobile phone, live further away from a bank, and need more support to open and effectively use a financial account.[40] Populations that are harder to reach would benefit from a more inclusive access to mobile phones.

3. *Promoting interoperability between different providers* (both financial institutions and mobile money providers) *and user identification mechanisms.* Figure 22 in the ICT section above illustrates how mobile subscriptions are relatively high even in LDCs. This may explain why mobile money has become overwhelmingly predominant in 'under-banked' areas, including in the majority of Africa as illustrated in Figure 23 below. Mobile money refers to payment services operated through a mobile device, without credit or debit cards, and without the need to connect the phone to an existing bank account.[41] The absence of interoperable payment solutions prevents business, especially MSMEs, from making the most of global trade and the digital

---

40   A. Demirgüç-Kunt, L. Klapper, D. Singer and S. Ansar, "The Global Findex Database 2021: Financial Inclusion, Digital Payments, and Resilience in the Age of Covid-19", *World Bank*, 2022, p.XVI.

41   As described by the IMF, the services that offer mobile phones as just another channel to access a traditional banking product are considered mobile banking, not mobile money. A bank account is not required to use mobile money services. Mobile money is a "pay-as-you-go digital medium of exchange and store of value using mobile money accounts, facilitated by a network of mobile money agents." *See*, International Monetary Fund, *FAS: What is mobile money? How is it different from mobile banking?*, available at: https://datahelp.imf.org/knowledgebase/ articles/1906552-fas-what-is-mobile-money-how-is-it-different-fro, accessed 1 September 2022.

economy. Interoperability may imply three aspects: technical, regulatory and usage interoperability.[42]

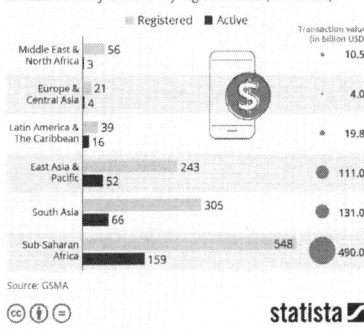

Fig. 23: Mobile money accounts by region in 2020 (millions) and transaction value (in billion USD).[43]

4. *Encouraging a low-cost 'switch' for financial products and services.* Switching costs in the banking context may be incurred by a consumer as a result of changing financial products or service. Such costs are mostly monetary, but may also be psychological as well as time- or effort-based. The ability, relative ease and willingness of consumers to 'switch' are conditions for well-functioning markets. Should it be discouraged or hindered, however, both the demand and supply side could be negatively impacted.

---

42   World Economic Forum, Defining and Measuring Payment Interoperability, White Paper, 2022.

43   F. Zandt, "Where Money Goes Mobile", *Statista*, available at: https://www.statista.com/chart/25713/mobile-money-accounts-by-region-in-2020/, accessed 1 September 2022.

Customs and trade facilitation

Trade facilitation relies on the proper operation of customs which is conditioned by the infrastructure of crossing points at the border, the receipt and consideration of customs declarations and other documents, mandatory preliminary information, control, clearance, testing, inspection and certification or accreditation to demonstrate a product's full compliance with target market requirements. Adhering to customs regulations is crucial as goods can only be released after verification of customs documentation and to enable import and export clearance. The latter depends on the submission of multiple paper documents or their electronic equivalents. In the EU for instance, this may include, among others, a commercial invoice,[44] an Authorised Economic Operator status,[45] a Proof of Origin,[46] a Binding Tariff Information,[47] a Binding Origin Information,[48] as well as additional documents that may differ depending on the mode of transport (e.g. a Bill of Lading[49]), inspection certifications (e.g. for

---

44 A commercial invoice contains general information about the goods (e.g. reason for export, shipping date, description, selling price, packaging, quantity, value, weight).

45 The Authorised Economic Operator status provides certain benefits (e.g. easier admittance to customs simplifications, priority treatment if selected for control, etc.). It is granted by the competent customs authority and recognised by customs authorities in all EU member states.

46 A proof of origin is a certificate declaring that the goods being shipped are manufactured and processed in the said country.

47 A Binding Tariff Information is a legal decision by the customs authorities on the tariff classification of the goods, and it is binding in the European Union.

48 A Binding Origin Information is a written decision that certifies the origin of the goods, and it is binding in the European Union.

49 A Bill of Lading is a document issued by the shipping company to the operating shipper, acknowledging that the goods were received on board.

food products health and/or veterinary certificates) and a CITES import certificate.[50]

A wide array of actors may also come into play: freight forwarders and other logistics service providers, customs brokers, operators in seaports, airports and rail-terminals, stevedores and handling agents, warehouse operators, testing and inspection companies and IT services, to name a few. Whenever one of the parties within the chain is required to submit relevant documents or information to customs authorities, this generates costs.[51]

Direct costs cover, for instance: costs related to the collection, production, transmission, posting/faxing and processing of information needed to prepare and submit relevant documents; fees and other charges associated with setting up and financing customs bonds and guarantees, inspections, testing; charges levied by intermediaries and many more.

Indirect costs cover, for instance, insufficient, unclear, contradictory or inconsistent information, documentation or customs procedures and requirements; backlog at inspection facilities and other delays at the border, among others.

Still, as illustrated in Figure 24, there are many legitimate reasons for having thorough checks and customs procedures at the border.

Hence, it is crucial for customs infrastructure to be as efficient as possible to ensure the right balance between the protection of legitimate interests – be it government revenue collection or enforcing safety and security requirements – and the need to seek simplified and harmonised customs procedures.

This was the aim behind the WTO's Trade Facilitation Agreement (TFA), which came into force in 2017. A 2015 study by the WTO estimated that the full implementation of the TFA may reduce trade

---

50   A CITES certificate is the confirmation by the issuing authority that the conditions for authorising the trade of regulated specimens of species are fulfilled.

51   A. Grainger, "Trade Facilitation and Import-Export Procedures in the EU: Striking the Right Balance for International Trade" *European Parliament*, Policy Department External Policies, Briefing Paper, 2008, p.10.

Regulatory Category	Examples of related activity
Revenue Collection	Collection of Customs duties, excise duties and other indirect taxes; payment of duties and fees; management of bonds and other financial securities
Safety and Security	Security and anti smuggling controls; dangerous goods; vehicle checks; immigration and visa formalities; export licences
Environment and Health	Phytosanitary, veterinary and hygiene controls; health and safety measures; CITES controls; ships' waste
Consumer Protection	Product testing; labelling; conformity checks with marketing standards (e.g. fruit and vegetables)
Trade Policy	Administration of quota restrictions; refunds; suspensive regimes

Fig. 24: Examples of international trade related regulatory activity.[52]

costs on average by 14.3%, mostly benefitting the poorest countries.[53] The TFA has already provided a framework for global administrative and regulatory standards, thus increasing business transparency and predictability as well as trust among trading partners.

In addition, resilience has to be factored into the implementation efforts of the TFA. Members that underwent trade facilitation reforms were better able to adapt and respond to changes in trade volumes and regulatory controls during the pandemic.[54] Over 40 members – including the EU – are seeking an accelerated implementation of the TFA in light of the Covid-19 pandemic.[55] The EU should continue to ensure and promote a forward-looking implementation of the TFA, whilst supporting countries that require technical assistance to comply with it and improve their customs processes and infrastructure accordingly.

---

52 A. Grainger, "Supply Chain Security: Adding to a Complex Operational and Institutional Environment", *World Customs Journal*, Vol. 1 N°2, 2007.

53 World Trade Organization, World Trade Report 2015: Speeding Up Trade: benefits and challenges of implementing the WTO Trade Facilitation Agreement, 2015, p.7.

54 World Trade Organization, *members mark 5th anniversary of Trade Facilitation Agreement, share experiences on impact*, 2022, https://www.wto.org/english/news_e/news22_e/fac_04jul22_e.htm, accessed 1 September 2022.

55 WTO document G/TFA/W/25, and subsequent revisions.

In the context of customs and trade facilitation, an emphasis should also be placed on non-tariff measures (NTMs) which, as detailed in Part I, have become symbolic of governments' turn towards 'precautionism'. EU exporters have been experiencing difficulties meeting technical and conformity assessment requirements imposed by third country trade partners. The bulk of NTMs reported related to technical barriers to trade, sanitary and phytosanitary measures as well as rules of origin.[56] Quality infrastructure is needed to enable businesses to meet these various standards without constituting a barrier to trade. NextGen trade agreements should also go beyond traditional trade facilitation and leverage available digital tools. This includes paperless trading, electronic certificate of origin systems, 'single window' platforms to receive customs documents via single entry points, automated customs operation systems, online publication of essential information, etc. As illustrated in Figure 25, the gains from a digitalisation of customs documentation are clear.

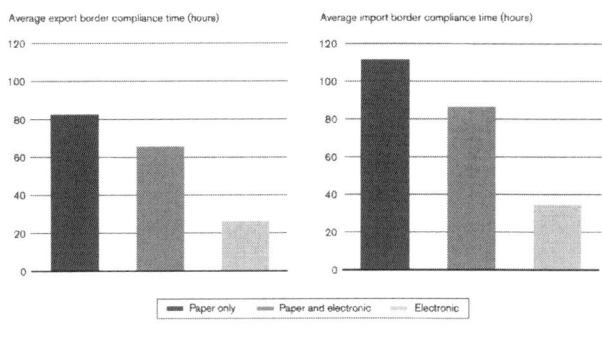

Source: World Bank (2017).

Fig. 25: Gains from the digitalisation of customs documentation.[57]

56 European Commission and International Trade Centre, Navigating Non-Tariff Measures: Insights from a Business Survey in the European Union, 2016, p.X.

57 World Trade Organization, World Trade Report 2018: The Future of World Trade: How Digital Technologies are Transforming Global Commerce, 2018, p. 71.

Finally, in order to address burdensome and inefficient processes, building capacity and developing human resources both at the business and state level (including customs and labs) remains of the utmost importance. EU exporters tend to be more affected when exporting to developing countries and economies in transition compared to developed countries.[58]

Trade policy enforcement mechanisms with teeth and muscles

The EU has a robust network of trade agreements: nearly 50 trade deals with close to 80 partners – and more are on the way.[59] But once deals are struck, what can ensure that their content is abided by? What tools are in the EU's arsenal to enforce what was agreed both within the EU itself and in its export markets? What could be improved in that regard?

Having an assertive trade policy is about ensuring that trade partners honour their commitments. This section emphasises that the enforcement of trade rules requires mechanisms with teeth and muscles in order to be effective. It is with this mindset that in 2020 the EU Commission created the new role of Chief Trade Enforcement Officer (CTEO).[60] Indeed, this constitutes a step forward in terms of strengthening the EU's capacity to enforce its agenda and to ensure that Europeans and their businesses obtain the best out of the Union's trade deals. The CTEO carries this responsibility in several ways, including by: (i) strengthening the implementation of multilateral, regional and bilateral trade agreements; (ii) ensuring that

58   European Commission and International Trade Centre, Navigating Non-Tariff Measures: Insights from a Business Survey in the European Union, 2016, p.5.

59   European Commission, *Questions and Answers: An open, sustainable and assertive trade policy*, 2021, https://ec.europa.eu/commission/presscorner/detail/en/qanda_21_645, accessed 1 September 2022.

60   European Commission, *European Commission appoints its first Chief Trade Enforcement Officer*, 2020, https://ec.europa.eu/commission/presscorner/detail/en/IP_20_1409, accessed 1 September 2022.

partners keep their markets open to EU exporters and investors, and respect trade commitments that benefit EU business; (iii) managing the single entry point where European market actors (business, trade organisations, NGOs) can submit complaints on the trade barriers and the lack of implementation of commitments in non-EU countries; (iv) coordinating dispute settlement proceedings.

The section dives deeper into the issue of enforcement by focusing on the importance of having a protective policy environment for the EU, its businesses, its citizens, for incentivising innovation and responding to threats. It also considers the question of improving existing dispute settlement mechanisms to make them more efficient, resilient and inclusive.

A protective environment

Making use of trade defence instruments in line with EU values

When international trade distortions and so-called 'unfair trade practices' are hurting EU businesses and production, one should recall that governments can have recourse to the islands of protective exceptions which were covered in Part II.

Such tools may also be a way for the EU to show its commitment to open and fair trade. In particular, the use of trade defence instruments such as anti-subsidy (i.e. countervailing) duties and anti-dumping duties is required to restore fairness and a level playing field in trade relations with the partner hurting the EU's domestic industry. This also applies to coercive practices (including threat of coercion) by other countries who disapprove of EU policy choices or of those of its member states.

In this light, the EU modernised its trade defence policies in 2018.[61] Investigations were made faster and more efficient, allowing for provisional measures to be imposed within approximately seven months, a two-month gain compared to previous practice. Moreover, the EU Commission has to provide information on its intention to

---

61   European Commission, *EU modernises its trade defence instruments*, 2018, https://ec.europa.eu/commission/presscorner/detail/en/ MEMO_18_396, accessed 1 September 2022.

apply provisional measures at least three weeks prior to their due date. This allows businesses to adapt to new market situations.

Trade defence should also uphold the EU's values, particularly that of inclusiveness, so as to use these tools in a manner consistent with the needs of different market players, be it smaller business-es or workers. Trade unions – which represent European workers whose jobs may be affected by unfair foreign trade practices – can fully participate in relevant investigations. These advancements are in line with the goal of addressing the distributional effects of trade openness and integration outlined in Part I, combined with the am-bition to make trade happen.

Dialogue – be it bilaterally or in a multilateral forum – should always remain the preferred approach; it is a first step towards de-escalation and the end of coercive or 'unfair' practices. Countermeasures and trade defence instruments should be used only as last resort, when there is no alternative manner to address economic intimidation or to level the playing field. The 2021 European Commission's proposal for new instrument to counter the use of economic coercion by third countries follows this philosophy by favouring negotiations and giv-ing ample opportunity for the third country to reconsider its hurtful and undesirable actions.[62]

Protecting EU innovators and innovations

Affordable and protective intellectual property rights (IPR), as stressed in the section on industrial entrepreneurship policies, are essential to promote European creativity and innovations. IPRs help generates jobs and provide businesses with tools to enhance their global competitiveness. IPRs enable creators and inventors and oth-er IPR users to reap the benefits of their work when their creations or inventions are being used. In doing so, IPRs also contribute to the enrichment of cultural heritage and diversity, in particular in the creative sectors (music, films, publishing) but also in certain manu-factures requiring specific know-how.

---

62   European Commission, *Protection Against Coercion*, https://policy.trade. ec.europa.eu/enforcement-and-protection/protecting-against-coercion_ en, accessed 1 September 2022.

Counterfeiting, piracy and other types of IP abuse hurts EU businesses through unfair competition and also risk endangering consumers inside and outside of Europe, for instance when safety standards are not be respected. Such practices also have disastrous effects on the job market. Some estimates mention global job losses of well above 2 million in 2013, and around 5 million by 2022.[63] Enforcing IPRs (e.g. trademarks and designs) with respect to such products may help prevent their entry into the EU market and enhance consumer trust and safety; meaning that they can rely on qualitive, genuine products made by the original manufacturer. In December 2021, the European Commission (EC) launched a public consultation, requesting contributions from all stakeholders, to identify online service providers as well as physical marketplaces outside the EU which are engaging in substantial IPR infringements. Consequently, towards the end of 2022, the EC intends to publish a revision of its Counterfeit and Piracy Watch List. As in the previous 2020 watch list, online service providers and marketplace operators should continue to outline the steps and actions they have taken to address IPR infringements. This will help pin down the most mischievous marketplaces and to engage in a dialogue with these operators and local authorities to stop such harmful practices. It could also provide an opportunity for the latter to inform the EU on difficulties they may be encountering in the implementation process.

Geographical indications (GI) are another means, this time specifically linked to the origin of a product, to guarantee the authenticity, characteristics and quality of goods. Typically, GIs are used for agricultural goods, foodstuffs, wines and spirits, with the aim to prevent competitors from exploiting the reputation and technique developed to create top-notch products. Negotiations on GI launched at the WTO under the Doha agenda have stalled for more than a dec-

---

63   Frontier Economics, *The Economic Impacts of Counterfeiting and Piracy: Report Prepared for BASCAP and INTA*, 2016, p.8. Available at: https://iccwbo.org/publication/economic-impacts-counterfeiting-piracy-report-prepared-bascap-inta/, accessed 1 September 2022.

ade.[64] Two topics were mandated: (i) the creation of a multilateral register for wines and spirits; and (ii) extending the higher level of protection (under Article 23 of the TRIPS Agreement) beyond wines and spirits. The EU has been a major proponent for these GI reforms at a multilateral level. Whilst it seems unlikely for WTO members to get back to the negotiating table in the short term, the EU continues to seek enhanced GI protection for its products in export markets under downsized fora, including in its bilateral trade agreements. Seeking a level of protection in the territory of the trade partner at a level comparable to that of the EU is a priority pursued by Europe. In that regard, a clear list of GI-protected products is established in trade agreements. Adequate enforcement mechanisms are also agreed in case of breach, and after dialogue has not proved successful. For instance, administrative enforcement via measures at the border as well as dispute settlement may be considered. The idea of enlarging geographical indications to craft and industrial products is also gaining ground in the EU – from Limoges porcelain manufacturers to Murano glass masters. This was the idea behind the deal struck between the European Parliament and Council in May 2023, with a view to broaden the scope of GI protection to such products.[65]

> *"The value of an idea lies in the using of it."*
> Quotation attributed to Thomas A. Edison

Emphasis should also be placed on the role played by IPRs in protecting and enabling MSMEs. Knowledge-based capital is not only becoming an increasing source of economic growth for them globally, but it is also shedding light on emerging business opportuni-

---

64   World Trade Organization, *TRIPS: Geographical Indications, Background*, https://www.wto.org/english/tratop_e/trips_e/gi_background_e.htm, accessed 1 September 2022.

65   European Council, Council and Parliament strike provisional deal to protect geographical indications for craft and industrial products, 2 May 2023, https://www.consilium.europa.eu/en/press/press-releases/2023/05/02/council-and-parliament-strike-provisional-deal-to-protect-geographical-indications-for-craft-and-industrial-products/, accessed 10 May 2023.

ties, such as IPR-based debt. The above quote by Thomas Edison can therefore be considered in its literal sense here. Access to finance is a major area of concern for smaller businesses. IPRs are instrumental in that respect and they may indeed be used as collateral – especially for start-ups – to obtain financing. This represents an attractive opportunity both for start-ups and venture capitalists for several reasons: (i) start-ups generally lack sales records, hence the importance of meeting patentability criteria to prove that their ideas have value which will help them be successful in piquing investors' interest; (ii) patents protect them from being copied by other businesses, and; (iii) if a start-up defaults, investors can sell or license patents to limit their losses.[66]

The protection of IPRs has to be balanced with other, welfare-enhancing principles. First, this requires facilitating the transfer of technology to developing countries that need it and particularly to LDCs. In this regard, the most recent mention of technology transfer in a major multilateral outcome is contained in the June 2022 WTO Ministerial Declaration on the WTO Response to the Covid-19 Pandemic and Preparedness for Future Pandemics. In paragraph 15, members "recognize that increasing the level of global preparedness to Covid-19 and future pandemics requires strengthened productive, scientific and technological capacity across the world. [Members] also recognize that such capacity is instrumental for developing solutions to public health crises beyond Covid-19, including those relating to HIV/AIDS, tuberculosis, malaria and other epidemics, as well as neglected tropical diseases, and for diversifying manufacturing locations. In line with WTO rules, [Members] underscore the importance of promoting technology transfer that contributes to building capacity in related sectors."[67] The transfer and dissemina-

---

66   A. Radauer, "Opportunities to Reap Financing Through IP for Innovation", in S. Dutta, B. Lanvin and S. Wunsch-Vincent (eds.), *Global Innovation Index 2020: Who Will Finance Innovation?*, 13th edition, 2020, p. 193.

67   Ministerial Declaration on the WTO Response to the Covid-19 Pandemic and Preparedness for Future Pandemics, World Trade Organization, 2022, WTO document WT/MIN(22)/31 - WT/L/1142.

tion of technology is an objective enshrined in the 1994 WTO TRIPS Agreement. More specifically, it requires developed members to provide incentives for their businesses to promote the transfer of technology to LDCs.[68]

Second, there is an urgent need to deliver on the imperative contained in the 2015 UN Sustainable Development Goal (SDG) 3.8 to achieve "access to safe, effective, quality and affordable essential medicines and vaccines for all". International trade policy has a role to play in this respect, e.g. through trade-facilitating measures like tariff reductions, by financing North-South partnerships to strengthen local health, pharmaceutical systems and infrastructure, and by promoting dialogue with various stakeholders (international organisations, development agencies, LDCs, healthcare industrials, civil society).

Protecting the EU, its citizens and businesses from undesirable foreign investments

Business may have a security component; the war in Ukraine is yet another example of this increasingly intertwined relationship. In April 2022, two months after the conflict's military escalation, the European Commission published a communication to guide EU member states regarding foreign direct investment (FDI) from Russia and Belarus in view of their actions and of the relevant economic and diplomatic sanctions adopted by the EU as a response.

The EU has sought to be adequately equipped to pinpoint, evaluate and address potential menaces to its security and public order, without scaring away investors and by remaining open, transparent and inclusive in welcoming foreign investments.

The EU's foreign investment screening mechanism became fully operational in 2020, with two main pillars:

1. Cooperation: Within the EU, member states and the Commission can exchange best practices and information as well as raise concerns where appropriate. Cooperation also makes sense outside the EU, especially with key partners.

---

68   Article 66.2, Agreement on Trade-Related Aspects of Intellectual Property Rights (TRIPS).

2. Guidance: The Commission can issue opinions should a potential FDI risk undermining EU security or public order, or that of a member state, bearing in mind the need to respect business-friendly timeframes and confidentiality requirements. The framework also outlines certain requirements for EU member states who set out to adopt or maintain their domestic screening mechanisms.

After one year of existence, this new tool had screened four hundred FDIs,[69] and all member states uniformly considered the cooperation mechanism as valuable for gaining a comprehensive overview of FDI into the EU, including particular investment targets and investor profiles.[70] Albeit a growing number of initiatives within member states to develop FDI screening frameworks, in 2022 several were still "planning to adopt" or "in the process of adopting" such a mechanism (see the illustration in Figure 26). A couple of members are still "without any legislative developments" on this front (Cyprus and Bulgaria). Security considerations are also being invoked to develop mechanisms to control not only inbound but also outbound investment flows.

---

69   European Commission, *Trade and security: Commission highlights work to defend EU interests and values*, 2021, https://ec.europa.eu/commission/presscorner/detail/en/ip_21_6226, accessed 1 September 2022.

70   European Commission, Report from the Commission to the Parliament and the Council: First Annual Report on the Screening of Foreign Direct investments into the Union, 2021, p.15.

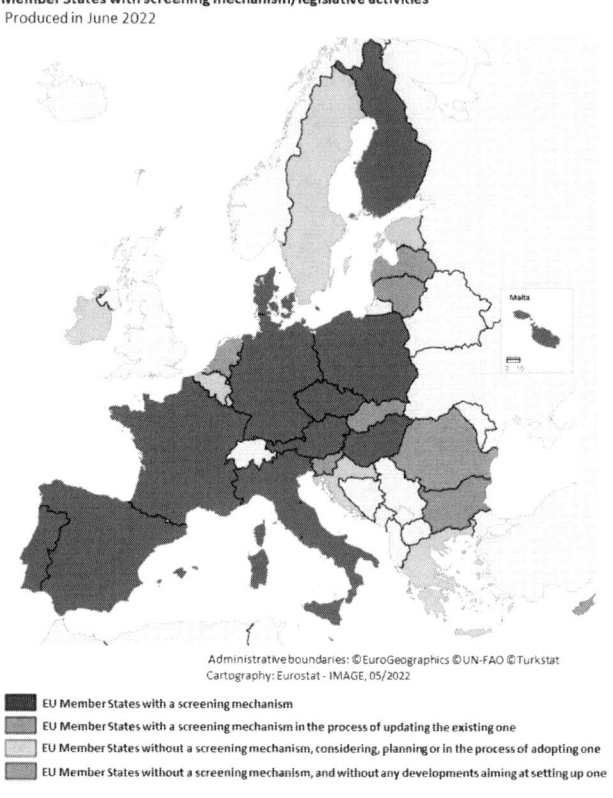

Member States with screening mechanism/legislative activities
Produced in June 2022

Administrative boundaries: © EuroGeographics © UN-FAO © Turkstat
Cartography: Eurostat - IMAGE, 05/2022

■ EU Member States with a screening mechanism

■ EU Member States with a screening mechanism in the process of updating the existing one

□ EU Member States without a screening mechanism, considering, planning or in the process of adopting one

■ EU Member States without a screening mechanism, and without any developments aiming at setting up one

Member States' notifications to the European Commission

Fig. 26: EU member states with an investment screening mechanism or relevant legislative activities.[71]

---

71   European Commission, Report from the Commission to the Parliament and the Council: First Annual Report on the Screening of Foreign Direct investments into the Union, 2021, p. 8.

Dispute settlement
Trade disputes

The role of dispute settlement is paramount in safeguarding the rule of law in international trade relations and in providing business with legal certainty and predictability. Part II emphasised the role of the WTO dispute settlement system as a means for WTO members to address situations where they consider there has been a violation of WTO Agreements and/or when a specific action from another member is injurious. It also recalled some major challenges, including the absence of a fully functioning two-tier system, as originally intended. Moving forward, two major objectives for the EU can be set regarding the settlement of trade disputes.

First, WTO negotiations to restore the Appellate Body (AB) are still on the way as of September 2022, but whether they will lead to a solution and, if so, when and in what exact form, are questions that nurture uncertainty. As the AB continues to be dysfunctional, there is a risk of appeals being sent into the void. To remedy legal loopholes, the European Commission proposed to broaden the scope of the 'Enforcement Regulation' (Regulation (EU) No 654/2014) in an amendment entered into force in February 2021 (Regulation (EU) 2021/167). The objective is the protection of the Union's interests under international trade agreements in situations when third countries simultaneously adopt or maintain illegal measures and block a dispute settlement process. This allows the EU to take a tougher stance on the enforcement of international trade law, allowing to exercise action (i.e. adopt countermeasures) even in such situations where a dispute settlement procedure has not been exhausted.

Second, the EU continues to build on the work accomplished in less-than-multilateral initiatives. In that regard, the Multi-Party Interim Appeal Arbitration Arrangement (MPIA) – as detailed further in Part II – constitutes a plurilateral stop-gap response to the absence of a second tier in the WTO dispute settlement system. Efforts are underway to expand on this temporary arrangement.

Ad hoc appeal arbitration agreements under the WTO framework are also a possibility for those members that are not a part of the

MPIA initiative but still wish to resolve their disputes in a two-tier process. The EU and Turkey (which is not part of the MPIA) participated in the very first WTO appeal in more than two years due to the AB paralysis. On 25 July 2022, under an ad hoc procedure agreed in advance by both parties, the very first appeal arbitration award under Article 25 of the WTO Dispute Settlement Understanding was adopted.[72] The rules and procedures contained in this ad hoc agreement were very similar to those in the MPIA, which may perhaps illustrate the importance of ad hoc solutions to gradually build support around a broader MPIA initiative.

Finally, in parallel, all EU trade agreements (bilateral and regional) also contain provisions governing the settlement of trade disputes. This has become even more important given the AB paralysis. In fact, the EU has remained particularly active in the bilateral dispute context by launching four disputes between 2018 and 2022.[73]

Investment disputes

International investment dispute settlement has a role to play in encouraging and retaining investments both in and out of Europe. The system of investor-state dispute settlement (ISDS) has stemmed from, and been guaranteed by, an ever-expanding network of investment treaties since the 1980s. This is true for bilateral investment treaties and other agreements which contain chapters on investment protection (e.g. NAFTA, later replaced by the USMCA, and the Energy Charter Treaty).

However, in the past decade, concerns have been voiced both on input and output legitimacy issues under the current ISDS system.

---

72   DS583 Turkey – Certain Measures concerning the Production, Importation and Marketing of Pharmaceutical Products. *Also see*: European Commission, *EU wins WTO case against Turkey's discriminatory practices on pharmaceuticals*, 2022, https://ec.europa.eu/commission/presscorner/detail/en/IP_22_4670, accessed 1 September 2022.

73   European Commission, *Bilateral disputes*, https://policy.trade.ec.europa.eu/enforcement-and-protection/dispute-settlement/bilateral-disputes_en#:~:text=The%20EU%20includes%20a%20dispute,the%20WTO%20dispute%20settlement%20system, accessed 1 September 2022.

Some issues identified include the duration and costs of proceedings; transparency; consistency of case law; limited review of decisions and the absence of appellate mechanism; issues relating to the appointment of arbitrators (especially the perceived lack of transparency, diversity and inclusiveness).[74]

Shedding light on inclusiveness, many studies continue to indicate a clear diversity deficit. Although over the last decades the appointment of female arbitrators has been on the rise, significant improvements are still required. In February 2022, the International Centre for Settlement of Investment Disputes (ICSID), the world's leading institution devoted to ISDS, released its caseload statistics for 2021. Overall, women accounted for only 27% of appointments; a low number but still an improvement over the 23% and 19% they accounted for in 2020 and 2019 respectively.[75]

The United Nations Commission on International Trade Law (UNCITRAL) has been conducting work on ISDS reform since 2017 in its Working Group III.[76] Moreover, both the EU-Canada Comprehensive Economic Trade Agreement (CETA) and the EU-Vietnam FTA contain a reference to a possible future permanent multilateral mechanism for settling investment disputes. The EU has also been including similar provisions in all of its ongoing negotiations which have an investment component. As work on a more desirable approach to investment dispute settlement is carried forward, it is in the EU's interest to ensure in the meantime that the resolution of such disputes operates in an effective, coherent manner, and in line with its core values.

---

74   Y. M. Bourgeois, "International Investment Arbitration: Legitimacy Challenges and Prospects for Future Reforms", *Sorbonne Student Law Review*, Vol. 2 No. 2, 2019.

75   International Centre for Settlement of Investment Disputes, *ICSID Releases 2021 Caseload Statistics*, 2022, https://icsid.worldbank.org/news-and-events/comunicados/icsid-releases-2021-caseload-statistics, accessed 1 September 2022.

76   United Nations Conference on International Trade Law, *Working Group III: Investor-State Dispute Settlement Reform*, available at: https://uncitral.un.org/en/working_groups/3/investor-state, accessed 1 September 2022.

The EU Commission, the Council and Parliament have all been pointing towards the same direction: a multilateral reform of ISDS would be more desirable than bilateral reforms; indeed, a collective approach is the way to go. Building consensus for a fully-fledged, permanent Multilateral Investment Court would allow for a more coherent, unified and effective policy on resolving investment disputes. The phase of exploratory work needs to shift gears into concrete actions for a healthier ISDS. In this process, a clear 'code of conduct', or guidelines, for arbitrators should be agreed on; with an emphasis on avoiding risks of conflicts of interest, on independence and increased inclusiveness (including gender-based), and to reflect the imperatives of human rights and environmental sustainability.

Part IV: making trade work for all – ensuring long-term social gains

At this juncture, it should be recalled that trade-led growth and development have contributed to an unprecedented reduction of poverty levels on a global scale. The goal set out by the United Nations of halving extreme poverty between 1990 and 2015 was met five years ahead of schedule.[1] The question now however is whether we can meet the new target set under the 2015 UN Sustainable Development Goals which call for an end to extreme poverty by 2030. It is also essential to contrast this initial achievement with legitimate concerns about aggravated climate pressures and rising inequality. As Part I made clear, trade comes with benefits as well as costs and risks. Trade can – and has – caused inequalities, as has technological progress. There have been losers in this process, people on the wrong side of widening economic inequality, and entire regions that have borne the brunt of import competition and technological change without being able to tap into the resulting opportunities. There are also sustainability challenges, linked to the environmental impact of more trade and economic growth. Trade and increased output can – and have – caused greater pollution and has damaged our environment. Serious action is necessary to tackle these downsides for trade to work for all people, not just some or most.

We have not all been equal in the face of these major challenges, even among nations subject to a comparable level of exposure to globalisation and technological advancements. For instance, inequality gaps have not been uniform across the globe – showing that some

---

1   United Nations, *Millenium Development Goals, Goal 1: Eradicate Extreme Poverty and Hunger*. Available at: https://www.un.org/millenniumgoals/poverty.shtml#:~:text=Target%201.A%3A,of%20extreme%20poverty%20since%201990, accessed 1 September 2022.

regions have coped better with distribution consequences than others. Another example, some countries have done a much better job at decoupling their economic activities from carbon emissions and other resource use. Countries do not stand helpless before these imperfections: they can act, primarily in the realm of domestic policy. Countries can also act at the international level – through cooperation on tax, on accords to deal with climate change and sustainability, on trade and other agreements to advance the social inclusion and environmental agendas.

The EU Commission laid out its vision for EU trade policy in a 2015 in a paper entitled "Trade for All".[2] It signals (i) the need for a more transparent EU trade policy, (ii) the fact that Europeans do not believe that open markets should require the EU to compromise on core principles such as sustainable development and human rights, and (iii) that trade policy should not only safeguard the European social and regulatory acquis at home but also project relevant interests and values abroad. One should not minimise the role already played by the EU as a global leader in helping people participate in, and reap the benefits of trade. But moving forward also means going beyond trade, including by enhancing the credibility of the 'trade ands' (environment, gender, education, tech, human rights, etc.) and by increasing accountability in the implementation of key standards.

As with any transition, though, and in order to leave no one behind, there are significant costs which ought to be managed. This is the main topic of the first section. It is important to note that any transition towards broad societal improvements is a multifaceted process, involving multiple sectors and actors. The notion of 'costs' should also be factored into any transition process. This includes costs relating to the actual investment aspect of a transition, as well as the 'costs' relating to distribution, sustainability and resilience. A second section covers the role of tax in making trade work for all, to address inequalities and also to help power up the EU's ability to operate major transitions and develop its strategic autonomy. In this

---

2   European Commission, Trade for All: Towards a more responsible trade and investment policy, 2015.

respect, the journey towards EU fiscal integration is difficult but necessary. Global efforts are also needed as the issue of tax avoidance or evasion is a transnational one. Countries are often experiencing decreased public tolerance regarding the perceived unfair nature of their respective tax systems. At the same time, however, corporate income taxes – especially for multinational companies – continue to generate a relatively small share of tax revenue in Europe, compared to individual income taxes, social insurance and consumption taxes. Third, making trade work for all entails enhancing the green lens of trade. Part II emphasised the important role of the WTO – and of trade and climate diplomacy in general – in making greener trade possible on a global scale. In order to actually make it happen and work for all, however, Part IV dives deeper into the discussion on how trade policies can contribute to addressing issues of the global commons such as environmental sustainability. This *Handbook* also outlines some different narratives that exist in relation to trade and environmental sustainability. The focus should also be placed on how to leverage the next generation (NextGen) of trade agreements to make them better tools to enforce trade and sustainable development standards. It is also crucial to discuss the European Green Deal, and the role played by EU trade and domestic policies in addressing sustainability issues. The fourth and final section focuses on the key role played by trade agreements, in particular those concluded by the EU, in promoting labour standards with trading partners. In addition, given the strong connection between trade, skills, growth, employment, education and skills, policies will have to be adjusted if trade is to work for every member of society, leaving no one behind.

Managing the transition costs

In the 1960s, American economist Walt Whitman Rostow worked on the concept of 'transition' from an economic lens and suggested a typology of transitions.[3] According to Rostow, countries pass

---

3   W. W. Rostow, "The Stages of Economic Growth", *The Economic History Review*, New Series, Vol. 12 N°1, 1959, p.1-16.

through five stages of development: (i) traditional society, where barter trading is still practiced and where output is consumed by producers rather than traded; (ii) a second stage laying the foundations for a 'take-off'; implying a move to commercial farming and increased specialisation where surpluses may be traded; (iii) a 'take-off' stage, indicating increased industrialisation and a move from agriculture to the manufacturing sector; (iv) the 'drive to maturity', suggesting diversification in new industries, with an increase in the services sector, and; (v) the stage of 'mass consumption', where the services sector is dominant, and the economy is geared towards it.

More than sixty years later, one could point out the limitations of this concept, including from a development point of view. A transition towards broad societal improvements is a multi-faceted, multi-domain, multi-actor and multi-level process. This *Handbook* has already hinted at a transition to a more open, resilient, greener, digitally ready and inclusive global economy.

The quest for improvements in such areas implies a set of interconnected changes which may take place in different areas, e.g. the economy, technology, institutions, culture, demography, the environment, belief systems. In order to support complex decision-making and in order to manage a transition and its costs, different aspects ought to be considered. For instance, a transition process may have implications at different levels: (i) a micro level, i.e. at the level of individuals and local practices and/or; (ii) a meso level, i.e. that of companies, organisations, institutions and their policies, rules, social norms and beliefs, and/or; (iii) a macro level, i.e. in macro economy, political culture, demography, natural environment, and worldviews and paradigms. Additionally, the speed, the size and the time period for a given transition (i.e. a temporal dimension) should also be considered.[4]

---

4   J. Rotmans and R. Kemp, "Managing Societal Transitions: Dilemmas and Uncertainties: The Dutch energy case-study", *Organisation for Economic Cooperation and Development*, Working Party on Global and Structural Policies, OECD Workshop on the Benefits of Climate Policy: Improving Information for Policy Makers, 2003.

The notion of 'costs' should be factored into any transition process. One could approach this issue in two main ways. First, there are the costs, meaning the investments, needed to successfully conduct a transition process. For instance, a 2022 study by McKinsey[5] estimated that, to achieve a global economy with net-zero emissions by 2050, more than USD 9 trillion would be needed in annual average spending on physical assets for the next thirty years. This includes spending on energy, mobility, industry, buildings, agriculture, forestry, and other land use. Second, another aspect of the notion of costs was already outlined in Part I, that is costs relating to distribution, sustainability and resilience. These are some of the major costs associated with global trade and integration, and any transition process will necessarily entail costs of this nature. Such costs can be monetary, environmental or social. Distributional costs, for instance, may be gendered or of a geographic nature (e.g. rural vs. urban), and may be reflected in the difficulties one has to participate in or benefit from a transition (e.g. compensation, access to essential resources).

With respect to the costs for people in the EU, the Union should endeavour to make any transition process socially legitimate. This includes managing the various costs borne by citizens, avoiding the exacerbation of existing imbalances and addressing them. For instance, a transition to net-zero emissions by 2050 necessarily entails that all EU member states, all sectors of the economy and all economic agents are bound to be impacted in one way or another, either directly or indirectly. This net-zero objective was set out in the EU's Green Deal approved in 2020.[6] No one should be left behind in the process, hence the existence of a Just Transition Mechanism (JTM) which aims to provide focused financial support in the regions most impacted by the transition (e.g. coal mining regions).

---

5   McKinsey, The net-zero transition: What it would cost, what it could bring, 2022.

6   European Commission, *Delivering the European Green Deal*, https://ec.europa.eu/info/strategy/priorities-2019-2024/european-green-deal/delivering-european-green-deal_en, accessed 1 September 2022.

Turning back to the above-mentioned levels which are relevant in any given transition process, the JTM aims to address various costs at various levels.[7]

- At the micro level, this means protecting individuals most vulnerable to the transition, including by: facilitating employment opportunities in new sectors and those in transition; offering re-skilling opportunities; improving energy-efficient housing; investing to fight energy poverty; facilitating access to clean, affordable and secure energy.
- At the meso level, this means supporting companies and sectors most active in carbon-intensive industries, including by: supporting the transition to low-carbon technologies and economic diversification based on climate-resilient investments and jobs; creating attractive conditions for public and private investors; providing easier access to loans and financial support; investing in the creation of new firms, MSMEs and start-ups; investing in research and innovation activities.
- At the macro level, this means assisting member states and regions highly dependent on fossil fuel or carbon intensive industries, including by: supporting the transition to low-carbon and climate-resilient activities; investing in public and sustainable transport; investing in renewable energy sources; improving digital connectivity; providing affordable loans to local public authorities; improving energy infrastructure, district heating and transportation networks.

A transition such as the green transition may be pictured as a set of cogwheels that ought to engage with one another in order to drive change. Given their complex interconnectedness, these cogwheels (individuals, civil society, businesses, member states and the EU) ought to have a common purpose and direction if they are to be mu-

---

7 European Commission, *The Just Transition Mechanism: making sure no one is left behind*, https://ec.europa.eu/info/strategy/priorities-2019-2024/european-green-deal/finance-and-green-deal/just-transition-mechanism_en, accessed 1 September 2022.

tually reinforcing. Should one cog be defective, then the transition process may be hindered.

Going beyond a JTM-like approach may be desirable to ensure a smooth and fair transition process for all, including women and rural populations, to take two examples.[8]

Fair taxation to address inequalities and power up the EU's 21st century transitions

Domestic taxes are an essential policy tool to address major inequalities and to mitigate distributional costs associated with trade. Under other sections in this *Handbook*, relevant forms of tax are covered including taxes pursuing environmental and digital aims or social inclusion. Taxation in a broad sense may also refer to customs duties which are charged on products shipped across international borders. These are also a major tool to achieve such objectives. Reducing tariffs on green goods as well as imposing carbon duties to pay a price on GHG emissions are examples of tax-oriented responses to environmental sustainability challenges. Governments' respective tax systems for energy products must also support the green transition by providing the appropriate incentives, while also bearing in mind the potential social impact of such taxes and the need to support vulnerable sections of the population. The Carbon Border Adjustment Mechanism is yet another example of taxes used with a view to address sustainability and trade issues.

Empirical research points to how inequality spikes have not been uniform across the globe, or even across regions subject to a comparable exposure to the forces of globalisation and technology, and sharing similar levels of development. For instance, Figure 27 shows that the inequality gap with respect to income shares in North America has been relatively wider than in Europe. In Europe, the top 10% capture around 36% of national income, whereas in North America, their share is around 45%. Also in Europe, the bottom 50%

---

8   J. Clancy and M. Feenstra, "Women, Gender Equality and the Energy Transition in the EU", *European Parliament*, 2019.

capture close to 20% of national income, whereas in North America, their share is just above the 10% mark.

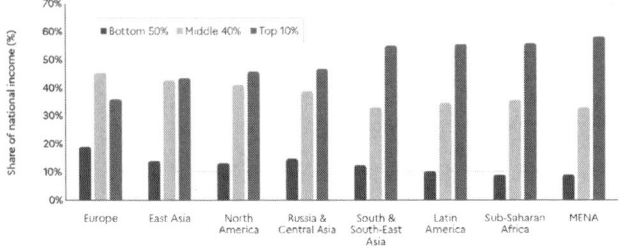

Interpretation: In Latin America, the top 10% captures 55% of national income, compared to 36% in Europe. Income is measured after pension and unemployment contributions and benefits paid and received by individuals but before income taxes and other transfers. **Sources and series:** *www.wir2022.wid.world/methodology.*

Fig. 27: The poorest half lags behind: Bottom 50%, middle 40% and top 10% income shares across the world in 2021.[9]

This goes to show that individual countries have a lot within their power to correct the downsides of trade, including distributional costs and inequalities. In fact, Europe has been a world leader in doing so, with European countries being among the leaders in spending on active labour market policies (ALMPs), as shown in Figure 28. ALMPs may focus on public employment services and other publicly funded services for jobseekers such as training, job search assistance and entrepreneurship support programmes, among others. These elements highlight the important role national policies and institutions play in shaping inequality. More resources available for ALMP systems also means more resilience to labour market shocks in times of increased pressure on the system.[10]

But managing transition costs and funding policies for the green, resilient, digital and fair NextGen EU agenda will not come cheap. Hence, all actors need to contribute. In this respect, the race to the bottom on taxing multinational enterprises (MNEs) has been harm-

---

9   L. Chancel, T. Piketty, E. Saez and G. Zucman, *World Inequality Report 2022*, 2022, p.11.

10   Organisation for Economic Cooperation and Development, OECD Employment Outlook 2021: Navigating the Covid-19 crisis and recovery, 2021, p.163.

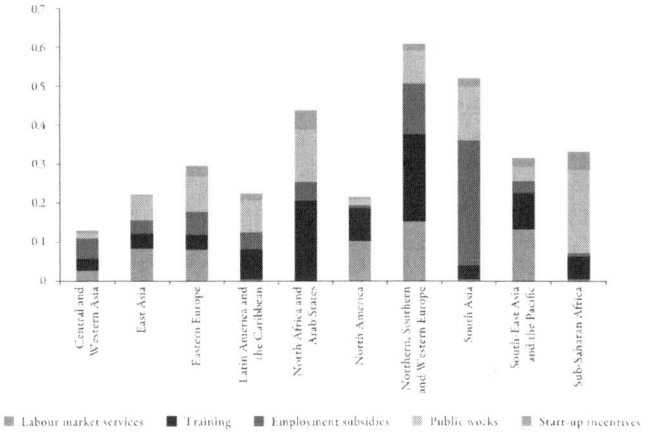

Note: The analysis refers to different years depending on data availability in the specific countries. Please refer to table A.1 in Pignatti and Van Belle (2018) for details on the countries and years covered.
Source: ILO calculations based on Pignatti and Van Belle (2018).

Fig. 28: Spending on ALMPs as a percentage of GDP, by type of measure, across regions, various years.[11]

ful and will continue to be so if left unaddressed. Given the transnational and global nature of tax avoidance and fraud, not everything can be resolved at country level. Some countries have tried to address revenue losses caused by such practices, but they have largely been stuck taxing relatively immobile workers by way of higher income and consumption taxes; all this while globalisation's biggest beneficiaries – MNEs and their shareholders – have kept their profits mobile, avoiding taxation in the process. In this regard, the OECD/ Group of 20 (G20) initiative on an Inclusive Framework on Base Erosion and Profit Shifting (described below under 'Tax considerations') is an instance of deeper cooperation for better globalisation. It led to a historic outcome indeed, but it needs to be effectively implemented and further international efforts will be required.

11   International Labour Organization, *What Works: Promoting Pathways to Decent Work*, 2019, P.76.

Taxation has been subject to major debates in Europe. There has been a longstanding confrontation of views about whether the EU should possess a strong fiscal capacity, or whether this should be a prerogative left to member states. The highly integrated economic and monetary union stands in stark contrast to the EU's current fiscal and budgetary framework, which bodes ill for achieving its strategic autonomy objectives and much-needed digital, green and social transitions. With this in mind, at the EU level, a lot has to do with pursuing the Union's journey towards greater fiscal integration and strengthening its capacity to mitigate profit shifting and the negative spillovers of tax competition.

The difficult journey towards EU fiscal integration

Direct taxation (on income and corporate taxes) remains the sole responsibility of member states, meaning that the EU does not have a direct role in collecting taxes or setting tax rates. Yet, the EU has established certain standards for business and personal taxation across the Union, and certain joint efforts have been made by EU member states to prevent tax avoidance and fraud, as well as double taxation.

With respect to indirect taxation, which affects the free movement of goods and the freedom to provide services across the EU single market, the Union's activities are generally aimed at coordination and harmonisation. This includes Value Added Taxes (VAT) and excise duties on specific goods (e.g. alcohol, tobacco and energy). This is important as variations in indirect taxation rates may distort the EU internal market and create unfair competition by giving businesses in one EU member state an unfair advantage over others.

In 1992, the Maastricht treaty created an economic and monetary union without coupling it with a fiscal union. In the EU, fiscal matters and finances (e.g. EU budget, the multiannual financial framework)[12] are still among those that require unanimity of all 27

---

12   The Multiannual financial framework (MFF) sets out the annual ceilings of expenditure that can be spent on various policy areas. The current framework runs for the period 2021-27. In exceptional circum-

member states, placing them in the same ranks as EU foreign and security policy and EU citizenship (e.g. granting any new rights to EU citizens). The latter requires for member states in the euro area and euro candidate countries to demonstrate sound public finances reflected in two criteria: (i) the budget deficit must not exceed 3% of GDP, and (ii) public debt must not exceed 60% of GDP. When assessed, certain flexibilities may be applied if, for instance, deficits rise above the 3% target in circumstances of economic downturn.

In 1997, the Stability Growth Pact (SGP) sees the light of day. With the SGP, members agreed to strengthen the monitoring and coordination of national fiscal and economic policies and to enforce the deficit and debt limits established by the Maastricht Treaty. Subsequently, the SGP was strengthened and readjusted throughout the years. A set of preventive rules were added (e.g. budgetary objectives, surveillance and monitoring via stability and convergence programmes), as well as corrective rules (excessive deficit procedures), and other amendments and guidance including to better consider individual national circumstances and to strengthen the SGP (more coordination, new monitoring tools).[13]

In 2011, the European Council discussed the adoption of a 'Fiscal Compact' – i.e. the requirement to have a balanced budget rule in domestic legal orders – as a response to the Eurozone sovereign debt crisis. All EU member states were on board, but one. The United Kingdom vetoed, and the others had no choice but to adapt. In 2012, they adopted an inter-governmental agreement outside the EU institutional framework, while still conferring powers to EU institutions: the Treaty on Stability, Coordination and Governance in the Economic and Monetary Union (TSCG). Today, all but Czech Republic

---

stance, flexibility mechanisms allow for additional spending. For more information, see the EUR-Lex, *Multiannual financial framework (MFF)*, https://eur-lex.europa.eu/EN/legal-content/glossary/multiannual-financial-framework-mff.html, accessed 1 September 2022.

13 European Commission, *History of the Stability and Growth Pact*, https://economy-finance.ec.europa.eu/economic-and-fiscal-governance/stability-and-growth-pact/history-stability-and-growth-pact_en, accessed 1 September 2022.

and Croatia have signed the accord. The TSCG limits signatories' deficit size per year to 0.5% of their GDP and calls for the establishment of automatic correction policies in the event of significant deviations from the objective. It complements fiscal rules set out in the 1992 Maastricht Treaty.

There is a long-standing debate as to whether the EU should be given a fiscal capacity of its own as well as a bigger budget, a borrowing and a lending capacity. Some see the Covid-19 pandemic as a potential turning point in that respect. The above-mentioned fiscal rules were 'suspended' during the EU-wide severe economic downturn caused by the pandemic. The general escape clause was activated and allowed the Commission and the Council to depart from the budget requirements that would normally apply. Many member states also triggered national escape clauses to suspend national budget rules.[14] In addition, many consider the common EU debt issued to finance the 'NextGenerationEU' recovery fund in response to Covid-19 as a first step towards an EU fiscal union, which would co-exist with the current highly integrated economic and monetary union. These responses feed into the ongoing debate about whether more ambitious fiscal steps could also be taken in the coming years.

There are two main opposing views regarding the future of EU fiscal policy. On the one hand, some consider that NextGenerationEU and the suspension of the deficit criteria were only temporary solutions to a temporary crisis. They wish to see the SGP returning to quasi back-to-normal conditions in 2023, with a return to the Maastricht fiscal rules (i.e. no fiscal deficits over the stipulated 3% of GDP and swiftly reducing debt-to-GDP levels in excess of 60%).

On the other hand, some are defending the view that shortcomings to the EU fiscal framework pre-existed the pandemic which further exposed them. This approach does not necessarily aim at scrapping the SGP entirely, but it wants to see EU fiscal policy take

---

14   European Parliament, *Implementation of the Stability and Growth Pact under pandemic times*, Briefing, 2021, https://www.europarl.europa.eu/RegData/etudes/BRIE/2020/659618/IPOL_BRI(2020)659618_EN.pdf, accessed 1 September 2022.

into account new realities and imperatives. Its proponents believe that the EU fiscal framework and policies should be reformed in a way that supports the ambitions of NextGenEU. The EU must be able to budget accordingly to achieve the twin transition objectives of sustainability and digitalisation, and to reinforce its capacity to achieve its strategic autonomy objectives. This means building on the momentum achieved during the EU's pandemic experience by enhancing fiscal solidarity and integration, including via mutual borrowing.[15] What is considered by some as a temporary approach may in fact shed light on the untapped potential of the EU's common debt solution. It is worth recalling the NextGenerationEU fund represents 5% of EU GDP whereas EU member states debt-to-GDP ratio is, on average, of about 90%.[16] Strengthened fiscal and budget capacity means more leeway for the EU to support investments in technology, decarbonisation, critical infrastructure, defense, research and development, etc. Achieving broader reform on tax and budget issues will certainly require efforts in consensus building across the EU membership.

Tax considerations to address distributional shortcomings

Multinational enterprises (MNEs) really matter in the global economy. They are productive, they provide many jobs, and they are highly profitable. Some have economic power comparable to certain middle-income countries. For instance, Cambodia's GDP amounted to over USD 26 billion in 2021,[17] a year in which the company Meta

---

15   A. Gonzalez Laya, "Europe's fiscal rules are holding it back", *Politico*, 2021, https://www.politico.eu/article/europe-fiscal-rules-holding-it-back/, accessed 1 September 2022.

16   Eurostat, *Euroindicators: Fourth quarter of 2021 Government debt down to 95.6% of GDP in euro area Down to 88.1% of GDP in EU*, 47/2022, 2022, https://ec.europa.eu/eurostat/documents/2995521/14497745/2-22042022-BP-EN.pdf/90896015-2ac1-081a-2eef-ad8d5f2c0da1, accessed 1 September 2022.

17   World Bank, *Data, GDP (current US$) – Cambodia*, https://data.worldbank.org/indicator/NY.GDP.MKTP.CD?locations=KH, accessed 1 September 2022.

made a profit of over USD 39 billion.[18] Consequently, MNEs' high profits also offer an opportunity for governments to generate tax revenue.

In this day and age, being mindful of major contemporary challenges that require the active contribution of all societal actors, one can question whether the corporate income tax system is still fit for purpose. The green, digital and inclusive agenda will not come cheap! This makes MNE tax considerations all the more important. Many MNEs declare a disproportionate share of profits in certain tax havens with the aim of reducing their total tax payments. They do so by exploiting gaps and mismatches between countries' respective tax systems. It is estimated that these practices cost jurisdictions USD 100 to 240 billion in foregone revenue every year.[19]

The related revenue losses are even more damaging now given the devastating economic impact of the pandemic and the severe stress it has put on many countries' public finances. Rising global awareness on this topic and the existing international tax policy debate reflect the urgency of fundamentally reviewing corporate income taxation. Countries have seen their population become less lenient vis à vis the perceived unfairness of respective tax systems. For example, certain EU member states (including Belgium, Denmark, France, and Poland) announced they would deny Covid-19 tax reliefs for companies registered or doing business with low-tax jurisdictions.[20] Additionally, the European Commission recommended that member states refrain from granting financial support to companies with links to countries on the "list of non-cooperative tax jurisdictions".[21]

18   W. Daniel, "Apple was the most profitable company on the Fortune 500 list this year. These are the biggest profit generators, and what that means about American business", *Fortune*, 2022, https://fortune.com/2022/05/24/fortune-500-most-profitable-companies-apple-berkshire-amazon-google-microsoft/, accessed 1 September 2022.

19   Organisation for Economic Cooperation and Development, *International collaboration to end tax avoidance – Understanding Tax Avoidance*, https://www.oecd.org/tax/beps/, accessed 1 September 2022.

20   International Monetary Fund, *Taxing Multinationals in Europe*, 2021, p.2.

21   European Commission, *Daily News 14/07/2020*, 2020, https://ec.europa.eu/commission/presscorner/detail/en/mex_20_1349, accessed 1 Septem-

In 2021, more than 130 jurisdictions signed a deal in the context of the OECD/G20 Inclusive Framework on Base Erosion and Profit Shifting (BEPS) to ensure that MNEs with global turnover above EUR 750 million will be subject to a minimum 15% tax rate from 2023 (although there have since been delays in the implementation process).[22] Furthermore, if the effective tax rate in a country is below the minimum rate, the differential may be taxed by other jurisdictions. The aim: ensuring a more equitable distribution of profits and of taxing rights among countries with respect to the largest and most profitable MNEs. Annually, this is expected to generate around USD 150 billion in additional global tax revenues. In proportion to existing revenues, developing country revenue gains through this framework are expected to be greater than those in developed economies.

Given the transnational nature of tax challenges, the EU needs to continue to support international cooperation and outcomes targeting unfair tax practices. This also entails encouraging and assisting EU member states in their full implementation of the global BEPS outcome, to finally put a brake on excessive tax competition and move to a more equitable taxation of economic activities in Europe. At the same time, deeper coordination among EU member states may be needed in this regard to address the challenges of profit shifting and tax competition at the EU level. How much governments collect through corporate income taxes varies considerably across European member states, in large part due to tax competition, domestic tax base erosion and profit shifting. Furthermore, tax competition has led governments to become increasingly reliant on consumption and labour income taxes, prompting feelings of unfairness amongst citizens. Corporate income taxes, compared to individual taxes, social insurance contributions and consumption taxes, generate a relatively small share of tax revenue in Europe. Figure 29 illustrates the compelling case for a bigger portion of corporate income taxes in

---

ber 2022.

22   Organisation for Economic Cooperation and Development, *International community strikes a ground-breaking tax deal for the digital age*, 2021, https://www.oecd.org/tax/international-community-strikes-a-ground-breaking-tax-deal-for-the-digital-age.htm, 1 September 2022.

the future tax 'mix' of European member states. Yet, the continuous downward trend of corporate income tax rates in past years seems to indicate a 'race to the bottom' in European corporate taxation. This entails significant government revenue losses – revenue which could be used to power up EU efforts to operate major transitions.

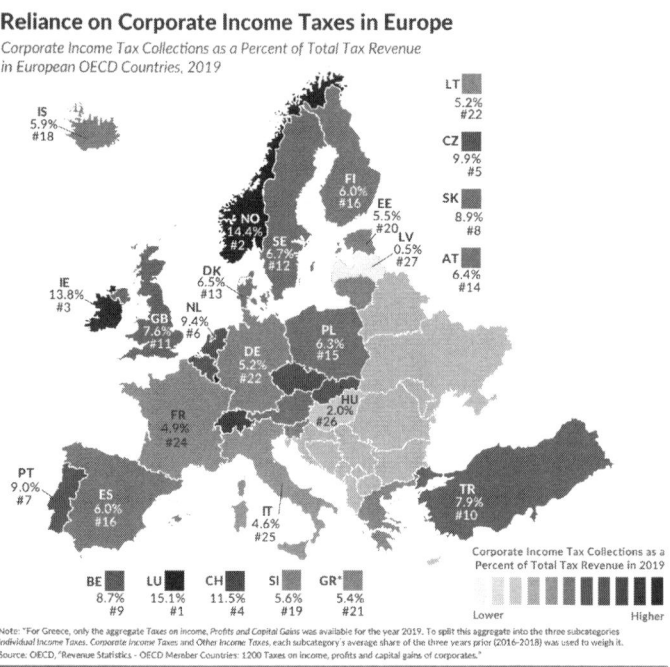

Reliance on Corporate Income Taxes in Europe

Corporate Income Tax Collections as a Percent of Total Tax Revenue in European OECD Countries, 2019

Note: *For Greece, only the aggregate Taxes on Income, Profits and Capital Gains was available for the year 2019. To split this aggregate into the three subcategories Individual Income Taxes, Corporate Income Taxes and Other Income Taxes, each subcategory's average share of the three years prior (2016-2018) was used to weigh it.*
Source: OECD, "Revenue Statistics - OECD Member Countries: 1200 Taxes on income, profits and capital gains of corporates."

TAX FOUNDATION   @TaxFoundation

Fig. 29: Reliance on corporate income taxes (CIT) in Europe. CIT collections as a percent of total tax revenue in European OECD Countries, 2019.[23]

23   E. Asen, "Reliance on Corporate Income Tax Revenue in Revenue", *Tax Foundation*, 2021, https://taxfoundation.org/reliance-on-corporate-income-taxes-in-europe-2021/#:~:text=In%202019%E2%80%94the%20 most%20recent,from%20corporate%20income%20taxes, accessed 1 September 2022.

Making trade work for the environment in the EU and beyond

Climate change is one of the greatest challenges facing the international community. It threatens peace, development, prosperity, lives and livelihoods the world over. Failure on this front means everyone may lose. A 2018 assessment by the Intergovernmental Panel on Climate Change (IPCC) stressed that human-induced warming has already reached approximately 1°C above pre-industrial levels in 2017, increasing at a rate of approximately 0.2°C per decade. Ambitious mitigation action is thus required to limit warming to 1.5°C – as set out in the 2015 Paris Climate Agreement discussed further below. Climate change adaptation will be less of a grueling task for society if this objective is met.[24]

In Part I, we saw that different narratives for trade and related challenges could be adopted. Part IV outlines some different narratives regarding the trade and environment discussion, whether about the impact of the former or about its role in helping address climate change. Going beyond these narratives, it is pertinent to discuss the role of climate change and trade. Part II highlighted that the role of multilateral cooperation and commitments should not be weakened, including in the context of the United Nations Framework Convention on Climate Change and of the World Trade Organization. On the contrary, this role should be reinforced. Climate change and its consequences (on food security for instance) are issues of the global commons; they must therefore be addressed through global efforts. This multilateral framework makes addressing trade and climate change issues possible on a global scale, but for greener trade to actually happen and work for all, more concrete and targeted efforts are required. At a smaller – yet crucial – scale too, governments should endeavour to strengthen the enforceability of trade and sustainable development standards. EU trade agreements

---

24   Intergovernmental Panel on Climate Change, *Special Report on Global Warming of 1.5 °C (SR15)*, 2018, Available at: https://www.ipcc.ch/sr15/, accessed 1 September 2022.

can play a key role in this respect, if the chapters on environmental and labour rights and standards are combined with the necessary guarantees to ensure compliance. Finally, this section dives into some of the main elements the EU has been seeking to implement via its Green Deal strategy presented in 2019. In this context, trade and domestic policies have a role to play in addressing environmental sustainability issues. Some of these policies are not only relevant within EU borders, but also beyond, such as the Carbon Border Adjustment Mechanism which seeks to address carbon leakage. EU efforts are focusing on several key areas to achieve its sustainability objectives. This includes healthy and resilient agriculture; inclusive green transport; renewable, affordable and secure energy; circularity, and; sustainable competition.

Which narrative for trade and the environment?

One cannot categorically deny the impact of open trade on the environment. Trade affects greenhouse gas (GHG) emissions in multiple ways. For instance, in past decades it has represented on average 20 to 30% of global GHG emissions, with a few sectors, energy and transportation in particular, accounting for the vast majority of these trade-related emissions.[25] However, does addressing this issue necessarily mean that trade should be restricted?

Different schools of thought have different perspectives on growth and ecology. Some preconise 'doughnut economics', a visual doughnut-shaped framework for sustainable development which aims to illustrate a middle ground between "planetary and social boundaries" in which "humanity can thrive".[26] Some talk about 'post-growth' or

25   A. Xu, E. Tresa, M. Bacchetta, F. Bellelli and J-A. Monteiro, "Carbon Content of International Trade", *World Trade Organization*, Trade and Climate Change, Information Brief N°4, revised 9 November 2021, https://www.wto.org/english/news_e/news21_e/clim_03nov21-4_e.pdf, accessed 1 September 2022.

26   K. Raworth, Doughnut Economics: Seven Ways to Think Lika a 21st-century Economist, Chelsea Green Publishing: 2017.

'agrowth', i.e. about the need to be agnostic about growth and to 'de-couple' well-being from economic growth.[27]

'Degrowth' is another narrative that involves shrinking rather than growing economies with the belief that this would help them become more sustainable. It stresses the need to move away from the assumption that growth is necessarily good and also suggests the end of GDP as an indicator of economic progress. It may imply buying less as well as producing and consuming locally. Premised in the 1970s, this concept started making more noise in the early 2000s, pushed by increasing awareness and concern about climate change. According to degrowthers, agrowthers, postgrowthers, or other such schools of thought alike, economic growth is not sustainable and, if it continues to be the default goal, it may be impossible achieve the objectives set out in the Paris Climate Agreement.[28] However, as of yet, many voters and policymakers around the world have not found degrowth to be appealing; preferring the 'green growth' pathway which perhaps evokes fewer images of scarcity and loss. According to the OECD, green growth refers to "fostering economic growth and development while ensuring that natural assets continue to provide the resources and environmental services on which our well-being relies".[29]

---

27   T. Wiedmann, M. Lenzen, L. T. Keyßer and J. K. Steinberger, "Scientists' Warning on Affluence", *Nature Communications*, 2020, https://www.nature.com/articles/s41467-020-16941-y.pdf, accessed 1 September 2022. *Also see* J. C. J. M. van den Bergh, "A third option for climate policy within potential limits to growth", *Nature Climate Change*, 2017, https://edisciplinas.usp.br/pluginfile.php/4203641/mod_label/intro/van%20den%20Bergh%20-%20Nature%202017.pdf, accessed 1 September 2022.

28   V. Masterson, "Degrowth – what's behind the economic theory and why does it matter right now?", *World Economic Forum*, 2022, https://www.weforum.org/agenda/2022/06/what-is-degrowth-economics-climate-change/, accessed 1 September 2022.

29   Organisation for Economic Cooperation and Development, "What is green growth and how can it help deliver sustainable development?", https://www.oecd.org/greengrowth/whatisgreengrowthandhowcanithelpdeliversustainabledevelopment.htm, accessed 1 September 2022.

Furthermore, many also question the viability of degrowth-like perspectives in bringing solutions to address the climate question. In fact, the IPCC emphasises that equity, sustainable development, and poverty eradication are mutually supportive and co-achievable within the context of climate action.[30] We saw earlier how important trade-led growth is to significantly curb poverty on a global scale. Is it not thanks to economic development that people today enjoy the benefits of less poverty, of electricity, longer life expectancies, cures against illnesses, etc.?[31] Is degrowth feasible, and if so, is it desirable? Should countries suddenly stop trading, would they be able to produce everything they need for their domestic consumption with existing technologies and capabilities? Would we all be equal in the degrowth process, bearing in mind the existing uneven distribution of resources, demographics, geographic constraints and exposure to natural disasters? Would degrowth prove to be a resilience-building approach for small island developing states and net-food importing countries, or would it rather weaken their resilience? How would one go about imposing that private individuals suddenly stop trading? Would degrowth not in fact lead to an overall loss of efficiency, and thus consuming more energy/resources to produce less? Increased trade has proven to also lead to technological advancements, and to the dissemination of greener technologies; would such advancements be halted due to degrowth?[32]

Whatever term is used, whatever policies are adopted, trade must always adopt a green lens as well as a social/development one. Today, the green lens of trade and growth remains insufficient. How, in the decades to come, will it be enhanced? Any feasible pathway towards avoiding the global warming threshold will necessarily involve syner-

30   Intergovernmental Panel on Climate Change, *Special Report on Global Warming of 1.5 °C (SR15)*, 2018, Available at: https://www.ipcc.ch/sr15/, accessed 1 September 2022.

31   K. Piper, "Can we save the planet by shrinking the economy?" *Vox*, 2021, https://www.vox.com/future-perfect/22408556/save-planet-shrink-economy-degrowth, accessed 1 September 2022.

32   World Trade Organization, Short Answers to Big Questions on the WTO and the Environment, 2020, p.3.

gies, trade-offs and coherence. Seizing economic opportunities must be done in concert with supporting development and addressing environmental pressures, thus ensuring a 'triple win', as illustrated in the graphical representation below (Figure 30). This entails a holistic approach comprised of the environment, development and the economy. It means that policymakers should take full consideration of the potential social impacts of any efforts towards a green transition. Together, the 1992 Rio Declaration and the 2000-2015 United Nations Millennium Development Goals, subsequently replaced by the 2015-2030 Sustainable Development Goals, were foundational to the adoption of a such a holistic perspective given the completeness of their coverage. At the WTO's Fourth Ministerial Conference in Doha, Ministers had already embedded a triple-win approach to the activities of the organisation. They instructed its Committee on Trade and Environment to pursue work in particular on situations relating to the elimination or reduction of trade restrictions or distortions that would benefit trade, the environment and development.

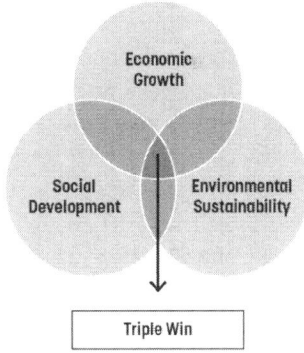

Source : Inspired by the Doha Ministerial Declaration (2001).

Fig. 30: A graphical representation of triple-win between the social, economic and environmental dimensions of sustainable development.[33]

---

33   *See* M. A. J. Teehankee, "Trade and Environment Governance at the World Trade Organization Committee on Trade and Environment", *Global Trade Law Series*, vol. 53, 2020, p.201.

A related challenge is how welfare may be measured; and there is a long route ahead to achieve convergence on a global scale in that regard. Different cultures, regions, countries, continue to have different views about what is the desirable path to welfare, and we are still far from a shared "scale of values".[34] For instance, the interpretation of what constitutes a 'triple win' may be different depending on economic, environmental, developmental, social or political factors within a country. As such, a least-developed country will likely place greater emphasis and a higher threshold on the development side, whilst developed countries with higher environmental standards will focus more on the sustainability aspect in order to consider that a policy will bring about a 'triple-win'. Countries' environmental impact as well as their ambition relating to trade-caused GHG emissions will differ depending on several factors. This includes the size of their economy, their population, the sectoral composition of their foreign trade, their level of participation in the global value chains (GVCs), the modes of transportation used in imports and exports, their energy efficiency and whether they have access to technologies that may help lower emissions in production and transportation. Furthermore, rising geopolitical tensions do not augur well for international cooperation on climate and on trade issues. This geopolitical context also raises questions as to how the green transition will be negotiated by Europe and others, particularly in terms of energy (fossil fuels, renewable energy, nuclear energy, liquified natural gas, etc.). Poorer countries, smaller businesses and modest households will surely need funding and support to adapt in an effort to minimise any potential domestic and international political fallout.

It is true that, historically, economic growth has gone hand in hand with increasing GHG emissions. But several economies have shown that this trend was not irreversible by reducing their emissions whilst experiencing growth at the same time (see Figures 31 and 32). Going forward, more efforts must be made towards further 'decou-

---

34   P. Lamy, "Lamy addresses Collège Universitaire de Sciences Po", World Trade Organization, 2012, https://www.wto.org/english/news_e/sppl_e/sppl252_e.htm, accessed 1 September 2022.

pling' growth from environmental damage and towards harnessing the green potential of trade. Some economists continue to believe that no absolute decoupling can be achieved on a global scale.[35]

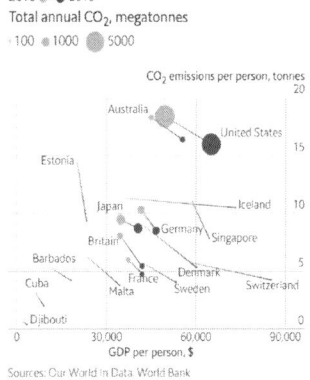

Fig. 31: Selected countries, GDP per person growth and CO2 emissions reductions (2010-2019).[36]

In the process of decoupling, it is important to bear in mind emissions occurring within national borders (territorial emissions), as well as consumption-related emissions. Indeed, production chains often extend across borders and emissions associated with the production of a good or service may arise in several countries. In order to get the full picture, it is important to take into account off-shored production, i.e. emissions transferred to other manufacturing, often still developing, economies. Consumption-based emissions have also fallen in many of these decoupling economies, showing that it is wrong to assume that emissions reductions are only tied

35   M. A. J. Teehankee, "Trade and Environment Governance at the World Trade Organization Committee on Trade and Environment", *Global Trade Law Series*, vol. 53, 2020, p.207 and p.209. For example, M. A. J. Teehankee mentions J. Hickel and G. Kiallis, "Is Green Growth Possible" *New Political Economy*, Vol. 25, N°4, 2020.

36   The Economist, *Several rich countries have decoupled GDP growth from emissions*, 2021, https://www.economist.com/graphic-detail/2021/11/11/several-rich-countries-have-decoupled-gdp-growth-from-emissions, accessed 1 September 2022.

to off-shored production and thus outsourced carbon footprint. For example, see Figure 32 showing Denmark's evolution of per capita CO2 emissions and per capita GDP. A similar evolution can be found for the United Kingdom, France, Germany, Sweden, Italy, Romania, Canada, Australia and the United States, among others.

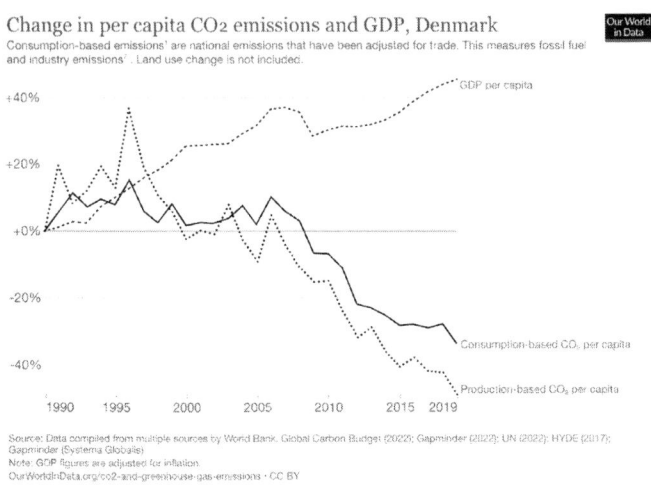

Change in per capita CO2 emissions and GDP, Denmark

Consumption-based emissions¹ are national emissions that have been adjusted for trade. This measures fossil fuel and industry emissions². Land use change is not included.

Source: Data compiled from multiple sources by World Bank, Global Carbon Budget (2022); Gapminder (2022); UN (2022); HYDE (2017); Gapminder (Systema Globalis)
Note: GDP figures are adjusted for inflation.
OurWorldInData.org/co2-and-greenhouse-gas-emissions • CC BY

1. **Consumption-based emissions:** Consumption-based emissions are national or regional emissions that have been adjusted for trade. They are calculated as domestic (or 'production-based' emissions) emissions minus the emissions generated in the production of goods and services that are exported to other countries or regions, plus emissions from the production of goods and services that are imported. Consumption-based emissions = Production-based − Exported + Imported emissions.

2. **Fossil emissions:** Fossil emissions measure the quantity of carbon dioxide (CO₂) emitted from the burning of fossil fuels, and directly from industrial processes such as cement and steel production. Fossil CO₂ includes emissions from coal, oil, gas, flaring, cement, steel, and other industrial processes. Fossil emissions do not include land use change, deforestation, soils, or vegetation.

Fig. 32: Change in per capita CO2 emissions and GDP, Denmark (1990-2019).[37]

This decoupling can be explained by the fact that such countries have been replacing fossil fuels as a means of energy to power growth, by energy with lower carbon emission. Another reason is efficiency in the use of energy, by increasing GDP whilst keeping a stable energy con-

---

37   H. Ritchie, "Many countries have decoupled economic growth from CO₂ emissions, even if we take off-shored production into account", *Our World in Data*, 2021, https://ourworldindata.org/co2-gdp-decoupling, accessed 1 September 2022.

sumption or even by reducing it. A key question is: how can this decoupling be accelerated, accentuated and extended to other economies?

Even in the unlikely event that it is possible for the EU to be a green island in a dirty world, this would do nothing to achieve the EU's own environmental objectives. The EU's great ambition for a green transition cannot be advanced in a silo. This 'green ambition' will only be successful to the extent that trade, domestic and external policies, investments, aid and partnerships are all helping and driving other regions around the globe to also address environmental and sustainability challenges at their own level. Above all, a clear and unambiguous determination on the part of policymakers, businesses and civil society will be required.

Enforcing trade and environmental standards in NextGen trade agreements

Since the 2011 EU-South Korea trade agreement, all the EU's trade agreements, including those with Canada, Japan, Singapore and Vietnam as well as the recently concluded negotiations with Mexico, Mercosur, the United Kingdom, and the investment deal with China,[38] now feature a trade and sustainable development (TSD) chapter which provides for environmental and labour commitments. The combination of dispute settlement mechanisms and TSD provisions in all EU trade agreements is essential to make trade work for the environment and for people. Assertive TSD policies are about ensuring that partners can honour their commitments, an objective which goes hand in hand with the enhanced enforcement efforts already covered in Part III.

Can the EU show more ambition in the enforcement of TSD provisions with respect to environment sustainability? Many authors have recommended linking the TSD chapter to the dispute settlement pro-

---

38   European Commission, *Panel of experts confirms the Republic of Korea is in breach of labour commitments under our trade agreement*, 2021, https://ec.europa.eu/commission/presscorner/detail/en/ip_21_203, accessed 1 September 2022.

cedure. They also suggest establishing a more effective enforcement mechanism, implying economic consequences or sanctions. Now, would trade partners still be willing to strike deals if the EU were to make new trade agreements conditional on including harder enforcement mechanisms for TSD? Harder mechanisms may be adopted for developed trade partners. On the other hand, in deals with developing countries, softer enforcement mechanisms via cooperation may arguably be more inclusive and effective in the long run to generate consensus and thus improve compliance. In a June 2022 communication, the European Commission unveiled a bolder approach.[39] Among other aspects, it provides for the application of sanctions as a last resort for breaches of the 2015 Paris Climate Agreement and ILO fundamental labour principles. Of course, in the interest of coherence, the EU must also accept that others impose sanctions in the event of European non-compliance with these provisions.

EU trade agreements explicitly refer to relevant international instruments that the parties commit to effectively implement. The 2018 EU-Japan agreement does so regarding the 2015 Paris Climate Agreement,[40] but the EU could also go beyond and systematically refer to relevant multilateral sustainability and labour instruments that ought to be implemented in NextGen trade agreements. There could be a systematic reference to the 1992 Convention on Biological Diversity, the 1997 Kyoto Protocol to the UNFCC, the 1973 Convention on International Trade in Endangered Species of Wild Fauna and Flora (CITES), to name a few. It is also worth making NextGen trade agreements future-proof. This not only entails mentioning and reflecting the recent outcomes such as that achieved at the 2021 COP 26 (i.e. the Agreement on the Paris Rulebook as well as the Glasgow Climate Pact), but also any subsequent MEA or relevant international instruments that may eventually see the light of day in the coming years.

---

39 European Commission, *Commission unveils new approach to trade agreements to promote green and just growth*, 2022, https://ec.europa.eu/commission/presscorner/detail/en/ip_22_3921, accessed 1 September 2022.

40 Agreement between the European Union and Japan for an Economic Partnership, 2018. *See* Article 16.4.4.

It may also be useful to complement the above points by including a clause in NextGen trade agreements establishing a Trade and Sustainable Development (TSD) Committee to examine the implementation of the TSD chapter or lack thereof. Finally, in the context of dispute settlement, the recommendations adopted by the panel of experts could be systematically included on the agenda of the TSD Committee for their reviewing and to provide parties with an opportunity to raise concerns in case of non-compliance. Such additions may enhance the credibility of NextGen trade agreements regarding the implementation of key TSD standards. Cooperation should remain the desired approach, but continued failure to uphold commitments should allow for a form of sanction as a last resort.

The European Green Deal, EU trade policy and sustainability

The European Green Deal (EGD) was presented by the European Commission in 2019. It is the EU's flagship strategy to address climate change. The EU Parliament also adopted the EU Climate Law in June 2021, which makes legally binding a target of reducing emissions 55% by 2030 and to achieve climate neutrality by 2050. One could also say that this law further compels the EU to meet its environmental engagements.

The EGD represents a shift in the EU's policy agenda with implications for trade. In 2021, the European Commission also presented a new strategy for "an open, sustainable and assertive trade policy". It aims to further integrate EU trade policy within its priorities reflected in the Green Deal, as well as regarding the EU's Digital strategy, its quest for open strategic autonomy, recovery from the pandemic, and its geopolitical ambitions.

EGD policies must support a transition towards a climate neutral economy, along with higher social standards both in the EU and globally – paving the way for a triple-win: (i) accelerating investments in cleaner energy and promoting circular value chains; (ii) promoting responsible and sustainable business practices, compliant with environmental, human rights and labour standards and; (iii) creating the requisite conditions and opportunities for sustainable goods and services to thrive. In this light, individual EU measures, such as the Carbon Border Adjustment Mechanism, will play an important role.

The example of the Carbon Border Adjustment Mechanism

The EU's Carbon Border Adjustment Mechanism (CBAM) is a case-in-point of a local measure with a global impact. When countries have strict environment policies, businesses may decide to offshore their production to another country with more 'tolerant' policies. The additional greenhouse gas emissions resulting from this move is considered 'carbon leakage'. Indeed, adopting stricter pollution regulations may come at the risk of losing business and thus jobs to competing nations with more lax policies. But by putting a price on imports of a targeted selection of products which have a high environmental cost, one can alleviate carbon leakage.

The idea behind the CBAM – as well as other similar existing systems – is to encourage non-EU producers to green their production processes. It is also hoped that the CBAM will encourage other jurisdictions to increase the ambition of their climate policies standards. How so? By making EU importing countries buy carbon certificates equal to the carbon price they would have paid if the goods had been produced under the EU's carbon pricing rules. However, if the non-EU producer demonstrates that they already have paid a price to offset the carbon used in the production process in a third country, then the relevant cost will be deduced for the EU importer.

How will the CBAM interact with the existing EU Emissions Trading System (ETS)? The EU ETS is the first, and one of the two largest, carbon-pricing systems in the world with China's recently adopted ETS. The EU CBAM will function in parallel with the EU ETS; they will be mutually supportive. The ETS applies the 'polluter pays principle': the costs of pollution must be borne by those who create it. It sets a 'cap and trade' system, i.e. it limits the total volume of GHG emissions that installations in a covered sector can emit cumulatively. The cap is divided into pollution permits ('allowances'), on the basis of one EU allowance per tonne of CO_2 equivalent emissions. Companies can obtain allowances via different channels, such as auctions organised by the European Energy Exchange or on the open, 'secondary' market (on trading platforms operated by ETS operators and financial institutions). Companies can then trade these allowances, for instance by selling spare credits due to a successful and ahead-of-schedule reduction of GHG emissions. There is a risk of carbon leakage, however, when putting a price on carbon within a territory, such as the EU. In its ETS, the EU mitigated this risk through free allocations of allowances to certain industries at high risk of carbon leakage – another channel through which companies may receive such allowances. As the CBAM starts being implemented, and as it is also a tool to address carbon leakage, the EU aims to gradually phase out this free allocation method. The CBAM will thus somewhat complement the EU ETS.

On 10 May 2023, the CBAM Regulation was signed by the co-legislators. However, the contours of the CBAM and its application are still being discussed by the EU institutions at the time of drafting this *Handbook*. This means that some major elements are yet to be defined, such as the set of rules and requirements for the reporting of emissions. This will be further specified in an implementing act adopted by the Commission, in consultation with the CBAM committee, composed of EU member states' respective experts.[41] Below are some of the major aspects of the CBAM which ought to be considered:

1. **Scope of product coverage:** the CBAM targets imports of some of the most carbon-intensive products into the EU and may include cement, aluminium, fertilisers, electric energy

---

41   European Commission, *Questions and Answers: Carbon Border Adjustment Mechanism (CBAM)*, 10 May 2023, https://taxation-customs. ec.europa.eu/system/files/2023-05/20230510%20Q%26A%20CBAM.pdf, accessed 12 May 2023. *Also see* J. Titievskaia and H. Morgado Simões with A. Dobreva, "EU carbon border adjustment mechanism Implications for climate and competitiveness" European Parliament, Briefing – EU Legislation in Progress, 2022, https://www.europarl.europa.eu/ RegData/etudes/BRIE/2022/698889/EPRS_BRI(2022)698889_EN.pdf, accessed 1 September 2022.

production, iron and steel products, as well as plastics, organic chemicals, hydrogen and ammonia in the first instance.

2. Scope of emissions coverage: how will the CBAM cover direct emissions (generated directly by the company and its activities, e.g. production, factories, company-owned vehicle fleets, etc.), indirect emissions (those associated with the company's energy consumption, mainly electricity, heat or steam), or other indirect emissions which go beyond (e.g. outsourced activities, waste disposal, business travel, freight transport, etc.)?

3. Transitional period and full implementation: the CBAM is intended to enter into force in its transitional phase as of 1 October 2023, but in its first phase importers will have to report emissions embedded in their goods without paying a financial adjustment just yet. January 2026 is the date frequently brought forward for the full and permanent implementation of the CBAM.

4. Governance: the European Council and Parliament expressed preference for a centralised administration with the creation an EU CBAM authority, unlike the Commission's proposal, which envisaged decentralised administration by each member state.

5. *De minimis:* the European Council considered a minimum threshold which would exempt from the CBAM obligations consignments below EUR 150 to reduce unnecessary administrative burden. Approximately one third of consignments to the EU would be concerned; their aggregate value and quantity supposedly represents an insignificant part of GHG emissions of total imports the covered products into the EU.

6. Financial assistance to LDCs: CBAM-generated revenues will feed the EU budget, but the EU must subsequently provide technical support to LDCs' efforts towards greening their manufacturing industries; support equivalent in value to the revenue generated by the sale of CBAM certificates.

The answers to some of these questions ultimately depend on the desired level of ambition – already unparalleled in the international arena – and on the overall EU strategy. For instance, the European Green Deal proposes to increase the binding target of renewable sources in the EU's energy mix to 40%, as discussed in the next section. This includes the promotion of renewable fuels, such as renewable hydrogen, ammonia and other derivatives in 'hard-to-green' sectors such as transport, in replacement of fossil-based energy sources. Would extending the CBAM's scope to hydrogen and ammonia – an option which was still under consideration at the time of drafting this *Handbook* – help or rather hinder members' ability to reach this target?

At the COP26 in Glasgow (2021), the WTO Director-General stressed that multilateral trade rules do not constitute a barrier to ambitious environmental policies, including CBAM-like systems. However, in the spirit of having open, transparent and fair global markets, it is key that such a mechanism is not protectionism in disguise. Furthermore, it is also important to support developing countries and LDCs throughout the low-carbon transition process. Indeed, some have warned against the risks of the CBAM unfairly penalising developing countries' exports, and that poorer countries should not face the same burden as more advanced economies.[42] For these reasons, the best solution to address carbon leakage is a global one, with the inclusion of weaker economies in shaping up international carbon tax standards and recommendations.

The keys to NextGen EU's sustainable economy

What are some of the policies that will help the EU achieve its sustainability objectives? Certain issues such as trade finance, the importance of digitalisation, incentivising and protecting innovation are of a cross-cutting nature. The purpose of this section and Figure 33 is rather to focus on more targeted policies and to discuss their potential impact. Throughout, reference will be made to certain proposals contained in the EGD.

---

42   S. Lowe, "The EU's carbon border adjustment mechanism: How to make it work for developing countries", *Centre for European Reform*, 2021, https://www.cer.eu/sites/default/files/pbrief_cbam_sl_21.4.21.pdf, accessed 1 September 2022.

Fig. 33: The keys to help the EU achieve its sustainability objectives.

🔑 HEALTHY AND RESILIENT AGRICULTURE

Efforts are needed to support the EU agricultural and agri-food sector, noting that it is primarily composed of small and medium enterprises. Several elements can help them become flag-bearers of the EU's sustainable agricultural practices globally. In the face of climate change and biodiversity loss, the EU should also aim to reduce its agro-related environmental and climate footprint. This implies adapting the EU's Common Agricultural Policy to the EGD. 'Eco-schemes' may be further implemented to reward the greenest farmers, those with environmentally friendly production systems (e.g. organic farming, agroecology, agroforestry). By 2030, the EGD's 'Farm to Fork' strategy is aiming for one quarter of the EU agricultural land to be under organic farming. Funds targeting rural development are also useful to improve green infrastructure, digitalisation (e.g. faster broadband) to optimise agricultural processes, knowledge transfer, education and innovation.

Sustainable agriculture also means concrete actions for enhanced animal welfare.

Promoting European green agricultural products on the internal market and in third countries will require promotion actions and information campaigns. Labelling also plays a major role in informing and guiding consumers in the EU and abroad towards the most sustainable (and healthiest) products.

Finally, global food security should remain a top priority. The EU's objective to strengthen its relationship with Africa, notably by supporting the implementation of the AfCFTA, may be accomplished via the promotion of sustainable investment in agriculture. A fully operational AfCFTA is expected to boost intra-African agricultural trade, which is currently estimated to be less than 20% of total agricultural trade.[43]

🔑 INCLUSIVE GREEN TRANSPORT

Transport should aim to facilitate international trade but it should also contribute to emission reductions in the long run. This means promoting the growth of the zero- and low-emissions vehicles market and ensuring that greener mobility be inclusive; even the most remote areas should be offered the opportunity to benefit from clean, accessible and affordable transport. This discussion is closely tied with that on sustainable energy and industrial entrepreneurship.

Batteries play an increasingly indispensable role as an energy source for cars. Although they are expected to significantly decrease emissions overall, batteries also have an environmental downside which ought to be mitigated. The EU must ensure that they can be repurposed, remanufactured or recycled at the end of their life. Incentives and funding can further enhance European electro-mobility.[44]

Mobility is also a central concept. The EGD will have to bring changes to the way citizens move around, which includes modernising the transport system, improving connections, infrastructure and promoting green modes of transport to shape NextGen Europe's mobility habits. Executive Vice President for the European Green Deal Frans Timmermans mentions: "faster European rail connections

43   Food and Agriculture Organization, "The African Continental Free Trade Area Agreement and agricultural development: challenges and prospects", *FAO Global Forum on Food Security and Nutrition*, 2020, https://www.fao.org/fsnforum/consultation/AFCFTA, accessed 1 September 2022.

44   European Court of Auditors, *Infrastructure for charging electric cars is too sparse in the EU*, Special Report 05/2021, 2021, https://op.europa.eu/webpub/eca/special-reports/electrical-recharging-5-2021/en/, accessed 1 September 2022.

with easy-to-find tickets and improved passenger rights support for cities to increase and improve public transport and infrastructure for walking and cycling, and making the best possible use of solutions for smart and efficient driving."[45]

RENEWABLE, AFFORDABLE AND SECURE ENERGY

The EGD proposes to increase the binding target of renewable sources to 40% in the EU's energy mix. As such, the EU seeks to further promote and enable the use of renewable fuels, such as hydrogen in energy-intensive industries and transport. In this respect, there is a need to scale up the development of hydrogen infrastructure and support hydrogen uptake in the EU.

Energy poverty is another menace to the green transition.

The quest for energy efficiency is also a fountainhead of local job creation, for instance in construction to meet the growing demand for more efficient buildings. The European Commission highlights that energy renovation will not only reduce GHG emissions but also create up to 160,000 new green jobs may be created in the construction sector by 2030.[46] Electrifying the EU's economy is also a key factor in meeting emission reduction targets.

CIRCULARITY

A range of actions may be undertaken to support a circular model of production and consumption in the EU, i.e., one that involves reuse, repair, sharing, recycling, refurbishment, etc. A 2021 survey provides that half of German, British and

---

45   European Commission, *New transport proposals target greater efficiency and more sustainable travel*, 2021, https://transport.ec.europa.eu/news/efficient-and-green-mobility-2021-12-14_en, accessed 1 September 2022.

46   European Commission, *Delivering the European Green deal*, https://ec.europa.eu/info/strategy/priorities-2019-2024/european-green-deal/delivering-european-green-deal_en, accessed 1 September 2022.

French consumers have purchased second-hand items over the course of a year.[47] There is a growing demand; the offer should follow-through. European companies should view the adoption of a circular business model as an opportunity for growth, innovation and job creation rather than a threat. Such a mind-set is key to reducing large-scale waste.

There are multiple aspects to a circular economy. It may imply sectorial efforts, including in the area of plastics, electric batteries, textiles and other consumer goods (fashion and luxury, electronics, home and living, non-food fast-moving consumer goods, sustainable toys, entertainment, among others). A major aim to ensure is the optimisation of a product's life cycle, including how they are designed, produced, marketed, and consumed. This means discouraging premature obsolescence of products, i.e., those specifically designed to have a limited lifespan to incite consumers to buy them again.

The EU Commission's Circular Economy Action Plan contains several relevant suggestions in that respect, including working towards the establishment of a "right to repair", for example regarding access to and availability of repair services and spare parts.[48] It is also important for consumers to have access to clear information about a product's characteristics and circularity, including its lifespan, repair modalities, and sustainability labels with ambitious minimum requirements. Digital technologies ought to be leveraged to guide European consumer choices with key data such as through product e-passports, resource mapping, tags, and watermarks (for online marketing).

47 S. Gatzer, S. Helmcke and D. Roos, "Playing offense on circularity can net European consumer goods companies €500 billion", McKinsey & Company, 2022, https://www.mckinsey.com/industries/consumer-packaged-goods/our-insights/playing-offense-on-circularity-can-net-european-consumer-goods-companies-500-billion-euros, accessed 1 September 2022.

48 European Commission, A new Circular Economy Action Plan For a cleaner and more competitive Europe, COM(2020) 98 final, 2020.

Another aspect of a circular economy is about restoring nature and enabling biodiversity to thrive once more. In this respect, sustainable forest management, strong forest protection, afforestation, will help increase carbon absorption, enhance climate change resilience, and protect EU Member States' biodiversity.

🔑 SUSTAINABLE, ETHICAL AND DIVERSE VALUE CHAINS

A better future through trade – leaving no one behind – cannot become a reality without the promotion of more sustainable, ethical and diverse value chains. Businesses will play a vital part in building a fairer and more sustainable economy. Greater attention should be placed on fostering greener and more responsible corporate behaviour throughout GVCs. To achieve these objectives, in 2022 the European Commission adopted a proposal for a Directive which lays down certain due diligence requirements that companies must follow.[49] It requires them to identify and, where necessary, prevent, end or mitigate the adverse impacts of their activities. These impacts may be twofold: (i) on human rights (e.g. regarding forced labour, child labour, exploitation of workers, inadequate workplace health and safety), and; (ii) on the environment (e.g. with respect to greenhouse gas emissions, pollution, or biodiversity loss and ecosystem degradation). The proposal still needs to be debated with Parliament and EU member states.

🔑 SUSTAINABLE COMPETITION

Circularity is also essential for long-term competitiveness, but there are several other competition aspects to consider.

---

49   European Commission, Proposal for a Directive of the European Parliament and of the Council on Corporate Sustainability Due Diligence and amending Directive (EU) 2019/1937, COM(2022) 71 final, 2022.

For instance, sustainability may boost the competitiveness of certain products, including food, as highlighted in the EGD's ambition to lead a "global transition towards competitive sustainability from farm to fork".[50] It could also entail preserving the EU's climate ambition by tackling unfair foreign competition from actors who are unlikely to be subject to stringent environmental protection rules. In this regard, the utility of the CBAM should be recalled.

The competition element of green public procurement (GPP) is also noteworthy as it provides opportunities for a competitive bidding process to achieve lower prices, but also greener results. Indeed, public authorities may be seen as major consumers, and they can combine their purchasing power with green objectives. It may be possible to fully unlock GPP potential as a tool to support the EGD,[51] perhaps by working towards ensuring that green purchasing requirements are compatible between member states and encouraging GPP as a best practice and introducing compulsory reporting to better monitor GPP uptake.

Finally, in June 2022 the European Council and the European Parliament reached a provisional political agreement on a corporate sustainability reporting directive (CSRD). The CSRD will allow the NextGen EU competition environment to factor in not only environmental but also social, human rights and governance factors by requiring more detailed reporting requirements for large companies and certain MSMEs (taking into account their characteristics), and

---

50   European Commission, *Farm to Fork Strategy: For a Fair, Healthy and Environmentally-Friendly Food System*, 2020, https://food.ec.europa.eu/system/files/2020-05/f2f_action-plan_2020_strategy-info_en.pdf, accessed 1 September 2022.

51   A. Sapir, T. Schraepen and S. Tagliapietra, "Green Public Procurement: A Neglected Tool in the European Green Deal Toolbox?", *Intereconomics*, Vol. 57, Number 3, 2022, https://www.intereconomics.eu/contents/year/2022/number/3/article/green-public-procurement-a-neglected-tool-in-the-european-green-deal-toolbox.html, accessed 1 September 2022.

this under the control of an accredited independent auditor or certifier. This is also coupled with the need to improve the accessibility of company-related information via the publication of their management reports.[52]

Making trade advance decent work in the EU and beyond

It is not uncommon to hear that workers are crucial to help keep the economy going. However, this should not be a one way street. The economy and trade must work for workers too, ensuring decent working conditions worldwide and allowing for increased social welfare through adequate policies.

The ILO promotes a decent work agenda via its Declaration on Fundamental Principles and Rights at work adopted in 1998, committing members to respect principles and rights in four areas: (i) freedom of association and the effective recognition of the right to collective bargaining; (ii) the elimination of all forms forced or compulsory labour; (iii) the effective abolition of child labour and; (iv) the elimination of discrimination in respect of employment and occupation. In 2022, the Declaration was amended to add a fifth category: (v) the right to a safe and healthy working environment.[53] It is worth noting that ILO member states (totalling 187 at the time of writing this *Handbook*) have committed to respect these principles whether or not they have ratified the relevant ILO Conventions.

In addition, the UN SDGs which frame the global development agenda until 2030 call for the promotion of sustained, inclusive and

---

52   European Council, New rules on corporate sustainability reporting: provisional political agreement between the Council and the European Parliament, 2022, https://www.consilium.europa.eu/en/press/press-releases/2022/06/21/new-rules-on-sustainability-disclosure-provisional-agreement-between-council-and-european-parliament/, accessed 1 September 2022.

53   International Labour Organization, *International Labour Conference adds safety and health to Fundamental Principles and Rights at Work*, 2022, https://www.ilo.org/global/about-the-ilo/newsroom/news/WCMS_848132/lang--en/index.htm, accessed 1 September 2022.

sustainable economic growth, full and productive employment and decent work for all by 2030. SDG Target 8.7 further calls for effective measures to eradicate forced labour, end modern slavery and human trafficking, and end child labour in all its forms.

First, Trade and Sustainable Development (TSD) chapters in trade agreements as well as the EU's Generalised Schemes of Preferences (GSP) are crucial tools to help uphold labour standards globally. In addition, increased focus on trade and skills policies for decent work and better jobs is essential to allow equal opportunities for all.

Enforcing trade and labour standards in NextGen trade agreements

The fact that there is an enduring tension between trade and labour, and therefore between multilateral efforts in the WTO and the ILO, must be recalled. In this respect, the EU has decided to go beyond the scope of the WTO on labour issues. This section echoes the one relating to the enforcement of trade and environment standards in NextGen agreements, covered above.

Most EU trade partners have ratified the fundamental ILO conventions.[54] Where this is not the case, however, the relevant trade deal commits the parties to making "continued and sustained efforts" towards ratifying the outstanding fundamental ILO Conventions.[55]

Since 2011 trade deals concluded by the EU have consistently included TSD chapters which provide for labour commitments on top of those relating to the environment. In their agreement, both parties commit to uphold international core labour rights and standards, including by putting in place domestic legal guarantees to ensure compliance with such standards as defined by the ILO, such as the freedom of association. In 2018 the EU launched its first ever

---

[54] The International Labour Organization's website lists the ILO fundamental conventions. *See* International Labour Organization, *Conventions and Recommendations*, https://www.ilo.org/global/standards/introduction-to-international-labour-standards/conventions-and-recommendations/lang--en/index.htm, accessed 1 September 2022.

[55] For instance, *see* Free Trade Agreement between the EU and its member states and the South Korea, 2011, Article 13.4.

bilateral trade dispute settlement process on a sustainable development commitment. It considered that the action taken by Korea to implement the provisions in the aforementioned agreement were insufficient. Three years later, the independent panel concluded that Korea needed to adjust its labour laws and practices and to swiftly continue the process of ratifying relevant ILO Conventions in order to comply with the agreement.

It is also worth looking at the EU's unilateral Generalised Scheme of Preferences (GSP). The regular strand of the GSP seeks to partially or fully remove import duties on two-thirds of tariff lines for products coming into the EU market from vulnerable economies. GSPs therefore constitute a platform to increase trading opportunities for these countries, to create growth, jobs and reduce poverty. The EU's ability to go beyond in terms opening its market to foreign countries goes hand in hand in with the protection of core labour standards and other values. This is clearly the case for its 'GSP+' feature as well as the 'Everything But Arms' which is the specific GSP scheme for the world's poorest countries.

Both are deemed special incentive arrangements in favour of sustainable development and good governance. 'GSP+' aims to further reduce the same tariffs as those contained in the regular GSP strand to 0% for vulnerable low- and lower-middle income partners, as long as they implement a series of international conventions on issues relating to labour and human rights, environmental and climate protection, and good governance. 'Everything But Arms' schemes provide relevant partners with duty-free quota-free access to EU markets for all products but arms and ammunitions, also in exchange of respecting a set of core international conventions. In 2020, the EU decided to suspend part of its trade preferences accorded to Cambodia through the Everything But Arms scheme over continued concerns expressed about human rights and labour violations.[56] This is

---

56   European Commission, *Cambodia loses duty-free access to the EU market over human rights concerns*, 2020, https://ec.europa.eu/commission/presscorner/detail/en/IP_20_1469, accessed 1 September 2022.

an example of how the EU GSP can be leveraged to promote labour and environment standards in trading partners' domestic systems.

Education and skills policies: an equal opportunity for all

Principle 1 of the European Pillar of Social Rights (EPSR), set out in 2017, underlines the significance of education and skills:

Everyone has the right to quality and inclusive education, training and lifelong learning in order to maintain and acquire skills that enable them to participate fully in society and manage successfully transitions in the labour market.

Part I highlighted some of the major changes in the global economy, including the rise of services, global value chains, sustainable trade, green goods and services, digitalisation etc. These transformations and transitions have resulted in changes at the levels of the market, in firms, for workers, for consumers, and more broadly for individuals and communities. It is interesting to note that, as consumers, individuals have in general benefited from lower prices, better quality goods and wider product variety. As workers, however, the above-mentioned evolutions may have costs within and among countries; they may be forced to leave their jobs and subsequently may find it difficult to access these various opportunities.

What exactly is the relationship between skills and trade, and how can the former help remedy shocks connected to the latter? Beyond the social aspect, what is the economic incentive for having skilled workers? What skills policy directions may be considered in Next-Gen EU to create an 'equal-opportunity-for-all' environment?

The connection between trade, skills and employment: from shocks to mutual benefits

Despite the impressive poverty reduction linked to trade-led growth, many people, communities, businesses and regions feel left out. In some of the world's richest countries, many people have failed to share in the gains from trade, openness, integration and technology. These workers feel left behind and they often blame globalisation for it. This fuels dissatisfaction, frustration, anger which may translate into domestic electoral consequences and, ultimately, pose a political threat to the open global economy. In addition, a much bigger group of people in developing countries have also failed to share in these gains. For instance, many countries, particularly in Africa, were left out of the global value chain revolution, except perhaps as raw materials suppliers. One should also pay attention to the role of technology as a source of anxiety for many workers, including the impact and shocks resulting from the ongoing artificial intelligence revolution.

With this in mind, when setting out to shape skills-based responses to trade-linked problems, policymakers may consider several motivational aspects (which may be cumulative).

1. Objective: nurturing a comparative advantage

An economy's ability to seize new opportunities and reap the broader benefits of trade, sustainability or of technology is conditioned by its capacity to adjust. Domestic policies may reduce adjustment costs and spread these benefits more inclusively. Reducing the number of those that are left behind means, as a corollary, enhanced contribution to the economy leading to bigger net gains from trade and technology, improved overall efficiency and higher income.[57] Skills development programmes may be more or less targeted towards developing a comparative advantage in specific activities or sectors, so as to strengthen the country's performance. As such, skills development systems and institutions should, across the board, be as responsive as possible to existing and upcoming skills needs of the market.

2. Objective: addressing employment shocks

Skills supply and skills policies have an important role to play in facilitating adjustments to trade-connected shocks. They may help smoothen transition of workers to higher-skill and productivity jobs in exporting firms and in up-and-coming sectors. Of course, the need to adjust to and mitigate such shocks is more important in LDCs. But even for developed countries there are major challenges to adjusting

---

57   International Labour Organization and World Trade Organization, *Investing in Skills for Inclusive Trade*, 2017, p.19.

to employment shocks which may heighten the priority that ought to be placed on skills development.

3. Objective: addressing wage inequality

Wage inequality may be exacerbated as a result of trade. A higher demand for certain skills may lead to a skill premium which may widen the wage inequality gap, especially in developing countries where it is already significant. The effect of the skill premium – the difference between the wage of high- and low-skilled workers – may be even more important if the skills supply is unresponsive.[58] Increasing the supply of marketable, in-demand skills may limit these gaps by democratising better-paid jobs, making them more accessible for more workers.

Looking beyond these different considerations, be it to address wage inequality, shocks or comparative advantage shortcomings, one can also examine the mutually beneficial relationship between trade and skills. A more specific focus is required on accessible high-quality education and skill policies which are instrumental to enabling and empowering those that have been left behind.

Skills policies matter for trade, efficiency and growth as well as for social imperatives. They equip workers to thrive in a changing economy whilst allowing the economy to further thrive in return by benefitting from top-notch workers. However, this is not automatic. According to the International Labour Organization (ILO): "effective skills development policies need to be integral components of national development strategies in order to prepare the workforce and enterprises for new opportunities and adopt a forward-looking approach to dealing with change".[59] At the international level, the ILO's Skills for Trade and Economic Diversification (STED) programme is also relevant to support countries' efforts to achieve decent work creation in key sectors for the future; those that have the potential to increase exports and contribute to growth. It aims to

---

58   International Labour Organization and World Trade Organization, *Investing in Skills for Inclusive Trade*, 2017, p.70.

59   International Labour Organization, Conclusions on Skills for Improved Productivity, Employment Growth and Development (International Labour Conference, 2008), 2008.

provide technical assistance on identifying, at sector level, some of the skills development strategies for future success in global trade.[60]

Trade and skills policies for EU workers: leaving no one behind

The EU's Social Rights Pillar proclaimed at the 2017 Gothenburg Summit sets out 20 principles and rights key for fair and well-functioning labour markets and social protection systems.[61] The Social Rights Pillar Action Plan – launched four years later in the midst of the Covid-19 pandemic – is designed to shape the actions to be taken by the Commission to effectively implement the principles of the Pillar.[62] The plan contains three main goals to be reached by 2030:

1. At least a 78% employment rate in the EU
2. At least 60% of adults attending training courses every year
3. Reducing by at least 15 million the number of people at risk of social exclusion or poverty, including 5 million children

The central role of skills and inclusive training to reach these objectives cannot be overstated. Within the Social Rights Pillar, active labour market policies (ALMPs) may enable public institutions to intervene and target specific groups of persons who are experiencing difficulties integrating or navigating the labour market. For instance, ALMP's include public employment services and other publicly funded services for jobseekers (training, job search assistance, entrepreneurship support programmes, among others).

The Action Plan is expected to undergo a review in 2025 and, in addition to the Commission's initiatives, other players, in particular individual EU member states, are encouraged to implement the suggested measures in their areas of competence. In the meantime,

---

60   C. Gregg, B. Tumurchudur Klok, "Rapid STED: A Practical Guide", *International Labour Organization*, 2020.

61   European Commission, *The European Pillar of Social Rights in 20 Principles*, https://ec.europa.eu/info/strategy/priorities-2019-2024/economy-works-people/jobs-growth-and-investment/european-pillar-social-rights/european-pillar-social-rights-20-principles_en, accessed 1 September 2022.

62   Ibid.

it is useful to turn to Joint Employment Report (JER)[63] published on a yearly basis and prepared by the European Commission and the Council to monitor the EU Employment Guidelines, and thus the employment situation in the Union. Most importantly, given existing synergies, the report's 2022 edition had an increased focus on the European Social Rights Pillar, including the content of the Action Plan, as well as the commitments made by EU leaders in May 2021 in the Porto Social Commitment. The signatories (the Portuguese Presidency of the European Council, the European Commission, the European Parliament and social partners) all agreed that "it is time to deliver in order to collectively ensure and support an ambitious agenda for economic and social recovery and modernisation", one that is "strong, sustainable and inclusive, so that all citizens can benefit from the twin green and digital transitions and live with dignity". The commitment suggests joining forces in order to implement policies aimed at inclusion, sustainability and job creation.

More specifically, one can look at the JER's review of the implementation of the employment guideline recommending that member states enhance labour supply and improve access to decent work, skills and competence (guideline no. 6). Several key findings and areas in need of improvement are highlighted in Figure 34:

2022 Joint Employment Report: selected excerpts.[64]

*"Participation in **early childhood education** and care has continued to increase in recent years, although significant*

---

63   European Commission, *Joint Employment Report 2022: As adopted by the Council on 14 March 2022*, 2022, available at: https://ec.europa.eu/social/main.jsp?catId=738&langId=en&pubId=8476&furtherPubs=yes, accessed 1 September 2022. The Commission's proposal for the report is part of the European Semester Autumn package; following exchanges between the Commission and its preparatory bodies the final text will be adopted by the Employment, Social Policy, Health and Consumer Affairs (EPSCO) Council.

64   European Commission, Joint Employment Report 2022: As adopted by the Council on 14 March 2022, 2022.

differences remain across Member States in terms of accessibility and quality."

*"The share of **early leavers from education and training** has decreased significantly, although the positive trend has slowed down and differences remain across countries."*

*"The share of early leavers from education and training is significantly higher among **non-EU-born pupils**."*

*"After years of steady progress, the share of 15- year-old pupils showing underachievement in basic skills is again on the rise, and students with **lower socio-economic backgrounds** face particularly difficult circumstances."*

*"Significant efforts are necessary to boost **pupils' digital skills** across the EU. [...] [T]he **pupils' socioeconomic or migrant background** remains a strong predictor of their level of digital skills. [...] EU Member States have recorded **limited progress in providing basic digital skills for adults**, and significant further efforts are needed on advanced digital skills."*

*"**Young persons with disabilities** still face difficult labour market prospects as a result of higher early school leaving and lower levels of tertiary educational attainment. [...] In 2019, at EU level about 21.8% of young persons with disabilities (aged 18-24) were early school leavers compared to 9.7% for those without."*

*"The existing **skills shortages in the EU labour markets are likely to persist and grow larger in some sectors and occupations**. [...] Eurofound reported increasing job vacancy rates in the construction, health care and information and communication sectors, where skills shortages were a structural problem already before the pandemic."*

*"**Adult skills development** remains far from standard practice throughout the EU. [...] In 2019, the participation rate of adults (aged 25-64) in learning activities (over the previous*

> *four weeks) reached 10.8%. In the context of the pandemic, in 2020, this rate dropped to 9.2%. [...] Adult learning participation among the low qualified remains significantly below the average."*

> *"The pandemic has significantly **increased the online share of adult learning**. [...] [However,] data point to **large cross-country differences** in online shares of adult learning, with **large gaps between women and men.**"*

> *"**Balancing work and parenting** obligations became relatively more difficult for women during the Covid-19 pandemic. [...] **Women's employment is strongly affected by access to quality and affordable early childhood education and care.**"*

Fig. 34: 2022 Joint Employment Report: selected excerpts.

Many governments, including in the EU, face constraints in their efforts to match the supply of skilled labour to the demand, noting that such constraints are often compounded in developing economies which tend to have more experience on this front as well as more robust education and training systems. Outlining the main constraints also helps set out some general considerations for coherent skills policymaking. These considerations are set out in Figure 35:

Some considerations for coherent skills policymaking.[65]
Anticipation:
1. Analysing skills needs may shed light on potential future skills development decision-making and may better inform on policy coherence and social dialogue.
2. Bearing in mind some previously mentioned trends, in particular sustainability and digitalisation, tomorrow's work-

---

65   V. Masterson, "These are the skills young people will need for the green jobs of the future", *World Economic Forum*, 2021, https://www.weforum.org/agenda/2021/08/these-are-the-skills-young-people-will-need-for-the-green-jobs-of-the-future/, accessed 1 September 2022.

ers will need certain skills for tomorrow's "green and digital jobs" (e.g., science, architecture, green engineering, agriculture, environmental justice, green energy, media, etc.).

3. Initial compulsory education is the starting point of coherent policymaking. Building strong core skills and knowledge during an individual's education cycle is crucial to strengthen skills quality assurance and pertinence to meet the needs of today and tomorrow.

4. Devising skills strategies may help build a comparative advantage, including in up-and-coming sectors.

Adaptation:

1. Continuous, life-long learning for workers at all skill levels underpins their ability to adapt.

2. Investing in training for workers may help business effectively implement strategies, to become more resilient to trade-connected shocks, to become more efficient, to create better managers, to increase compliance with regulations, to boost innovation, to become more sustainable, and to develop a more environmentally friendly and healthier work environment for its employees.

3. Combatting skills shortage may be done via reskilling (lateral learning experiences to acquire new skills) and upskilling (acquiring advanced skills with a view to doing a different job, as a steppingstone for career advancement). These are relevant for active workers and those who are or may risk being displaced, to strengthen their position on the job market.

Information and Dialogue:

1. Strengthening labour market information and employment services systems to provide and communicate the information needed by all, from governments to individual workers and students, to inform their decision-making.

2. Social dialogue is central to making skills systems responsive – both at national and sectoral level. Skills policies need to be connected to the needs of industries.

Inclusiveness:

1. Supporting MSMEs in their efforts to train their employees and have access to skilled workers.

2. Enhancing employability prospects and skills for people who are more vulnerable to trade-connected employment shocks, including women, youth, seniors, low-skilled workers.

3. Enhancing employability prospects and skills for people with disabilities, including by promoting equality, inclusion and diversity in learning programmes, recruitment processes, employment and business mindsets.

4. Employers must draw on the skills of all potential workers and learn to supervise and train employees with different characteristics.

5. Good practices for promoting LGBT+ inclusion within companies, including networks, charters and codes of conduct, awareness raising and training initiatives at the workplace.

E-Learning:

1. Due to social distancing and increased remote working, the Covid-19 pandemic emphasised the need to boost digital skills. Particular emphasis should be placed on computer literacy, which is now required in the vast majority of occupations. Digital learning from a young age but also for low-skilled workers and job-seekers with very few ICT skills is therefore essential.

Fig. 35: Some considerations for coherent skills policymaking.

Conclusion

Trade has a clear record in raising living standards and increasing prosperity in advanced and developing economies alike. Extreme poverty has been halved since 1990 and trade openness was instrumental in this achievement. Trading partners throughout the world stand to benefit from one another's respective strengths in the production of certain goods and services, following the principles of comparative advantage, specialisation, economies of scale and economic efficiency. The utilisation of these principles, along with globalisation and technological advancements, has built a global trade and economic integration system which is becoming more interconnected and intricate by the day. This system, however, has also been subject to legitimate concerns which must be remedied. Trade-related environmental harm, distributional aspects relating to unemployment or income, a decreased quality of certain goods, potential increases in prices, loss of resilience to shocks due to excessive dependence on trade partners – these are some of the main critiques that must be addressed. Given the EU's pre-eminent role in global trade and its allegiance to values, it is uniquely positioned to contribute to this task both at home and beyond. The European Union is the top foreign direct investment destination, the world's leading provider of official development assistance, the world's largest single market area, a trailblazer in deep economic integration; it possesses the world's largest trade agreements network covering an exceptional number of policy areas; it is the world's largest exporter of manufactured goods and services, and it is the largest export market for eighty countries, more than any other single market.

Despite its outstanding significance, trade must not be viewed in isolation. The challenge for policymakers lies in approaching trade with a comprehensive perspective, connecting the dots to adjacent policy areas. In order to promote to a greener, more inclusive and prosperous economy in the coming decades, adopting a trade-only lens is inadequate. Any path forward must imply a holistic approach. Seizing economic opportunities must be done in concert with supporting development and addressing social and environmental pressures.

The *Handbook* has shed light on some of the main trade trends with a focus on how to **make trade possible** – a must if a government is to conceive modern policies that are adapted to modern problems. Modern economies should know how to leverage global value chains, services and digitalisation. They should adopt technical measures to protect the health of their citizens whilst refraining from disguised protectionism. They should also leverage policy tools and trade in green goods and services to make trade greener and more inclusive. By moving beyond the traditional goods-and-tariffs policy areas, the next generation (NextGen) of trade agreements will help shape a better future.

The Multilateral Trading System (MTS), the system operated by the World Trade Organization (WTO), is crucial to maintaining a global trade environment that is more open, transparent, stable and predictable by: (i) facilitating the implementation of trade agreements and rules; (ii) providing a forum for negotiations between members; (iii) settling trade disputes; (iv) reviewing members' policies and; (v) cooperating with other international organisations, which proved paramount during the Covid-19 pandemic. Its 'sea of open trade' principles support trade and promote global economic welfare, including through non-discrimination, market access, transparency and notifications, special and differential treatment for developing and least developed countries, as well as continuing negotiations to expand open trade in new areas. However, its 'islands of protective exceptions' must not be submerged by open-trade-only perspectives, as they are also crucial to preserve major economic and non-economic principles (health, environment, security).

Downsized trade regimes and relations – be it bilateral, regional or plurilateral – may also constitute a way forward in the face of the several challenges affecting the MTS. Negotiations among like-minded groups of members are essential to advance work towards delivering timely and meaningful outcomes on 21st century issues (e-commerce, MSMEs, investment facilitation, environmental sustainability, etc.). The MPIA initiative also represents a plurilateral stop-gap solution to the paralysis of the WTO's Appellate Body. Nonetheless, any downsized initiatives must take into consideration associated risks of fragmentation and mind its legal architecture. Priority must therefore also be given to improving and strengthening the functioning of the MTS, as global problems require global solutions. How else would we address the gaping digital divide, worldwide pandemics and environmental imperatives?

The *Handbook* also focused on what is needed **to make trade happen**. Several elements are mentioned as conditions for a trade facilitating and welfare enhancing environment. Trade players need to harness available tools to help them make sound trade and market choices. There are countless tools out there by various agencies that may be leveraged by businesses and policymakers alike. Emphasis must especially be placed on how smaller businesses and developing countries can leverage these tools to increase their participation and tap into the benefits of global trade. Trade cannot happen without available resources to finance it. Inclusive access to trade finance is crucial, especially given that up to 80% of trade is financed by credit or credit insurance, often of a short-term nature due to the inherent risks linked to international trade. Trade finance gaps remain around the world, including in the EU within member states regarding smaller businesses and women, as well as among member states; some require more support in this respect than others. It is also more difficult for trade to happen without adequate infrastructure in place, and if that infrastructure does not leverage digital tools.

Making trade happen also requires adequate policy enforcement mechanisms. In addition, a protective environment must allow for the use of trade defence instruments against unfair trade practices that hurt businesses. Protecting innovators and their innovations should remain a top priority, especially as intellectual property rights protect and enable MSMEs' to grow. Foreign direct investment (FDI) is key to foster innovation and competitiveness but today it is also important to maintain a 'strategic conditional openness' approach to protect vital domestic security interests. Enforcement is also about dispute settlement. Here, trade dispute mechanisms ought to be repaired at the WTO, and strengthened in downsized dispute settlement systems (the MPIA, ad hoc appeals and bilateral and regional trade agreements). Arbitration of disputes between investors and states ought to continue the progress made towards becoming more inclusive, efficient and transparent as discussions for a Permanent Court are ongoing.

One should not forget about the 'losers' of globalisation, technology, trade and economic integration, notwithstanding their unique contribution to development and poverty reduction. Legitimacy of trade opening rests on **making trade work for all**. Concrete policies are needed to help manage various transition costs and to ensure that trade contributes to wider social inclusion and environmental agenda. A transition towards broad societal improvements is a multi-faceted, multi-domain, multi-actor and multi-level process.

Fair domestic tax policies and enhanced fiscal and budgetary capacity contribute to reducing inequalities. Empirical evidence shows that inequality spikes have not been uniform across the globe, even among regions subject to a comparable exposure to the forces of globalisation and technology. Europe has proven that governments have leverage to correct the downsides of trade, including via active labour market policies. International cooperation on corporate income taxation will be essential to address the loss of government revenue associated with profit shifting practices. In this respect, the OECD/G20 BEPS initiative is a tangible example of international efforts towards better globalisation; its outcome must be fully implemented.

On trade and environment, ambitious and meaningful action is required to limit global warming and adhere to the objectives and principles set out in multilateral environmental agreements. Different perspectives on growth and ecology exist, including some that involve shrinking rather than growing economies. But the importance of trade as a stepping stone for peace and as a driver for development and enhanced welfare the world over should be recalled. At the same time, adopting an environmental lens in trade and domestic policy is crucial to meet the environmental challenges of our time. International climate and trade diplomacy provides a vehicle to address issues of the global commons. But it will also be essential to ensure greater coherence with policies on agriculture, transportation, energy, value chain due diligence, circularity and competition, to name but a few.

Finally, for those who have found themselves on the wrong side of gaping economic inequality, skills and education policies must concentrate on leaving no one behind. There is a strong connection between trade, skills and employment.

In a nutshell, a progressive approach requires placing equal efforts on making trade possible, making it happen, as well as ensuring it works for the benefit of all.

The EU and global trade timeline

1941
The Atlantic Charter

Outlines objectives and principles of crucial importance to the UK and US for the post-WWII era. It underscores the key role to be played by trade and economic cooperation as a stepping stone for peace.

1947
Havana & the stillborn ITO

Havana hosts UN Conference on Trade and Employment. The ITO Charter is agreed on in March 1948 but ratification proves impossible in the US. Still, the General Agreement on Tariffs and Trade (GATT) lives on as the only multilateral instrument governing global trade.

1950
Schuman Declaration

French Foreign Minister Robert Schuman announces a plan for France and Germany to pool their coal and steel production, inviting other states to join them.

1944
Bretton Woods Agreement

Establishes a fixed currency exchange rate system using gold as a universal standard. Creates the IMF and World Bank, and also includes plans for an International Trade Organization (ITO).

1948
Start of the GATT years

From 1948 to 1995, the GATT provides the rules for much of world trade, despite being a provisional agreement at first. It is to evolve through successive rounds of negotiations which further open up trade.

1952
European Coal and Steel Community

The ECSC comes into being, based on the Schuman plan for deeper cooperation and integration of the coal and steel industries. Six countries take part: Belgium, France, (West) Germany, Italy, Luxembourg and the Netherlands.

1957
Two Rome Treaties

The six founding countries build on the success of the ECSC, expanding cooperation to other sectors. In 1957, the European Economic Community (EEC) and Euratom Treaties are signed.

1958
Birth of the EU Parliament

The European Parliamentary Assembly holds its first meeting, replacing the ECSC's Common Assembly. In 1962, it will formally change its name to European Parliament.

1960, May
EFTA is created

Some countries outside the EEC create the European Free Trade Association (EFTA) to promote their own economic integration. Founding countries are Austria, Denmark, Norway, Portugal, Sweden and the UK. By 2022, members include Iceland, Liechtenstein, Norway and Switzerland.

1960, Dec.
The OECD is Born

The Organisation for Economic Co-operation and Development (OECD) replaces its forerunner, the Organisation for European Economic Cooperation (OEEC). The definition of Official Development Assistance (ODA) adopted by its Development Assistance Committee (DAC) in 1969 becomes the "gold standard" of foreign aid.

1962
First European CAP

In the first European Common Agricultural Policy (CAP), the EEC six have joint control over food production. Later on, in the 1990s, surplus due to overproduction will require corrections for a more efficient CAP.

1967
Merging the three Communities

The Treaty merging the executives of the three communities (ECSC, EEC and Euratom) enters into force. The Commission and Council serve respectively as the administrative and the executive arm.

1971
End of the gold standard

US President Richard Nixon announces the end of the convertibility of the US dollar to gold. Until today, floating exchange rates are used; currencies reflect market conditions rather than being pegged to the value of gold.

1972
First World Conference on the Environment

The 1972 UN Conference on the Environment in Stockholm was the first world conference making the environment a major issue. Among other outcomes, it established the United Nations Environment Programme (UNEP).

1963
The EEC's first major international agreement

The Yaoundé Convention, signed by the EEC six with 18 recently independent African states, is the first association between Europe and Africa based on open trade and financial aid.

1968
Customs Union begins in Europe

All duties and restrictions are lifted among the EEC six, allowing free cross-border trade for the first time. They also apply common customs duties on goods from the rest of the world. However, some regulatory obstacles remain in the internal market.

1973, Jan.
First enlargement of the Communities

Denmark, Ireland and the United Kingdom formally join the European Communities, which now has nine members.

1973, Oct.
First global oil crisis

In the wake of the Fourth Arab-Israeli War, Arab oil exporters impose an embargo and price increases targeting countries that supported Israel, including certain European countries. In 1979, a second oil crisis hit the world in the aftermath of the Iranian revolution.

1981
Greece joins the EC

Greece joins the European Communities, becoming its tenth member.

1986
Spain and Portugal join the EC

Portugal and Spain join the European Communities, now composed of twelve members.

1988
IPCC established

The UN, via its World Meteorological Organization and UNEP, establishes the Intergovernmental Panel on Climate Change.

1979
First direct elections of the European Parliament

Prior to June 1979, members of the European Parliament were delegated by national parliaments. This is the first time European members of Parliament are directly elected by citizens of its now nine members.

1985
Schengen Agreement

The Schengen Area is established separately from the Communities due to divergences among members on the abolition of border controls. In 1985, half of them sign the agreement; as of 2022, it includes all bar Ireland which has opted out.

1987
Towards a Single Market

The Single European Act launches a process to sort out remaining regulatory differences so as to effectively create a single market. It also strengthens the competence and powers of the Communities.

1989
Fall of the Berlin Wall

The Berlin Wall falls on 9 November 1989. A year later, the Eastern half of Germany finally joins the European Communities.

1990
Europe's Gateway with Asia

Through the EU Gateway Programme, launched in 1990, the Union aims to deepen economic interaction and cooperation between Europe and Japan. The programme is later expanded to include other partners.

1992, Feb.
Maastricht Treaty

The Treaty on European Union (TEU) is signed in Maastricht. It formally establishes the European Union, composed of three pillars: the Communities, the common foreign and security policy (CFSP) and justice and home affairs (JHI).

1992, May
UNFCC adopted

The United Nations Framework Convention on Climate Change (UNFCC) is adopted at the UN Headquarters in New York.

1992, June
Earth Summit & Rio Declaration

The 1992 UN Earth Summit leads to the adoption of the Rio Declaration on Environment and Development. It is foundational in its adoption of a holistic perspective to sustainable development.

1993
Single Market established

Certain intangible barriers are finally replaced with mutually recognised standards and common regulations. The Single Market is hence established, along with its four freedoms: the free movement of people, goods, services and capital.

1994
Birth of the WTO

The end of the Uruguay Round of negotiations (1986-94) leads to the 1994 Marrakesh Agreement establishing the World Trade Organization. A year later, the WTO is operational, nearly 50 years after the failure of the ITO.

1995
Three new EU members

Austria, Finland and Sweden join the European Union (EU), which now has 15 members.

1997, Oct.
Treaty of Amsterdam signed

It reforms EU institutions, making substantial changes to the Maastricht Treaty, giving more powers to the Union (e.g. on employment and social matters, on police and judicial cooperation) and strengthening the EU Parliament's role.

1997, Dec.
Kyoto Protocol

At COP 3, countries achieve an important milestone with adoption of the world's first greenhouse gas emissions reduction treaty.

1999
The euro is born

Eleven countries adopt the euro, first for commercial and financial transactions only; euro bills and coins arrive in 2002. As of 2023, the Eurozone consists of 20 countries (Croatia being the latest country to have joined).

2001, Feb.
Treaty of Nice signed

The Nice Treaty is signed with the aim to reform the EU's institutional functioning and make the EU fit for further enlargement. It increases the EU Parliament's legislative and supervisory powers and extends the scope of qualified majority voting.

2001, Nov.
Doha Development Round

The Doha Round is launched at the WTO's Fourth Ministerial Conference, with development as its raison d'être and the aim to achieve major MTS reform by further opening up trade and creating rules in various areas.

2005, May
EU Constitution rejected

Voters in France and subsequently in the Netherlands reject the Treaty establishing a Constitution for Europe, signed by the 25 EU members the year before.

2007, Jan.
Two new EU members

Bulgaria and Romania join the EU which now has 27 members.

2008
At the heart of the Global Financial Crisis

Following a real estate market collapse in the United States, a major financial and economic crisis hits the world.

2004
Biggest EU enlargement

In 2004, 10 new countries join the EU which now has 25 members. Bar Cyprus and Malta, the newcomers are all Central and Eastern European countries (Czechia, Estonia, Hungary, Latvia, Lithuania, Poland, Slovakia and Slovenia).

2005, Dec.
Aid for Trade launched

The Aid for Trade initiative is launched at the Sixth WTO Ministerial Conference, and becomes a part of the OECD's ODA.

2007, Dec.
Lisbon Treaty signed

It amends previous treaties, giving Parliament the right to appoint the Commission's President, based on a proposal from the European Council which takes into account European Parliamentary elections results. Co-decision is extended to other areas.

2009
European Sovereign Debt Crisis Begins

Following the 2008 crisis, several EU countries face public finance challenges. The Eurozone debt crisis that ensues highlights the need for monetary governance improvements to make the euro work in the long run.

2012
European Monetary Stability, Coordination and Governance

A subset of EU members adopts the TSCG as a response to the debt crisis, outside the EU framework (due to a UK veto), while still conferring powers to EU institutions. As of 2022, all EU members but Czechia and Croatia signed the agreement.

2013, Sep.
Belt and Road Initiative

During an official visit to Kazakhstan in 2013, the Belt and Road Initiative (BRI) is unveiled by Chinese President Xi Jinping. Until 2015 it is known as "One Belt One Road".

2011
EU-South Korea trade deal

South Korea is the EU's first trading partner to ratify an agreement containing sustainable development obligations. From now on, all EU trade agreements are to include a trade and sustainable development chapter.

2013, July
A 28th EU member

Croatia joins the EU and becomes its 28th member.

2015
Paris Climate Agreement

Adopted at the COP 21, it is the first multilaterally binding treaty with the aim to combat climate change. It sets the goal to limit temperature rises to below 2°C with the target of 1.5°C by 2050.

2016, Jan.
UN Sustainable Development Goals come into force

The 17 SDGs are part of the 2030 UN Agenda for Sustainable Development adopted in 2015. The SDGs build on the UN Millennium Development Goals.

2016, June
Brexit

The United Kingdom votes to leave the EU by referendum. 52% vote in favour of the UK to leave. After 47 years in the Union, the UK officially leaves the EU as of February 2020.

2017
Launch of WTO plurilateral negotiations

Subsets of WTO members issue statements in 2017 and 2020 to launch plurilateral negotiations on major 21st century issues, including e-commerce, small enterprises, investment facilitation for development, sustainability.

2019, Nov.
Blue Dot Network

In 2019, the US, along with Japan and Australia, announce their own global infrastructure initiative: the Blue Dot Network.

2019, Dec.
European Green Deal

The European Commission presents its Green Deal strategy.

2020, Jan.
Covid-19

In January 2020, the WHO announces the spread of a coronavirus-related disease in Wuhan, China. Across the world, and in Europe, it triggers a major public health emergency and a historic economic slowdown.

2020, July
First EU sovereign debt bonds

The European Council agrees to issue EUR 750 billion worth of European sovereign bonds to support EU member states hit hard by the Covid-19 pandemic. The recovery package is coined 'Next Generation EU'.

2021, June
Build Back Better World

The Build Back Better World (B3W) initiative is proposed by the US at a Group of Seven (G7) Summit held in June 2021 and agreed upon. It builds on the progress and the principles of the Blue Dot Network.

2021, Nov.
EU Global Gateway

The EU Commission unveils its Global Gateway initiative which aims to be the European Union's contribution to narrowing the global investment gap.

2022, Feb.
Russia invades Ukraine

A sad day which sees war return in Europe. In response, the EU imposes sets of diplomatic and economic sanctions on Russia and Belarus as of April 2022. On 23 June 2022, the Council grants Ukraine the candidate status for EU accession.

2021, Nov.
First Global Tax Deal

An OECD/G20 initiative leads over 135 participants to join a plan to reform international taxation rules: the Inclusive Framework on BEPS (domestic tax base erosion and profit shifting). It aims to ensure that multinational enterprises pay a fair share of income tax wherever they operate.

2021, Nov.
COP 26 in Glasgow

The two major achievements: (i) The Agreement on the Paris Rulebook provides guidelines on the implementation of the 2015 Paris Climate Agreement. (ii) The Glasgow Climate Pact lists a series of non-binding resolutions including a first mention of phasing out coal and fossil fuel subsidies in a COP outcome document.

2022, June
Partnership for Global Infrastructure and Investment

G7 members unveil the PGII initiative. This project can be considered as another 'rebranded' version of the B3W initiative presented at the June 2021. The EU Global Gateway is also roofed by the PGII.

What's Next for the EU and Global Trade?

2022, June
WTO 12th Ministerial Conference

Despite ongoing and rising geopolitical tensions, WTO members agree to the Geneva Package which includes outcomes on response to emergencies (e.g. food insecurity and pandemics), on e-commerce, on fisheries subsidies WTO reform, etc.

Glossary

Active labour market policies (ALMPs)

Umbrella term for a variety of policies aiming to provide jobseekers with a more inclusive access to the labour market and better jobs. Such policies include public employment services, vocational training, job search assistance and entrepreneurship support, among others.

Aid for Trade (A4T)

The Aid for Trade initiative was launched at the Sixth WTO Ministerial Conference in December 2005. It aims to help developing and least developed countries engage in international trade – in particular by mobilising resources – to help address the obstacles they regularly encounter in the process (e.g. infrastructure and supply-side obstacles).

Anti-dumping duties

Tariffs levied on certain 'dumped' goods originating from a specific trading partner to offset the dumping margin (i.e. the difference between the import price and the normal value of the product in the exporting country).

Bilateral agreement

An agreement between two parties.

Circular economy

The circular economy is a model of production and consumption aimed at extending the life cycle of a given product and reducing waste as much as possible. Among other activities, it involves sharing, reusing, repairing, leasing, refurbishing and recycling existing materials and products.

Comparative advantage

Comparative advantage is the ability of a country or business to produce a particular good or service at a lower opportunity cost than others. It is an economic principle developed by David Ricardo which provides a strong argument in favour of specialisation and open trade for greater gains. Opportunity costs represent the potential losses of a country (or business) when choosing a course of action, foregoing other alternative options. The country with the greatest comparative advantage is that with the lowest opportunity costs in producing a good or service. For example, it would make sense for a country relatively better at producing wine than cars to specialise in wine making, investing more (resources, labour, equipment) in wine making and using profits from that sector to import cars instead.

Countervailing measures

Measures adopted by an importing country in the form of additional tariffs, with the aim to offset the subsidies given to exporters in the exporting countries.

Customs duties

Tariffs imposed at the border of a country on products when entering or leaving its territories. These charges are detailed in each country or customs territory's tariff schedule.

Deep trade agreements (DTAs)

DTAs are reciprocal trade agreements between countries that go beyond the traditional trade policy areas and also cover issues such as labour, sustainability, international investment flows and intellectual property rights, among others. These are still trade agreements but their goal is integration beyond trade, or 'deep integration'.

Dumping

Dumping occurs when a company exports a product at a price lower than the price it normally charges on its own home market. The WTO Anti-Dumping Agreement does not pass judgement on whether dumping is to be considered unfair competition. Its focus is rather on how members can or cannot react to this practice.

Economies of scale

The term economies of scale describes a situation in which, as a business grows, it may produce goods at a lower per-unit cost. Companies experience cost advantages as their production becomes more efficient and as costs can be spread over a larger amount of goods produced.

Efficiency (economics)

In the field of economics, efficiency is when all factors of production and resources in an economy (including goods, services, capital, land

and labour) are distributed or allocated to their most valuable uses, and thus where loss (or waste) is eliminated or minimized.

Foreign direct investment (FDI)

FDI refers to cross-border investments made by any kind of foreign investor with the aim to establish or maintain lasting interest in, and a significant degree of influence over an enterprise residing in another economy.

Global value chains (GVCs)

A value chain refers to all the activities and tasks required to bring a product from its conception to consumption by final consumers (including design, sourcing of components and materials to production, marketing, distribution and retail). A value chain does not need to be international. However, these processes have increasingly been happening across national borders and thus developing global traits.

Harmonised System (HS)

The HS has been set up by the World Customs Organisation to classify the different goods that are traded. Each participating member has to abide by the same classification system (including a six-digit code for each product) so as to facilitate customs related processes

Industrial entrepreneurship policies (IEPs)

For the purposes of this *Handbook*, what some authors refer to as 'new industrial policies' are here understood as 'industrial entrepreneurship policies'. This aims to better showcase the fact that a conducive, facilitating policy and infrastructure environment is required for entrepreneurs to be increasingly willing to bear the risks (and thus potentially enjoy the rewards) of seizing new business opportunities. IEPs can be considered as a 'package' of interactive strategies and measures aimed at fostering innovation, incentivising business and job creation and, in that regard, identifying what elements might inhibit open trade from realising its full potential, including enhanced welfare.

Integration

Economic integration is a process in which countries or territories reduce a variety of obstacles to advance a set of economic goals (e.g. increase trade between participants, reduce costs for producers and consumers) – albeit often motivated by political factors (e.g. a desire for enhanced political stability). There are different forms and levels of integration, ranging from economic collaboration to a highly complex and integrated economic and political space.

Although integration is first and foremost framed by members' trade relationships, it may gradually develop into an increasingly political relationship, eventually leading to what some may call a political union. This may entail a union of states that share some form of centralised decision-making, and which is recognised internationally as a single political entity.

The EU is a unique economic, monetary and political union. One example of this is the fact that European citizens are entitled to enjoy political rights (e.g. standing as a candidate and voting in elections to the European Parliament). In addition, the Charter of Fundamental Rights brings together personal, civic, political, economic and social rights enjoyed by people in the EU and which are guaranteed by the European Union, where EU law applies. Another example is the adoption of a common currency or monetary policy by EU member states which requires a certain convergence in macroeconomic policy and certain restraints on members' respective fiscal and expenditure policies. This may lead to a gradual blurring of the line between economic and political integration.

Different authors have adopted different perspectives when pointing to the levels and evolutions of integration. For instance, some refer interchangeably to 'common' and 'single' markets, others consider the latter to be a more integrated economic form. Below is an attempt to provide an overview of some of the main steps in the economic integration process, as relevant from the perspective of this *Handbook* and bearing in mind existing divergent views. This implies a journey from the most basic to the deepest forms of integration.

Preferential trade areas

Preferential trade agreements, unlike other trade agreements, can be unilateral. This means that the reduction of trade obstacles is not necessarily reciprocal.

Free trade areas

(i) Basic free trade areas mainly focus on traditional trade topics, i.e. goods and tariffs issues.

(ii) Deeper trade areas go beyond traditional trade topics to also cover regulatory issues such as subsidies and technical barriers to trade.

(iii) Deepest trade areas, as seen in the *Handbook*, cover policy areas beyond goods, including services, intellectual property, environment, labour, movement of people, consumer protection, research and technology as well as financial assistance.

Customs union

Groups of countries or territories form a customs union when they decide to apply a common system of procedures, rules and tariffs for all – or almost all – of their imports, exports and goods in transit. Participants in a customs union may also share common trade and competition policies.

Common market

The term 'common market' is often interchangeably referred to as 'single market' or 'internal market'. In addition to the removal of tariffs, a common market seeks to guarantee 'four freedoms' – the free movement of goods, services, people and capital – by removing relevant obstacles resulting from national borders.

Economic union

In addition to encompassing both a customs union and a common market, one could view an economic union as the close coordination of the national economic policies of the union's members.

Economic and monetary union

When an economic union involves monetary integration – be it through an agreed fixing of relative exchange rates or a common currency for some or all of its members – it becomes an economic and monetary union.

Complete economic integration

On top of all the elements of an economic union, complete economic integration implies a complete monetary union as well as a total harmonisation of fiscal policy (interchangeably referred to as a 'fiscal union').

Like product

A like product is a domestic product directly competitive or substitutable with a product under investigation. It therefore generally has the same or similar features to the investigated product. The scope of the term is likely to differ depending on the GATT article at issue (e.g. MFN, national treatment, dumping).

Market access

The ability of a company or country to sell goods and services across borders. More specifically, in a WTO context, it means the conditions (e.g. tariffs or non-tariff measures) agreed by members for the entry of goods and services into their domestic markets. Members' market access commitments are contained in their respective goods and services schedules.

Most-favoured-nation (MFN) principle

It is one of the non-discrimination pillars of the WTO, along with the national treatment obligation. According to the MFN principle, a WTO member is not allowed to discriminate between and among trading partners.

Multilateralism

In WTO parlance, 'multilateral' refers to activities on a global, or near-global, level. In particular, it covers issues of relevance to all WTO members, in contrast to regional or plurilateral work, i.e. work carried out by subsets of members.

National treatment principle

It is one of the non-discrimination pillars of the WTO, along with the most-favoured-nation clause. According to the national treatment principle, a member is not allowed to discriminate between products and services supplied by domestic entities and those supplied by foreign entities.

NextGen

For the purposes of this Primer, 'NextGen' refers mainly to the next generation of trade agreements or the next generation of the European Union. It aims to place emphasis on the role of the upcoming trade agreements as well as upcoming EU policies in shaping a better world including through increased consideration of elements which are essential to make trade happen (inclusive access to trade finance, aid for trade, digital infrastructure, etc.) and work for all (e.g. labour, sustainability, development).

Non-discrimination (ND)

Non-discrimination is a foundational pillar of the Multilateral Trading System. There are two basic ND principles: the most-favoured-nation (MFN) clause and national treatment.

Non-tariff measures (NTMs)

In WTO parlance, NTMs fall under the rubric of sanitary and phytosanitary (SPS) measures and technical barriers to trade (TBT). Generally, they are 'technical' measures (e.g. regulations, standards, testing, certification) but they may also be 'non-technical' (e.g. quotas, quantitative restrictions, and forced logistics or distribution channels).

Plurilateralism

In WTO parlance, this term refers to a 'less-than-multilateral' level, whereby a subset of WTO members will be conducting work and/or negotiations. It contrasts with multilateralism which refers to work carried out by the entirety of WTO members, hence on a global, or near-global, level.

Precautionism

Precautionist measures focus less on the protection of domestic firms but rather on efforts to protect people from various risks (consumer protection, health, safety, environment, etc.). The rise of precautionism, term coined by former WTO Director General and EU Commissioner for Trade Pascal Lamy, is made evident by the rise of non-tariff measures in trade relations.

Regional trade agreements (RTAs)

RTAs are a generic term often used in WTO parlance to refer to reciprocal agreements, including customs unions or free trade agreements, without necessarily including members from the same region (e.g. EU-Canada Comprehensive Economic).

Rules of origin

All goods traded internationally are required to have an origin (economic origin) when they are declared to customs at an import point. Rules of origin enable consumers and businesses to establish the origin of the good. The rise in global value chains and the increase in trade of components have made it increasingly difficult to attribute a single country of origin when several countries are involved in the chain of production.

Safeguards

Safeguard measures may be adopted by a WTO member to protect a specific domestic industry from a sudden and sharp increase in imports of any product causing, or threatening to cause, serious injury to its domestic industry. Generally, safeguards are characterised by temporary import restrictions of a given product.

Schedules

The schedules represent WTO members' market access commitments. Each member must have one schedule for goods and one for services. Goods schedules provide a tariff binding for each product, i.e. the duty level that a member is bound to respect. Services schedules contain requirements that a member applies to allow foreign services suppliers to supply services in their territory.

Servicification

Behind the term 'servicification' lies the observation that businesses, including the manufacturing sector, are increasingly dependent on services.

Single market

Trade bloc spanning over several countries that functions without border regulations (e.g. technical standards) and without tariffs which typically apply to trade relations between countries. The single market allows for the unrestricted movement of goods, services, capital and labour.

Special and differential treatment (SDT)

The WTO Agreements contain provisions which provide special rights to developing and least developed countries, i.e. 'special and differential treatment' provisions. For example, SDT measures may confer longer implementation periods, additional flexibility, support in the form of technical assistance and capacity building.

Subsidies

Grants or financial contribution given by a government – or any public body – within its territory which confers a benefit.

Trade in tasks

Trade in tasks generally refers to the 'outsourcing' of activities that a company initially provided in-house; or 'offshoring' if this implies relocation of such activities abroad to a foreign company. This enables companies to make use of a country's comparative advantage at the task level.

Trade intelligence

Trade intelligence is considered broadly in this *Handbook*. It refers to the strategies and technology tools used by various economic actors, governments or businesses, for example, for analysis, management and decision-making in a trade and business context.

Triple-win

Triple-win outcomes refer to outcomes that are beneficial at the same time for social development, economic growth and environmental sustainability.

List of abbreviations

A4T: Aid for trade

AB: Appellate Body (of the WTO)

ACCTS: Agreement on Climate Change, Trade and Sustainability

AfCFTA: African Continental Free Trade Area

ALMP: Active labour market policies

AML: Anti-money-laundering

APEC: Asia-Pacific Economic Cooperation

B3W: Build Back Better World initiative

BEPS: OECD/G20 Inclusive Framework on Base Erosion and Profit Shifting

BoP: Balance of payments

BRI: Belt and Road Initiative

CBAM: Carbon Border Adjustment Mechanism

CEE: Central and Eastern European

CETA: EU-Canada Comprehensive Economic Trade Agreement

CFT: Countering the financing of terrorism

COP: Conference of the Parties of the UNFCC

Covid-19: Coronavirus disease

CSRD: 2022 EU Corporate Sustainability Reporting Directive

CTE and CTESS: The WTO's Committee on Trade and Environment and its Special Session

CTEO: The European Commission's Chief Trade Enforcement Officer

DAC: The OECD's Development Assistance Committee

DSB: The WTO's Dispute Settlement Body

DSU: The WTO's Dispute Settlement Understanding

DTA: Deep trade agreement

EBRS: European Bank for Reconstruction and Development

EC: The European Commission

ECSC: European Coal and Steel Community

EEC: European Economic Community

EFTA: European Free Trade Association

EGA: WTO initiative on an Environmental Goods Agreement

EGD: European Green Deal

EGSS: Environmental goods and services sector

EIB: European Investment Bank

EIF: Enhanced Integrated Framework for Trade-Related Assistance for the Least Developed Countries

ESG: Environment, social and governance

EU: European Union

Euratom: European Atomic Energy Community

Eurofound: European Foundation for the Improvement of Living and Working Conditions

ETS: The EU's Emissions Trading System

FDI: Foreign direct investment

FEPS: Foundation for European Progressive Studies

FFSR: WTO initiative on Fossil Fuel Subsidy Reform

FTA: Free trade agreement

G7: Group of Seven intergovernmental forum

G20: Group of 20 intergovernmental forum

GATS: General Agreement on Trade in Services

GATT: General Agreement on Tariffs and Trade

GDP: Gross domestic product

GHG: Greenhouse gas

GI: Geographical indications

GPP: Green public procurement

GSP: WTO Generalised System of Preferences

GVC: Global value chain

HS: Harmonized system

ICC: International Chamber of Commerce

ICT: Information and communication technology

IDP: WTO Informal Dialogue on Plastics Pollution and Sustainable Plastics Trade

IEP: Industrial entrepreneurship policies

IFC: International Finance Corporation

ILO: International Labour Organization

IMF: International Monetary Fund

IPCC: Intergovernmental Panel on Climate Change

IPR: Intellectual property rights

ISDS: Investor-state dispute settlement

ITO: International Trade Organization

IUU fishing: Illegal, unreported and unregulated fishing

ITC: International Trade Centre

JER: Joint Employment Report by the European Commission and the European Council

JTM: Just Transition Mechanism

KYC: Know your customer

LDCs: Least developed countries, listed by the UN Economic Analysis and Policy Division's Committee for Development

LLDC: Landlocked developing country

MEA: Multilateral environmental agreement

MFN: Most favoured nation, international trade status

MNE: Multinational enterprise

MPIA: Multi-Party Interim Appeal Arbitration Arrangement

MSME: Micro, small and medium-sized enterprises

MTS: Multilateral trading system

NAFTA: North American Free Trade Agreement (1994-2020)

ND: Non-discrimination

NextGen: Next generation (NextGen EU, NextGen trade agreements, etc.)

NGO: Non-governmental organisation

NTB: Non-tariff barrier

NTM: Non-tariff measure

ODA: Official development assistance

OECD: Organisation for Economic Co-operation and Development

OEEC: Organisation for European Economic Cooperation

PGII: G7 Partnership for Global Infrastructure and Investment

PCO: Prudential carve-out

PPP: Public-private partnership

PTA: Preferential trade agreement

PV: Photovoltaic

QR: Quantitative restriction

RTA: Regional trade agreement

SGP: EU Stability and Growth Pact

TESSD: WTO Structured Discussion on Trade and Environmental Sustainability

TFA: Trade facilitation agreement

TPRB: The WTO's Trade Policy Review Body

TPRM: The WTO's Trade Policy Review Mechanism

TRIPS Agreement: The WTO Agreement on Trade-Related Aspects of Intellectual Property

TSCG: 2012 Treaty on Stability, Coordination and Governance in the Economic and Monetary Union

TSD: Trade and sustainable development

UK: United Kingdom

UN: United Nations

UNCITRAL: United Nations Commission on International Trade Law

UNCTAD: United Nations Conference on Trade and Development

UNEP: United Nations Environment Programme

UNFCC: United Nations Framework Convention on Climate Change

US: United States

USMCA: US-Mexico-Canada Agreement (successor to NAFTA)

SDG: Sustainable Development Goals

SDT: Special and differential treatment

SPS: Sanitary and phytosanitary

STO: Specific trade obligation

TBT: Technical barrier to trade

TFEU: Treaty on the Functioning of the European Union

TRTA: Trade-related technical assistance

WCO: World Customs Organization

WHO: World Health Organization

WIPO: World Intellectual Property Organization

WTO: World Trade Organization
WWII: Second World War

List of figures

Fig. 1: GDP per capita and world exports.   24

Fig. 2: Billions of extreme poor and share of population.   25

Fig. 3: Stages of production processes and reliance on services. The example of the servicification of Swedish manufacturing.   41

Fig. 4: Growth of world trade in goods and commercial services.   43

Fig. 5: Growth of e-commerce retail sales worldwide in billion USD, 2014-2025 (including future projections).   45

Fig. 6: Key indicators for the environmental economy and the overall economy, EU-27, 2000-2017.   46

Fig. 7: The number of RTAs with gender-related provisions has increased steadily.   49

Fig. 8: ePing SPS and TBT Platform – Number of SPS and TBT notifications per year since the creation of the WTO.   51

Fig. 9: Share of policy areas for different PTAs.   53

Fig. 10: The sea of open and regulated trade and its islands of protective exceptions.   74

Fig. 11: Excerpt taken from Canada's goods schedule.   78

Fig. 12: Excerpt taken from Mexico's services schedule.   79

Fig. 13: Recap of the islands of protective exceptions: what form of exception and what aim?   94

Fig. 14: Example of the fragmentation of the e-commerce governance network (2020).   101

Fig. 15: Application of the WTO moratorium on customs duties on electronic transmissions – example of the e-book.   112

Fig. 16: Share of global foreign direct investment (FDI) in 2018 (%).   122

Fig. 17: China, the US and the EU: trade and investment strategies.   125

Fig. 18: Sources of funding, by gender in the EU, ITC business survey (2019).   128

Fig. 19: Total ODA in USD billions from all DAC countries(1960-2021).   132

Fig. 20: EU & 27 EU member states' Aid for Trade action by
        geographical coverage (%).   133
Fig. 21: Transport and insurance costs of international trade
        across all transport modes and commodities.
        Percentage share of value of imports, 2006–2016.   139
Fig. 22: Estimated penetration of ICTs
        by level of development, 2016.   141
Fig. 23: Mobile money accounts by region in 2020 (millions)
        and transaction value (in billion USD).   145
Fig. 24: Examples of international trade related regulatory activity. 148
Fig. 25: Gains from the digitalisation of customs documentation.   149
Fig. 26: EU member states with an investment screening
        mechanism or relevant legislative activities.   158
Fig. 27: The poorest half lags behind: Bottom 50%, middle 40%
        and top 10% income shares across the world in 2021.   170
Fig. 28: Spending on ALMPs as a percentage of GDP, by type
        of measure, across regions, various years.   171
Fig. 29: Reliance on corporate income taxes (CIT) in Europe.
        CIT collections as a percent of total tax revenue in
        European OECD Countries, 2019.   178
Fig. 30: A graphical representation of triple-win between the social,
        economic and environmental dimensions of
        sustainable development.   183
Fig. 31: Selected countries, GDP per person growth and
        CO_2 emissions reductions (2010-2019).   185
Fig. 32: Change in per capita CO_2 emissions and GDP,
        Denmark (1990-2019).   186
Fig. 33: The keys to help the EU achieve its sustainability objectives. 193
Fig. 34: 2022 Joint Employment Report: selected excerpts.   209
Fig. 35: Some considerations for coherent skills policymaking.   211

Bibliography

#

2Zero Emission, *EGVIAfor2Zero – Private Side of the Partnership*, available at: https://www.2zeroemission.eu/, accessed 1 September 2022.

A

African Union, *African Union and European Union step up digital cooperation for Sustainable Development in Africa following EU-AU Summit*, 2022, https://au.int/en/pressreleases/20220323/african-union-and-european-union-step-digital-cooperation-sustainable, accessed 1 September 2022.

Agreement between the European Union and Japan for an Economic Partnership, 2018.

Agreement Between the World Intellectual Property Organization and the World Trade Organization, 1995.

Agreement on the Application of Sanitary and Phytosanitary Measures.

Agreement on Technical Barriers to Trade.

Anderson, J., and Caimi, G., "3 ways digital technology can be a sustainability game-changer", *World Economic Forum*, https://www.weforum.org/agenda/2022/01/digital-technology-sustainability-strategy/#:~:text=Todaypercent2Cpercent20digitalpercent20technologiespercent20arepercent20being,alsopercent20enablepercent20innovationpercent20andpercent20collabouration, accessed 1 September 2022.

Andrenelli, A., and López González, J., "Electronic transmissions and international trade – shedding new light on the moratorium debate", OECD, Trade Policy Papers, No. 233, *OECD* Publishing, Paris: 2019.

Ambroziak, Ł., "The CEECs in global value chains: The role of Germany", *Acta Oeconomica*, Vol. 68, Issue 1, 2018, p.1-29.

Asen, E., "Reliance on Corporate Income Tax Revenue in Revenue", *Tax Foundation*, 2021, https://taxfoundation.org/reliance-on-corporate-income-taxes-in-europe-2021/#:~:text=In%202019%E2%80%94the%20most%20recent,from%20corporate%20income%20taxes, accessed 1 September 2022.

Asian Development Bank, *Modernizing Sanitary and Phytosanitary Measures to Facilitate Trade in Agricultural and Food Products: Report on the Development of an SPs Plan for the CAREC Countries*, 2013.

Asian Development Bank and World Trade Organization, *The Global Value Chain Development Report 2021: Beyond Production*, 2021.

Asia-Pacific Economic Cooperation, Leaders' Declaration, 2012.

Auboin M., and Gonzalez Behar, V., "Why exporters need to mind the trade finance gap", *World Economic Forum*, 2020, https://www.weforum.org/agenda/2020/02/exporters-mind-trade-finance-gap/, accessed 1 September 2022.

Autor, D., Dorn, D., and Hanson, G.H., "On the Persistence of the China Shock", *NBER Working Paper Series*, Working Paper 29401, 2021, https://www.nber.org/system/files/working_papers/w29401/w29401.pdf, accessed 1 September 2022.

B

Baldwin, R., *The Globotics Upheaval: Globalization, Robotics and the Future of Work*, Oxford University Press: 2020, p.63.

Baldwin, R., "Global Supply Chains: Why they Emerged, Why they Matter, and Where they are Going", in D. K. Elms and P. Low, *Global Value Chains in a Changing World*, WTO Publications, 2013.

Baldwin, R., and Ito, T., "The Smile Curve: Evolving Sources of Value Added in Manufacturing", *Canadian Journal of Economics*, 54(4), 2022, p.1842-1880.

Banga, R., "Growing Trade in Electronic Transmissions: Implications for the South", *UNCTAD*, Research Paper No. 29, 2019.

BBC News, *AUKUS: Australia to pay €555m settlement to French firm*, 11 June 2022, https://www.bbc.com/news/world-australia-61770012, accessed 1 September 2022

Bellelli, F. S., and Xu, A., *How do environmental policies affect green innovation and trade? Evidence from the WTO Environmental Database (EDB)*, World Trade Organization, Staff Working Paper ERSD-2022-03, 2022, https://www.wto.org/english/res_e/reser_e/ersd202203_e.pdf, accessed 1 September 2022.

Bhagwati, J., "US Trade Policy: The infatuation with free trade agreements", *Columbia University*, Discussion Paper Series, No. 726, 1995.

Blake, H., and Bulman, T., "Surging energy prices are hitting everyone, but which households are more exposed?", *Organisation for Economic Cooperation and Development*, 2022, https://oecdecoscope.blog/2022/05/10/surging-energy-prices-are-hitting-everyone-but-which-households-are-more-exposed/, accessed 1 September 2022.

Bourgeois, Y. M., "International Investment Arbitration: Legitimacy Challenges and Prospects for Future Reforms", *Sorbonne Student Law Review*, Vol. 2 No. 2, 2019.

C

Cantore, C. M., *The Prudential Carve-Out for Financial Services: Rationale and Practice in the GATS and Preferential Trade Agreements*, Cambridge University Press: 2018

Campos, N. F., Coricelli, F., and Moretti, L., "Institutional integration and economic growth in Europe", *Journal of Monetary Economics*, Volume 103, May 2019, Pages 88-104.

Carrère, C., Olarreaga, M., and Raess, D., *Labour Clauses in Trade Agreements: worker protection or protectionism?*, 2017, available at: https://www.wto.org/english/res_e/reser_e/gtdw_e/wkshop17_e/rass_e.pdf, accessed 1 September 2022.

Carrière-Swallow, Y., Deb, P., Furceri, D., Jiménez D. and Ostry, J. D., "Shipping Costs and Inflation", *International Monetary Fund*, Working Paper WP/22/61, 2022.

Casarini, N., "Defend, Engage, Maximise: A Progressive Agenda for EU-China Relations", *Foundation for European Progressive Studies*, FEPS Policy Paper, 2019.

Cecchetti, S., and Schoenholtz, K., "Sudden stops: A primer on balance-of-payments crises", Vox EU, 2018, https://cepr.org/voxeu/blogs-and-reviews/sudden-stops-primer-balance-payments-crises, accessed 1 September 2022.

Cerdeiro, D. A., Mano, R., Eugster, J., Muir, D. V., and Peiris, S. J., "Sizing Up the Effects of Technological Decoupling", *International Monetary Fund*, Working Paper WP/21/69, 2021.

Chancel, L., Piketty, T., Saez, E., and Zucman, G., *World Inequality Report 2022*, 2022.

Charter of Fundamental Rights of the European Union, 2012, OJ C 326/02.

Clancy, J., and Feenstra, M., "Women, Gender Equality and the Energy Transition in the EU", *European Parliament*, 2019.

Clean Aviation, *Clean Sky 2*, available at: https://www.cleansky.eu/, accessed 1 September 2022.

Commission on Growth and Development, *The Growth Report: Strategies for Sustained Growth and Inclusive Development*, 2008.

Consolidated version of the Treaty on the Functioning of the European Union, OJ C 326/01.

Coy, P., "'Onshoring' is so Last Year. The New Lingo is 'Friend-Shoring'", Bloomberg, 2021, https://www.bloomberg.com/news/articles/2021-06-24/-onshoring-is-so-last-year-the-new-lingo-is-friend-shoring#xj4y7vzkg, accessed 1 September 2022.

D

Damen, M., "The European Union and its trade partners", European Parliament, Fact Sheets on the European Union, 2021, https://www.europarl.europa.eu/factsheets/en/sheet/160/the-european-union-and-its-trade-partners, accessed 1 September 2022.

Daniel, W., "Apple was the most profitable company on the Fortune 500 list this year. These are the biggest profit generators, and what that means about American business", *Fortune*, 2022, https://fortune.com/2022/05/24/fortune-500-most-profitable-companies-apple-berkshire-amazon-google-microsoft/, accessed 1 September 2022.

Demirgüç-Kunt, A., Klapper, L., Singer, D. and Ansar, S., "The Global Findex Database 2021: Financial Inclusion, Digital Payments, and Resilience in the Age of Covid-19", *World Bank*, 2022.

Devadas, S., and Loayza, N., "When is a Current Account Deficit Bad?", *World Bank*, Research Policy Briefs, No. 17, October 2018.

DIGITALEUROPE, *DIGITALEUROPE and global industry associations call on EU, US and Japanese ministers to take action on digital trade at WTO MC12*, 2022, https://www.digitaleurope.org/news/digitaleurope-and-global-industry-associations-call-on-eu-us-and-japanese-ministers-to-take-action-on-digital-trade-at-wto-mc12/, accessed 1 September 2022.

DS400 and DS401: European Communities – Measures Prohibiting the Importation and Marketing of Seal Products.

DS453: Argentina – Measures Relating to Trade in Goods and Services.

DS512: Russia – Measures Concerning Traffic in Transit.

DS544, 547, 548, 552, 554, 556 and 564: United States – Certain Measures on Steel and Aluminium Products.

DS567: Saudi Arabia – Measures concerning the Protection of Intellectual Property Rights.

DS583: Turkey – Certain Measures concerning the Production, Importation and Marketing of Pharmaceutical Products.

Dusek, M., "Business leaders embrace Europe's new green reality for investment and growth", *World Economic Forum*, 2020, https://www.weforum.org/agenda/2020/09/business-leaders-embrace-europe-s-new-green-reality-for-investment-and-growth/, accessed 1 September 2022.

E

The Economist, *The Great Teslafication*, 18 June 2022, https://www.economist.com/business/2022/06/12/how-supply-chain-turmoil-is-remaking-the-car-industry, accessed 1 September 2022.

The Economist, *Several rich countries have decoupled GDP growth from emissions*, 2021, https://www.economist.com/graphic-detail/2021/11/11/several-rich-countries-have-decoupled-gdp-growth-from-emissions, accessed 1 September 2022.

Eichengreen, B., *Globalizing Capital: A History of the International Monetary System*, Third Edition, Princeton University Press: 2019.

Ellerbeck, S., "The Great Resignation is not over: A fifth of workers plan to quit in 2022", *World Economic Forum*, 2022, https://www.weforum.org/agenda/2022/06/the-great-resignation-is-not-over/, accessed 1 September 2022.

Enhanced Integrated Framework, *Funding Partners*, available at: https://enhancedif.org/donors, accessed 1 September 2022.

EUR-Lex, *Multiannual financial framework (MFF)*, https://eur-lex.europa.eu/EN/legal-content/glossary/multiannual-financial-framework-mff.html, accessed 1 September 2022.

European Bank for Reconstruction and Development, *Trade Facilitation Programme: Overview*, https://www.ebrd.com/work-with-us/trade-facilitation-programme.html, accessed 1 September 2022.

European Commission, *A new Circular Economy Action Plan For a cleaner and more competitive Europe*, COM(2020) 98 final, 2020.

European Commission, *Access2Markets*, available at: https://trade.ec.europa.
eu/access-to-markets/en/content/about-access2markets, accessed 1 September 2022.

European Commission, *Annex to the Communication from the Commission to the European Parliament, the Council, the European Economic and Social Committee and the Committee of the Regions, Trade Policy Review – An Open, Sustainable and Assertive Trade Policy*, 2021, https://trade.ec.europa.eu/doclib/docs/2021/february/tradoc_159439.pdf, accessed 1 September 2022.

European Commission, *Batteries and accumulator*, https://environment.ec.europa.eu/topics/waste-and-recycling/batteries-and-accumulators_en, accessed 1 September 2022.

European Commission, *Bilateral disputes*, https://policy.trade.ec.europa.eu/enforcement-and-protection/dispute-settlement/bilateral-disputes_en#:~:text=The%20EU%20includes%20a%20dispute,the%20WTO%20dispute%20settlement%20system, , accessed 1 September 2022.

European Commission, *Cambodia loses duty-free access to the EU market over human rights concerns*, 2020, https://ec.europa.eu/commission/presscorner/detail/en/IP_20_1469, accessed 1 September 2022.

European Commission, *Commission unveils new approach to trade agreements to promote green and just growth*, 2022, https://ec.europa.eu/commission/presscorner/detail/en/ip_22_3921, accessed 1 September 2022.

European Commission, Communication, COM(2020) 456 final, 2020.

European Commission, *Count your transport emissions – "CountEmissions EU"*, https://ec.europa.eu/info/law/better-regulation/have-your-say/initiatives/13217-Count-your-transport-emissions-CountEmissions-EU_en, accessed 1 September 2022.

European Commission, *Daily News 14/07/2020*, 2020, https://ec.europa.eu/commission/presscorner/detail/en/mex_20_1349, accessed 1 September 2022.

European Commission, *Delivering the European Green Deal*, https://ec.europa.eu/info/strategy/priorities-2019-2024/european-green-deal/delivering-european-green-deal_en, accessed 1 September 2022.

European Commission, *EU 27 Trade in Goods and Services by Partner* (2021), Eurostat, https://trade.ec.europa.eu/doclib/docs/2006/september/tradoc_122530.pdf, accessed 1 September 2022.

European Commission, *EU Aid for Trade: Progress Report 2021*, 2021.

European Commission, *EU Gateway | Business Avenues supports European companies in Asia*, https://fpi.ec.europa.eu/stories/eu-gateway-business-avenues-supports-european-companies-asia_en#:~:text=The%20 Programme%20helped%20thousands%20of,%2C%20logistics%2C%20 and%20customised%20services, accessed 1 September 2022.

European Commission, *EU modernises its trade defence instruments*, 2018, https://ec.europa.eu/commission/presscorner/detail/en/MEMO_18_396, accessed 1 September 2022.

European Commission, *EU position in World Trade*, https://policy.trade. ec.europa.eu/eu-trade-relationships-country-and-region/eu-position-world-trade_en, accessed 1 September 2022.

European Commission, *EU trade agreements: delivering for Europe's businesses*, 2020, https://ec.europa.eu/commission/presscorner/detail/en/ ip_20_2091, accessed 1 September 2022.

European Commission, E*U wins WTO case against Turkey's discriminatory practices on pharmaceuticals*, 2022, https://ec.europa.eu/commission/press-corner/detail/en/IP_22_4670, accessed 1 September 2022.

European Commission, *European Commission appoints its first Chief Trade Enforcement Officer*, 2020, https://ec.europa.eu/commission/presscorner/ detail/en/IP_20_1409, accessed 1 September 2022.

European Commission, *The European Pillar of Social Rights in 20 Principles*, https://ec.europa.eu/info/strategy/priorities-2019-2024/economy-works-people/jobs-growth-and-investment/european-pillar-social-rights/european-pillar-social-rights-20-principles_en, accessed 1 September 2022.

European Commission, *European Semester Thematic Factsheet: Addressing Inequalities*, 2017, available at: https://ec.europa.eu/info/sites/default/files/ file_import/european-semester_thematic-factsheet_addressing-inequalities_en_0.pdf, accessed 1 September 2022.

European Commission, *Factual summary report of the online public consultation in support to the fitness check and revision of the EU animal welfare legislation*, Summary report Ares(2022)2359311, 2022, Available at: https://ec.europa.eu/info/law/better-regulation/have-your-say/initiatives/12950-Animal-welfare-revision-of-EU-legislation/public-consultation_en, accessed 1 September 2022.

European Commission, *Farm to Fork Strategy: For a Fair, Healthy and Environmentally-Friendly Food System*, 2020, https://food.ec.europa.eu/system/

files/2020-05/f2f_action-plan_2020_strategy-info_en.pdf, accessed 1 September 2022.

European Commission, *Foreign Direct Investment in the EU: Following up on the Commission Communication "Welcoming Foreign Direct Investment while Protecting Essential Interests" of 13 September 2017*, Commission Staff Working Document, 2019.

European Commission, *Foreign direct investment report: continuous rise of foreign ownership of European companies in key sectors*, 2019, https://ec.europa.eu/commission/presscorner/detail/en/IP_19_1668, accessed 1 September 2022.

European Commission, *G20 Leaders' Communique Hangzhou Summit*, Statement, 2016, https://ec.europa.eu/commission/presscorner/detail/en/STATEMENT_16_2967, accessed 1 September 2022.

European Commission, *History of the Stability and Growth Pact*, https://economy-finance.ec.europa.eu/economic-and-fiscal-governance/stability-and-growth-pact/history-stability-and-growth-pact_en, accessed 1 September 2022.

European Commission, *International Trade Centre's Market Analysis Tools now free for all EU users*, 2021, https://international-partnerships.ec.europa.eu/news-and-events/news/international-trade-centres-market-analysis-tools-now-free-all-eu-users-2021-07-22_en, accessed 1 September 2022.

European Commission, *Joint Employment Report 2022: As adopted by the Council on 14 March 2022*, 2022, available at: https://ec.europa.eu/social/main.jsp?catId=738&langId=en&pubId=8476&furtherPubs=yes, accessed 1 September 2022.

European Commission, *The Just Transition Mechanism: making sure no one is left behind*, https://ec.europa.eu/info/strategy/priorities-2019-2024/european-green-deal/finance-and-green-deal/just-transition-mechanism_en, accessed 1 September 2022.

European Commission, *Myth-busting: Five things you think you know about electric cars – but are not true*, 2021, https://europa.eu/climate-pact/news/myth-busting-five-things-you-think-you-know-about-electric-cars-are-not-true-2021-11-19_en, accessed 1 September 2022.

European Commission, *New transport proposals target greater efficiency and more sustainable travel*, 2021, https://transport.ec.europa.eu/news/efficient-and-green-mobility-2021-12-14_en, accessed 1 September 2022.

European Commission, *Panel of experts confirms the Republic of Korea is in breach of labour commitments under our trade agreement*, 2021, https://ec.europa.eu/commission/presscorner/detail/en/ip_21_203, accessed 1 September 2022.

European Commission, *Proposal for a Directive of the European Parliament and of the Council amending Directive 2011/83/EU concerning financial services contracts concluded at a distance and repealing Directive 2002/65/EC*, COM/2022/204 final, 2022.

European Commission, *Proposal for a Directive of the European Parliament and of the Council on Corporate Sustainability Due Diligence and amending Directive (EU) 2019/1937*, COM(2022) 71 final, 2022.

European Commission, *Proposal for a Regulation of the European Parliament and of the Council Establishing the Just Transition Fund*, COM/2020/22 final, 2020.

European Commission, *Protection Against Coercion*, https://policy.trade.ec.europa.eu/enforcement-and-protection/protecting-against-coercion_en, accessed 1 September 2022.

European Commission, *Questions and Answers: An open, sustainable and assertive trade policy*, 2021, https://ec.europa.eu/commission/presscorner/detail/en/qanda_21_645, accessed 1 September 2022.

European Commission, *Questions and Answers: Carbon Border Adjustment Mechanism (CBAM)*, 2023, https://taxation-customs.ec.europa.eu/system/files/2023-05/20230510%20Q%26A%20CBAM.pdf, accessed 12 May 2023.

European Commission, *Recovery Plan for Europe*, https://ec.europa.eu/info/strategy/recovery-plan-europe_en, accessed 1 September 2022.

European Commission, *Report from the Commission to the Parliament and the Council: First Annual Report on the Screening of Foreign Direct investments into the Union*, 2021.

European Commission, *REPowerEU: A plan to rapidly reduce dependence on Russian fossil fuels and fast forward the green transition*, 2022, https://ec.europa.eu/commission/presscorner/detail/en/IP_22_3131, accessed 1 September 2022.

European Commission, *Shaping and Securing the EU's Open Strategic Autonomy: By 2040 and beyond*, JRC Science for Policy Report, 2021.

European Commission, *Special Eurobarometer 491: European's Attitudes on Trade and EU Trade Policy*, Summary, May 2019, available at: https://europa.eu/eurobarometer/surveys/detail/2246, accessed 1 September 2022.

European Commission, *Statement by President von der Leyen on the occasion of the launch of the Partnership for Global Infrastructure and Investment at the G7 Leaders' Summit*, 2022, https://ec.europa.eu/commission/press-corner/detail/en/statement_22_4122, accessed 1 September 2022.

European Commission, *Study on switching of financial services and products: Final report*, 2019.

European Commission, *Trade and security: Commission highlights work to defend EU interests and values*, 2021, https://ec.europa.eu/commission/presscorner/detail/en/ip_21_6226, accessed 1 September 2022.

European Commission, *Trade defence*, https://policy.trade.ec.europa.eu/enforcement-and-protection/trade-defence_en, accessed 1 September 2022.

European Commission, *Questions and Answers: Carbon Border Adjustment Mechanism (CBAM)*, 10 May 2023, https://taxation-customs.ec.europa.eu/system/files/2023-05/20230510%20Q%26A%20CBAM.pdf, accessed 12 May 2023.

European Commission and Eurofound, *Employment and labour markets What just happened? Covid-19 lockdowns and change in the labour market*, 2021, https://www.eurofound.europa.eu/sites/default/files/ef_publication/field_ef_document/ef21040en.pdf, accessed 1 September 2022.

European Commission and International Trade Centre, *Navigating Non-Tariff Measures: Insights from a Business Survey in the European Union*, 2016.

European Council, *Council agrees on the Carbon Border Adjustment Mechanism (CBAM)*, 2022, https://www.consilium.europa.eu/en/press/press-releases/2022/03/15/carbon-border-adjustment-mechanism-cbam-council-agrees-its-negotiating-mandate/, accessed 1 September 2022.

European Council, *Council and Parliament strike provisional deal to protect geographical indications for craft and industrial products*, 2 May 2023, https://www.consilium.europa.eu/en/press/press-releases/2023/05/02/council-and-parliament-strike-provisional-deal-to-protect-geographical-indications-for-craft-and-industrial-products/, accessed 10 May 2023.

European Council, *Joint statement of the 20th EU-China Summit*, 2020, https://www.consilium.europa.eu/media/36165/final-eu-cn-joint-statement-consolidated-text-with-climate-change-clean-energy-annex.pdf, accessed 1 September 2022.

European Council, *New rules on corporate sustainability reporting: provisional political agreement between the Council and the European Parliament*, 2022, https://www.consilium.europa.eu/en/press/press-releases/2022/06/21/

new-rules-on-sustainability-disclosure-provisional-agreement-be-tween-council-and-european-parliament/, accessed 1 September 2022.

European Court of Auditors, *Infrastructure for charging electric cars is too sparse in the EU*, Special Report 05/2021, 2021, https://op.europa.eu/webpub/eca/special-reports/electrical-recharging-5-2021/en/, accessed 1 September 2022.

European Energy Research Alliance, *BatteRIes Europe*, available at: https://www.eera-set.eu/component/projects/projects/20-projects/69-batter-ies-europe.html, accessed 1 September 2022.

European Investment Bank, *Greece: EIB and Citi to release EUR 350 million to Greek export and import companies through Trade Finance Facilitation initiative*, 2022, https://www.eib.org/en/press/all/2022-084-eib-and-citi-to-release-eur-350-million-to-greek-export-and-import-companies-through-trade-finance-facilitation-initiative, accessed 1 September 2022.

European Parliament, *Implementation of the Stability and Growth Pact under pandemic times*, Briefing, 2021, https://www.europarl.europa.eu/RegData/etudes/BRIE/2020/659618/IPOL_BRI(2020)659618_EN.pdf, accessed 1 September 2022.

European Parliament, *New rules on batteries: MEPs want more environmental and social ambition*, 2022, https://www.europarl.europa.eu/news/en/press-room/20220304IPR24805/new-rules-on-batteries-meps-want-more-envi-ronmental-and-social-ambition, accessed 1 September 2022.

Eurostat, *Energy, Transport and Environment Statistics*, European Union, 2020.

Eurostat, *Euroindicators: Fourth quarter of 2021 Government debt down to 95.6% of GDP in euro area Down to 88.1% of GDP in EU*, 47/2022, 2022, https://ec.europa.eu/eurostat/documents/2995521/14497745/2-22042022-BP-EN.pdf/90896015-2ac1-081a-2eef-ad8d5f2c0da1, accessed 1 September 2022.

F

Fernandes, A. M., Rocha, N., and Ruta, M., eds., *The Economics of Deep Trade Agreements*, World Bank, 2021, p.131.

Food and Agriculture Organization, "The African Continental Free Trade Area Agreement and agricultural development: challenges and pros-pects", *FAO Global Forum on Food Security and Nutrition*, 2020, https://

www.fao.org/fsnforum/consultation/AFCFTA, accessed 1 September 2022.

Free Trade Agreement between the EU and its Member States and the Republic of Korea, 2011.

Frontier Economics, *The Economic Impacts of Counterfeiting and Piracy: Report Prepared for BASCAP and INTA*, 2016, p.8. Available at: https://iccwbo.org/publication/economic-impacts-counterfeiting-piracy-report-prepared-bascap-inta/, accessed 1 September 2022.

G

G20, *G20 Action Plan for Recovery and Reform, London Summit – Leaders' Statement*, 2 April 2009, https://www.oecd.org/g20/summits/london/G20-Action-Plan-Recovery-Reform.pdf, accessed 1 September 2022.

General Agreement on Tariffs and Trade, 1994.

Gatzer, S., Helmcke, S., and Roos, D., "Playing offense on circularity can net European consumer goods companies €500 billion", *McKinsey & Company*, 2022, https://www.mckinsey.com/industries/consumer-packaged-goods/our-insights/playing-offense-on-circularity-can-net-european-consumer-goods-companies-500-billion-euros, accessed 1 September 2022.

General Agreement on Trade-Related Aspects of Intellectual Property

Geneva Trade Platform, Multi-Party Interim Appeal Arbitration Arrangement (MPIA), https://wtoplurilaterals.info/plural_initiative/the-mpia/, accessed 1 September 2022.

Georgieva, K., Gopinath, G., and Pazarbasioglu, C., "Why we must resist geoeconomic fragmentation – and how", *International Monetary Fund*, Blog, 2022, https://blogs.imf.org/2022/05/22/why-we-must-resist-geoeconomic-fragmentation-and-how/, accessed 1 September 2022.

Global Trade Helpdesk, https://globaltradehelpdesk.org/en, accessed 1 September 2022.

González, A., *Trade Thoughts from Geneva, by Deputy Director-General A. Gonzalez: One year of exporting Covid-19 vaccines: what does the evidence show?*, World Trade Organization, 2022, https://www.wto.org/english/blogs_e/ddg_anabel_gonzalez_e/blog_ag_22feb22_e.htm, accessed 1 September 2022.

González Laya, A., "Europe's fiscal rules are holding it back", *Politico*, 2021, https://www.politico.eu/article/europe-fiscal-rules-holding-it-back/, accessed 1 September 2022.

González Laya, A., "Global Insecurity is No Reason to Divest from the WTO", *Financial Times*, 2022, https://www.ft.com/content/bb1fab70-02e0-4392-8fa5-e88c03398d44, accessed 1 September 2022.

Grainger, A., "Supply Chain Security: Adding to a Complex Operational and Institutional Environment", *World Customs Journal*, Vol. 1 N°2, 2007.

Grainger, A., "Trade Facilitation and Import-Export Procedures in the EU: Striking the Right Balance for International Trade" *European Parliament*, Policy Department External Policies, Briefing Paper, 2008, p.10.

Gregg, C., Tumurchudur Klok, B., "Rapid STED: A Practical Guide", *International Labour Organization*, 2020.

H

Herrero, A. G., and Xu, J., "Countries' Perceptions of China's Belt and Road Initiative: A Big Data Analysis", *Bruegel*, Working Paper, Issue 1, 2019, https://www.bruegel.org/wp-content/uploads/2019/02/WP-2019-01final.pdf, accessed 1 September 2022.

Hickel, J. and Kiallis, G., "Is Green Growth Possible" *New Political Economy*, Vol. 25, N°4, 2020.

I

Infrastructure Support Mechanism (ISM) Africa, *About us*, https://www.ism-africa.eu/about-us/, accessed 1 September 2022.

Intergovernmental Panel on Climate Change, *AR5 Climate Change 2014: Mitigation of Climate Change*, 2014.

Intergovernmental Panel on Climate Change, *Sixth Assessment Report: Mitigation of Climate Change*, 2022, available at: https://report.ipcc.ch/ar6wg3/pdf/IPCC_AR6_WGIII_FinalDraft_FullReport.pdf, accessed 1 September 2022.

Intergovernmental Panel on Climate Change, *Special Report on Global Warming of 1.5 °C (SR15)*, 2018, Available at: https://www.ipcc.ch/sr15/, accessed 1 September 2022.

International Chamber of Commerce, *The Business Case for a Permanent Prohibition on Customs Duties on Electronic Transmissions*, ICC Issues Brief N°2, ICC Working Group on E-commerce, 2019.

International Chamber of Commerce, *Global Industry Statement on the WTO Moratorium on Customs Duties on Electronic Transmissions*, 2022, https://iccwbo.org/content/uploads/sites/3/2021/11/icc-document-global-industry-statement-on-the-wto-moratorium-on-customs-duties-on-electronic-transmissions-2022.pdf, accessed 1 September 2022.

International Centre for Settlement of Investment Disputes, *ICSID Releases 2021 Caseload Statistics*, 2022, https://icsid.worldbank.org/news-and-events/comunicados/icsid-releases-2021-caseload-statistics, accessed 1 September 2022.

International Energy Agency, *Special Report on Solar PV Global Supply Chains*, 2022, https://www.iea.org/events/special-report-on-solar-pv-global-supply-chains, accessed 1 September 2022.

International Finance Corporation and World Trade Organization, *Trade Finance and the Compliance Challenge: A Showcase of International Cooperation*, 2019.

International Labour Organization, *Conclusions on Skills for Improved Productivity, Employment Growth and Development* (*International Labour Conference, 2008*), 2008.

International Labour Organization, *Conventions and Recommendations*, https://www.ilo.org/global/standards/introduction-to-international-labour-standards/conventions-and-recommendations/lang--en/index.htm, accessed 1 September 2022.

International Labour Organization, *Implementing new Labour Code will expedite Viet Nam's path to high income country*, 2020, https://www.ilo.org/hanoi/Informationresources/Publicinformation/Pressreleases/WCMS_765310/lang--en/index.htm, accessed 1 September 2022.

International Labour Organization, *International Labour Conference adds safety and health to Fundamental Principles and Rights at Work*, 2022, https://www.ilo.org/global/about-the-ilo/newsroom/news/WCMS_848132/lang--en/index.htm, accessed 1 September 2022.

International Labour Organization, *Trade Union Action on Disability and Decent Work: A Global Overview*, 2017.

International Labour Organization, *What Works: Promoting Pathways to Decent Work*, 2019.

International Labour Organization and World Trade Organization, *Investing in Skills for Inclusive Trade*, 2017.

International Monetary Fund, *FAS: What is mobile money? How is it different from mobile banking?*, available at: https://datahelp.imf.org/knowledge-base/articles/1906552-fas-what-is-mobile-money-how-is-it-different-fro, accessed 1 September 2022.

International Monetary Fund, *Taxing Multinationals in Europe*, 2021.

International Monetary Fund, World Bank and World Trade Organization, *Making Trade an Engine of Growth for All: The Case for Trade and for Policies to Facilitate Adjustment*, 2017.

International Renewable Energy Agency and World Trade Organization, *Trading into a Bright Energy Future: The Case for Open, High-Quality Solar Photovoltaic Markets*, 2021.

International Trade Centre, *ecomConnect*, https://intracen.org/resources/tools/e-commerce, accessed 1 September 2022.

International Trade Centre, *Export Potential Map*, https://exportpotential.intracen.org/en/, accessed 1 September 2022.

International Trade Centre, *From Europe to the World: Understanding Challenges for European Businesswomen*, 2019.

International Trade Centre, *Investment Map*, https://www.investmentmap.org/home, accessed 1 September 2022.

International Trade Centre, *LegaCarta*, https://legacarta.intracen.org/, accessed 1 September 2022.

International Trade Centre, *Market Access Map*, https://www.macmap.org/, accessed 1 September 2022.

International Trade Centre, *Market Price Information portal*, https://mpi.intracen.org/home, accessed 1 September 2022.

International Trade Centre, *Priority groups*, available at: https://intracen.org/our-work/priority-groups, accessed 1 September 2022.

International Trade Centre, *Procurement Map*, https://procurementmap.intracen.org/, accessed 1 September 2022.

International Trade Centre, *SDG Trade Monitor*, https://sdgtrade.org/en, accessed 1 September 2022.

International Trade Centre, *SheTrades*, https://www.shetrades.com/#/?lan=en, accessed 1 September 2022.

International Trade Centre, *SME Trade Academy*, https://learning.intracen.org/, accessed 1 September 2022.

International Trade Centre, *Sustainability Gateway*, https://www.sustainabilitygateway.org/, accessed 1 September 2022.

International Trade Centre, *Sustainability Map*, https://www.sustainabilit-ymap.org/home, accessed 1 September 2022.

International Trade Centre, *Trade Briefs*, https://intracen.org/resources/tools/trade-briefs, accessed 1 September 2022.

International Trade Centre, *Trade Map*, https://www.trademap.org/Index.aspx, accessed 1 September 2022.

International Trade Centre, *Youth and trade*, available at: https://intracen.org/our-work/topics/youth-and-trade, accessed 1 September 2022.

International Trade Centre, World Customs Organization and World Trade Organization, *Rules of Origin Facilitator*, https://findrulesoforigin.org/, accessed 1 September 2022.

Ionel, Z., "Labour Rights in EU Trade Agreements: Towards Stronger Enforcement", *European Parliament Research Service*, January 2022, https://www.europarl.europa.eu/RegData/etudes/BRIE/2022/698800/EPRS_BRI(2022)698800_EN.pdf, accessed 1 September 2022.

Inter-Parliamentary *Union, Parliamentary Conference on the WTO: Webinars in the context of the 12th Ministerial Conference*, https://www.ipu.org/event/parliamentary-conference-wto-webinars-in-context-12th-ministerial-conference, accessed 1 September 2022.

J

Jansen, M., "Defining the Borders of the WTO Agenda", in A. Narlikar, M. Daunton and R.M. Stern, eds., *The Oxford Handbook on the World Trade Organization*, online edn, Oxford Academic, 2012, p.161-183, https://academic.oup.com/edited-volume/28190/chapter/213121453, accessed 1 September 2022.

K

Krugman, P. R., "Increasing Returns, Monopolistic Competition, and International Trade", *Journal of International Economics*, Vol. 9, Issue 4, November 1979, p. 469-479.

Krugman, P. R., Obstfeld, M., and J. Melitz, M., *International Trade: Theory and Policy*, 11th Edition, Pearson: 2018.

Kuriyama, C., "A Review of the APEC List of Environmental Goods", *Asia-Pacific Economic Cooperation*, Policy Brief No. 41, 2021, https://www.apec.org/docs/default-source/Publications/2021/10/A-Review-of-the-

APEC-List-of-Environmental-Goods/221_PSU_Review-of-APEC-List-of-Environmental-Goods.pdf, accessed 1 September 2022.

L

Lamy, P., "Foreword", in Mattoo, A., Rocha, N., and Ruta, M., *Handbook of Deep Trade Agreements*, World Bank, 2020.

Lamy, P., in "Biennial Conference on Competition, Regulation and Development", organised by the CUTS International, November 2021, available at: https://cuts-ccier.org/precautionism-is-risking-open-trade-more-than-protectionism-pascal-lamy-2/, accessed 1 September 2022.

Lamy, P., "Lamy addresses Collège Universitaire de Sciences Po", World Trade Organization, 2012, https://www.wto.org/english/news_e/sppl_e/sppl252_e.htm, accessed 1 September 2022.

Lanz, R., Miroudot, S., and Nordås, H. K., "Trade in Tasks", *OECD Trade Policy Working Papers*, No. 117, OECD Publishing, 2011.

Le Point, *Fermeture de Bridgestone : le plan de sauvegarde de l'emploi a été signé*, 2021, https://www.lepoint.fr/economie/fermeture-de-bridgestone-le-plan-de-sauvegarde-de-l-emploi-a-ete-signe-13-02-2021-2413801_28.php#11, accessed 1 September 2022.

N. Lloyd, "Turning up the heat on Europe's fuel poverty crisis", *Euronews in partnership with the European Commission*, 2022, https://www.euronews.com/next/2022/01/26/turning-up-the-heat-on-europe-s-energy-poverty-crisis, accessed 1 September 2022.

Lowe, S., "The EU's carbon border adjustment mechanism: How to make it work for developing countries", *Centre for European Reform*, 2021, https://www.cer.eu/sites/default/files/pbrief_cbam_sl_21.4.21.pdf, accessed 1 September 2022.

M

V. Mallinckrodt, "How to achieve supplier diversity: 4 experts explain", *World Economic Forum*, 2021, https://www.weforum.org/agenda/2021/07/how-to-achieve-supplier-diversity-experts-explain-68df4f727b/, accessed 1 September 2022.

Marrakesh Agreement Establishing the World Trade Organization, 1994.

Marrakesh Ministerial Decision on Trade and Environment, 1994.

Masters, B., *US Baby Formula Crisis Highlights Risk of Reshoring*, Financial Times, 18 May 2022.

Masterson, V., "Degrowth – what's behind the economic theory and why does it matter right now?", *World Economic Forum*, 2022, https://www.weforum.org/agenda/2022/06/what-is-degrowth-economics-climate-change/, accessed 1 September 2022.

Masterson, V., "These are the skills young people will need for the green jobs of the future", *World Economic Forum*, 2021, https://www.weforum.org/agenda/2021/08/these-are-the-skills-young-people-will-need-for-the-green-jobs-of-the-future/, accessed 1 September 2022.

Mattoo, A., Rocha, N., and Ruta, M., *Handbook of Deep Trade Agreements*, World Bank, 2020.

Mavroidis, P. C., and Sapir, A., "All the Tea in China: Solving the 'China Problem' at the WTO", *Global Policy*, Volume 12, Supplement 3, April 2021, p.41-48, https://onlinelibrary.wiley.com/doi/epdf/10.1111/1758-5899.12925, accessed 1 September 2022.

McCabe, D., "How Frustration Over TikTok Has Mounted in Washington", *The New York Times*, 2022, https://www.nytimes.com/2022/08/14/technology/tiktok-china-washington.html, accessed 1 September 2022.

McKinsey, *The net-zero transition: What it would cost, what it could bring*, 2022.

Meltzer, J. P. and Kerry, C. F., "Cybersecurity and digital trade: Getting it right", *Brookings*, 2019, https://www.brookings.edu/research/cybersecurity-and-digital-trade-getting-it-right/, accessed 1 September 2022.

Memorandum of Understanding between the European Commission, the European Investment Bank together with the European Investment Fund, and the European Bank for Reconstruction and Development in respect of Cooperation Outside the European Union, 2012.

Miles, T., "EU blames China for WTO environmental trade talks collapse", *Reuters*, 2016, https://www.reuters.com/article/us-trade-environment-idUSKBN13T0MX, accessed 1 September 2022.

Ministerial Declaration of the Sixth Session of the Ministerial Conference of the World Trade Organization, "Hong Kong Ministerial Declaration", WTO document WT/MIN(05)/DEC, 2005.

Ministerial Declaration on the WTO Response to the Covid-19 Pandemic and Preparedness for Future Pandemics, World Trade Organization, 2022, WTO document WT/MIN(22)/31 - WT/L/1142.

Monteiro, J.A., *The Evolution of Gender-Related Provisions in Regional Trade Agreements*, World Trade Organization, Staff Working Paper ERSD-2021-

8, 2021, https://www.wto.org/english/res_e/reser_e/ersd202108_e.pdf, accessed 1 September 2022.

Mulabdic, A., Osnago A., and Ruta, M., *Deep integration and UK-EU trade relations*, World Bank, Policy Research Working Paper 7947, 2017, https://openknowledge.worldbank.org/bitstream/handle/10986/25956/WPS7947.pdf?sequence=1&isAllowed=y, accessed 1 September 2022.

N

New Zealand Government, *Joint Statement: Agreement on Climate Change, Trade and Sustainability (ACCTS) at MC12*, 15 June 2022, https://www.beehive.govt.nz/release/joint-statement-agreement-climate-change-trade-and-sustainability-accts-mc12, accessed 1 September 2022.

O

Organisation for Economic Cooperation and Development, *The Blue Dot Network: A Proposal for a Global Certification Framework for Quality Infrastructure*, 2022, https://www.oecd.org/daf/blue-dot-network-proposal-certification.pdf, accessed 1 September 2022.

Organisation for Economic Cooperation and Development, *China's Belt and Road Initiative in the Global Trade, Investment and Finance Landscape*, OECD Business and Finance Outlook, 2018, p.20.

Organisation for Economic Cooperation and Development, *Covid-19 and Global Value Chains: Policy Option to Build More Resilient Production Networks*, 2020.

Organisation for Economic Cooperation and Development, *Economic Outlook, Interim Report March 2022: Economic and Social Impacts and Policy Implications of the War in Ukraine*, 2022.

Organisation for Economic Cooperation and Development, *Global Value Chains: Efficiency and Risks in the Context of Covid-19*, 2021.

Organisation for Economic Cooperation and Development, *International collaboration to end tax avoidance – Understanding Tax Avoidance*, https://www.oecd.org/tax/beps/, accessed 1 September 2022.

Organisation for Economic Cooperation and Development, *International community strikes a ground-breaking tax deal for the digital age*, 2021, https://www.oecd.org/tax/international-community-strikes-a-ground-breaking-tax-deal-for-the-digital-age.htm, 1 September 2022.

Organisation for Economic Cooperation and Development, *OECD Employment Outlook 2021: Navigating the Covid-19 crisis and recovery*, 2021.

Organisation for Economic Cooperation and Development, *Official Development Assistance (ODA)*, available at: https://www.oecd.org/dac/financing-sustainable-development/development-finance-standards/official-development-assistance.htm, accessed 1 September 2022.

Organisation for Economic Cooperation and Development, "What is green growth and how can it help deliver sustainable development?", https://www.oecd.org/greengrowth/whatisgreengrowthandhowcanithelpdeliversustainabledevelopment.htm, accessed 1 September 2022.

Organisation for Economic Cooperation and Development", "Why governments should target support amidst high energy prices", *Policy Responses: Ukraine, Tackling the Policy Challenges*, 2022, https://www.oecd-ilibrary.org/docserver/40f44f78-en.pdf?expires=1662053440&id=id&accname=ocid195767&checksum=0F70A438C950BD0A466A32206AFC2082, accessed 1 September 2022.

Organisation for Economic Cooperation and Development and World Trade Organization, *Aid for Trade at a Glance 2017: Promoting Trade, Inclusiveness and Connectivity for Sustainable Development*, 2017.

Oxford English Dictionary, available at: https://www.oed.com/, accessed 1 September 2022.

Oxford Learner's Dictionaries, available at: https://www.oxfordlearnersdictionaries.com/, accessed 1 September 2022.

P

Pfizer, *An Open Letter from Pfizer Chairman and CEO to Colleagues*, 2021, https://www.pfizer.com/news/articles/why_pfizer_opposes_the_trips_intellectual_property_waiver_for_covid_19_vaccines, accessed 1 September 2022.

Piper, K., "Can we save the planet by shrinking the economy?" *Vox*, 2021, https://www.vox.com/future-perfect/22408556/save-planet-shrink-economy-degrowth, accessed 1 September 2022.

R

Radauer, A., "Opportunities to Reap Financing Through IP for Innovation", in Dutta, S., Lanvin, B., and Wunsch-Vincent, S., (eds.), *Global Innovation Index 2020: Who Will Finance Innovation?*, 13th edition, 2020

Raworth, K., *Doughnut Economics: Seven Ways to Think Lika a 21st-century Economist*, Chelsea Green Publishing: 2017.

Regulation (EU) 2019/881 of the European Parliament and of the Council of 17 April 2019 on ENISA (the European Union Agency for Cybersecurity) and on information and communications technology cybersecurity certification and repealing Regulation (EU) No 526/2013 (Cybersecurity Act).

Reinsch W. A., and Benson, E., "Environmental Goods Agreement: A New Frontier or an Old Stalemate?", *Centre for Strategic and International Studies*, 2021, https://www.csis.org/analysis/environmental-goods-agreement-new-frontier-or-old-stalemate, accessed 1 September 2022.

Reuters, *Europe wants to join China "Belt and Road" plan but needs reciprocity – Merkel*, 2019, https://www.reuters.com/article/france-china-merkel-idINKCN1R715U, accessed 1 September 2022.

Ricardo, D., 1772-1823. *On the Principles of Political Economy and Taxation*, London: John Murray, 1817.

Richardson, B., "Energy Dept. pushes heat pumps to reduce greenhouse emissions", *The Washington Post*, 2022, https://www.washingtonpost.com/business/2022/03/28/heat-pumps-energy/, accessed 1 September 2022.

Ritchie, H., "Many countries have decoupled economic growth from CO_2 emissions, even if we take off-shored production into account", *Our World in Data*, 2021, https://ourworldindata.org/co2-gdp-decoupling, accessed 1 September 2022.

Roberts, A., and Lamp, N., *Six Faces of Globalization: Who Wins, Who Loses, and Why it Matters*, Harvard University Press, 2021.

Rostow, W. W., "The Stages of Economic Growth", *The Economic History Review*, New Series, Vol. 12 N°1, 1959, p.1-16.

Rotmans, J., and Kemp, R., "Managing Societal Transitions: Dilemmas and Uncertainties: The Dutch energy case-study", *Organisation for Economic Cooperation and Development*, Working Party on Global and Structural Policies, OECD Workshop on the Benefits of Climate Policy: Improving Information for Policy Makers, 2003.

Ruehl, M., "EU deforestation law triggers ire of its trading partners", *Financial Times*, 2023, https://www.ft.com/content/c2f2eea9-1eb5-478f-ac53-5666776c0a35, accessed 18 June 2023.

S

Samuelson, P.A., "The Way of an Economist", in Samuelson, P.A., ed., *International Economic Relations: Proceedings of the Third Congress of the International Economic Association*, 1969, Macmillan: London, p.1-11.

Sapir, A., Schraepen T., and Tagliapietra S., "Green Public Procurement: A Neglected Tool in the European Green Deal Toolbox?", *Intereconomics*, Vol. 57, Number 3, 2022, https://www.intereconomics.eu/contents/year/2022/number/3/article/green-public-procurement-a-neglected-tool-in-the-european-green-deal-toolbox.html#:~:text=1%20Green%20public%20procurement%20is,function%20that%20would%20otherwise%20be, accessed 1 September 2022.

Skonieczna, A., and Castellano, L., "Gender Smart Financing, Investing In and With Women: Opportunities for Europe", *European Commission*, Discussion Paper 129, 2020.

Smeets, M., ed., *Adapting to the Digital Trade Era: Challenges and Opportunities*, World Trade Organization, 2021.

Statista, *Global retail e-commerce sales (2014-2025)*, available at: https://www.statista.com/statistics/379046/worldwide-retail-e-commerce-sales/, accessed 1 September 2022.

T

Teehankee, M. A. J., *Trade and Environment Governance at the World Trade Organization Committee on Trade and Environment*, Wolters Kluwer: Global Trade Law Series, vol. 53, 2020.

Titievskaia, J., and Morgado Simões, H., with Dobreva, A., "EU carbon border adjustment mechanism Implications for climate and competitiveness" European Parliament, Briefing – EU Legislation in Progress, 2022, https://www.europarl.europa.eu/RegData/etudes/BRIE/2022/698889/EPRS_BRI(2022)698889_EN.pdf, accessed 1 September 2022.

Thomas, J., «Bridgestone : direction et syndicats trouvent un compromis sur le plan social», *Le Monde*, 2021, https://www.lemonde.fr/economie/article/2021/02/12/bridgestone-direction-et-syndicats-trouvent-un-compromis-sur-le-plan-social_6069797_3234.html, accessed 1 September 2022.

Toye, R., "The International Trade Organization", in A. Narlikar, M. Daunton and R.M. Stern, eds., The Oxford Handbook on the World Trade Organization, online edn, Oxford Academic, 2012, https://doi.org/10.1093/oxfordhb/9780199586103.013.0005, accessed 1 September 2022.

Trade4MSMEs, https://trade4msmes.org/, accessed 1 September 2022.

Trade Obstacles Alert Mechanism, https://www.tradeobstacles.org/CountrySelection.aspx, accessed 1 September 2022.

Trade Policy Review Mechanism

U

Understanding on the Rules and Procedures Governing the Settlement of Disputes

Unibanco, I., "How a trade war would impact global growth", *World Economic Forum*, 2019, https://www.weforum.org/agenda/2019/01/how-trade-war-would-impact-global-growth-tariff/, accessed 1 September 2022.

United Nations, *Millenium Development Goals, Goal 1: Eradicate Extreme Poverty and Hunger*. Available at: https://www.un.org/millenniumgoals/poverty.shtml#:~:text=Target%201.A%3A,of%20extreme%20poverty%20since%201990, accessed 1 September 2022.

United Nations, *Rising inequality affecting more than two-thirds of the globe, but it's not inevitable: new UN report*, 2020, https://news.un.org/en/story/2020/01/1055681, accessed 1 September 2022.

United Nations, *The Sustainable Development Goals Report 2016: Leaving no one behind*, available at: https://unstats.un.org/sdgs/report/2016/leaving-no-one-behind, accessed 1 September 2022.

United Nations Conference on International Trade Law, *Working Group III: Investor-State Dispute Settlement Reform*, available at: https://uncitral.un.org/en/working_groups/3/investor-state, accessed 1 September 2022.

United Nations Conference on Trade and Development, *UNCTAD e-Handbook of Statistics 2021*, https://hbs.unctad.org/trade-structure-by-partner/#:~:text=Intrapercent2Dregionalpercent20tradepercent20waspercent20most,mostpercent20tradepercent20waspercent20extrapercent2Dregional, accessed 1 September 2022

United Nations Conference on Trade and Development, *Why and how to measure international transport costs*, Transport and Trade Facilitation Newsletter N°89, First Quarter 2021, 2020, https://unctad.org/news/why-and-how-measure-international-transport-costs, accessed 1 September 2022.

United Nations Environment Programme, *The Growing Footprint of Digitalisation*, Foresight Brief 27, November 2021.

United Nations Framework Convention on Climate Change, *Multilateralism Key to Achieving Climate Goals*, 2022, https://unfccc.int/news/multilateralism-key-to-achieving-climate-goals, accessed 1 September 2022.

United States Census Bureau, *Trade in Goods with China*, https://www.census.gov/foreign-trade/balance/c5700.html, accessed 1 September 2022.

The University of Adelaide, *Institute for International Trade: The Topology of E-commerce Governance*, https://iit.adelaide.edu.au/news/list/2021/09/16/the-topology-of-e-commerce-governance, accessed 1 September 2022.

V

van 't Wout, D., "The enforceability of the trade and sustainable development chapters of the European Union's free trade agreements", *Asia Europe Journal*, 2022, p.81-98.

van den Bergh, J. C. J. M., "A third option for climate policy within potential limits to growth", *Nature Climate Change*, 2017, https://edisciplinas.usp.br/pluginfile.php/4203641/mod_label/intro/van%20den%20Bergh%20-%20Nature%202017.pdf, accessed 1 September 2022.

Van den Bossche, P., and Akpofure, S., "The Use and Abuse of the National Security Exception under Article XXI(b)(iii) of the GATT 1994", *World Trade Institute*, Working Paper No. 03/2020, 2020, https://www.wti.org/media/filer_public/50/57/5057fb22-f949-4920-8bd1-e8ad352d22b2/wti_working_paper_03_2020.pdf, accessed 1 September 2022.

Van den Bossche, P., Zdouc, W., *The Law and Policy of the World Trade Organization: Text, Cases, and Materials*, Fifth Edition, Cambridge University Press: 2022.

VanGrasstek, C., *The History and Future of the World Trade Organization*, WTO, 2013.

Venkataramakrishnan, S., "National security concerns pile pressure on 'splinternet' cracks", *Financial Times*, 2021, https://www.ft.com/content/e4b87d3d-d2f4-4ba2-9602-6fd330bac6f6, accessed 1 September 2022.

W

White House, *Fact Sheet: President Biden and G7 Leaders Launch Build Back Better World (B3W) Partnership*, https://www.whitehouse.gov/briefing-room/statements-releases/2021/06/12/fact-sheet-president-biden-and-g7-leaders-launch-build-back-better-world-b3w-partnership/, accessed 1 September 2022.

Wiedmann, T., Lenzen, M., Keyßer, L. T., and Steinberger, J. K., "Scientists' Warning on Affluence", *Nature Communications*, 2020, https://www.nature.com/articles/s41467-020-16941-y.pdf, accessed 1 September 2022.

World Bank, *Air Freight: A Market Study with Implications for Landlocked Countries*, Transport Papers TP-26, 2009.

World Bank, *Data, GDP growth (annual %)*, https://data.worldbank.org/indicator/NY.GDP.MKTP.KD.ZG, accessed 1 September 2022.

World Bank, *Data, GDP (current US$) – Cambodia*, https://data.worldbank.org/indicator/NY.GDP.MKTP.CD?locations=KH, accessed 1 September 2022.

World Bank, *Global Economic Prospects and the Developing Countries 2002: Making Trade Work for the Poor*, 2001.

World Bank, *World Development Report 2020: Trading for Development in the Age of Global Value Chains*, 2020.

World Bank and World Trade Organization, *The Role of Trade in Developing Countries' Road to Recovery: Joint Policy Note*, 2022.

World Bank and World Trade Organization, *The Role of Trade in Ending Poverty*, 2015.

World Bank and World Trade Organization, *Women and Trade: The Role of Trade in Promoting Gender Equality*, 2020, p.95.

World Customs Organization, *What is the Harmonized System (HS)?*, http://www.wcoomd.org/en/topics/nomenclature/overview/what-is-the-harmonized-system.aspx, accessed 1 September 2022.

World Economic Forum, *Defining and Measuring Payment Interoperability*, White Paper, 2022.

World Economic Forum, *Markets of Tomorrow: Pathways to a New Economy*, Insight Report, 2020.

World Intellectual Property Organization, *WIPO IP Diagnostics*, https://www.wipo.int/ipdiagnostics/en/index.html, accessed 1 September 2022.

World Trade Organization, *Aid for Trade Global Review 2022: Empowering Connected, Sustainable Trade*, 2022.

World Trade Organization, *Annual Report 2022*, WTO, available at: https://www.wto.org/english/res_e/booksp_e/anrep_e/ar22_e.pdf,accessed 1 September 2022.

World Trade Organization, *Backbone of the multilateral trading system: WTO goods schedules*, https://www.wto.org/english/news_e/news17_e/mark_27jul17_e.pdf, accessed 1 September 2022.

World Trade Organization, *Coordinated global response key to MSMEs'
post-pandemic economic recovery — DDG Zhang*, 2021, https://www.wto.
org/english/news_e/news21_e/msmes_22oct21_e.htm, accessed 1 September 2022.

World Trade Organization, *Covid-19 and world trade*, https://www.wto.org/
english/tratop_e/covid19_e/covid19_e.htm, accessed 1 September 2022.

World Trade Organization, *The Crisis in Ukraine: Implications of the War for
Global Trade and Development*, 2022.

World Trade Organization, *Energy efficiency and illegal logging at centre of
discussions in environment committee*, 2015, https://www.wto.org/english/
news_e/news15_e/envir_22jun15_e.htm, accessed 1 September 2022.

World Trade Organization, *ePing – SPS & TBT Platform* (WTO, UN, ITC),
available at: https://eping.wto.org/en/FactsAndFigures/Notifications,
accessed 1 September 2022.

World Trade Organization, *Implementing the WTO Agreement on Fisheries
Subsidies: Challenges and Opportunities for Developing and Least-Developed
Country Members*, 2022.

World Trade Organization, I*n a world of polycrisis, Aid for Trade Global
Review focuses on recovery, resilience*, 2022, https://www.wto.org/english/
news_e/news22_e/aid_27jul22_e.htm, accessed 1 September 2022.

World Trade Organization, *Lamy says the Round's development potential
must be preserved*, 2005, https://www.wto.org/english/news_e/news05_e/
stat_lamy_28nov05_e.htm, accessed 1 September 2022.

World Trade Organization, *Members mark 5th anniversary of Trade Facilitation Agreement, share experiences on impact*, 2022, https://www.wto.org/
english/news_e/news22_e/fac_04jul22_e.htm, accessed 1 September 2022.

World Trade Organization, *National Foreign Trade Council: Strengthening the
WTO and the Global Trading System*, Remarks by Director General Okonjo-Iweala, 27 April 2022, https://www.wto.org/english/news_e/spno_e/
spno25_e.htm, accessed 1 September 2022.

World Trade Organization, *Trade Concerns Database*, https://tradeconcerns.
wto.org/en, accessed 1 September 2022.

World Trade Organization, *Trade finance and SMEs: Bridging the Gaps in
Provision*, 2016.

World Trade Organization, *TRIPS: Geographical Indications, Background*,
https://www.wto.org/english/tratop_e/trips_e/gi_background_e.htm,
accessed 1 September 2022.

World Trade Organization, *Understanding the WTO: Basics – What is the World Trade Organization*, https://www.wto.org/english/thewto_e/whatis_e/tif_e/fact1_e.htm, accessed 1 September 2022.

World Trade Organization, *Working group on small business welcomes three more members*, 2022, https://www.wto.org/english/news_e/news22_e/ms-mes_08feb22_e.htm, accessed 1 September 2022.

World Trade Organization, *World Trade Report 2009: Trade Policy Commitments and Contingency Measures*, 2009.

World Trade Organization, *World Trade Report 2015: Speeding Up Trade: benefits and challenges of implementing the WTO Trade Facilitation Agreement*, 2015.

World Trade Organization, *World Trade Report 2016: Levelling the Trading Field for SMEs*, 2016.

World Trade Organization, *World Trade Report 2018: The Future of World Trade: How Digital Technologies are Transforming Global Commerce*, 2018.

World Trade Organization, *World Trade Report 2019: The Future of Services Trade*, 2019.

World Trade Organization, *World Trade Report 2020: Government Policies to Promote Innovation in the Digital Age*, 2020.

World Trade Organization, *World Trade Report 2021: Economic Resilience and Trade*, 2021.

World Trade Organization, *World Trade Statistical Review 2021*, 2021.

World Trade Organization, *WTO Data – Information on trade and trade policy measures*, https://data.wto.org/en, accessed 1 September 2022.

World Trade Organization, *The WTO in Brief*, https://www.wto.org/english/thewto_e/whatis_e/inbrief_e/inbr_e.htm, accessed 1 September 2022.

World Trade Organization, *WTO Matrix on Trade-Related Measures Pursuant to Selected Multilateral Environmental Agreements (MEAs)*, https://www.wto.org/english/tratop_e/envir_e/envir_matrix_e.htm, accessed 1 September 2022.

World Trade Organization, *WTO members agree to extend TRIPS transition period for LDCs until 1 July 2034*, https://www.wto.org/english/news_e/news21_e/trip_30jun21_e.htm, accessed 1 September 2022.

WTO document G/TFA/W/25

WTO document GATS/SC/56/Suppl.2

WTO document INF/MSME/4

WTO document JOB/DSB/1/Add.12

WTO document TN/TE/26

WTO document WT/CTE/W/249

WTO document WT/GC/W/442

WTO document WT/GC/W/798

WTO document WT/GC/W/799/Rev.1

WTO document WT/GC/W/833

WTO document WT/GC/W/819

WTO document WT/LET/1469

WTO document WT/MIN(21)/6

WTO document WT/MIN(21)/8

WTO document WT/MIN(21)/9

WTO document WT/MIN(22)/W/16/Rev.1

WTO document WT/MIN(22)/24 – WT/L/1135

X

Xu, A., Tresa, E., Bacchetta, M., Bellelli, F., and Monteiro, J., "Carbon Content of International Trade", *World Trade Organization*, Trade and Climate Change, Information Brief N°4, revised 9 November 2021, https://www.wto.org/english/news_e/news21_e/clim_03nov21-4_e.pdf, accessed 1 September 2022.

Y

Ye! Community – https://yecommunity.com/, accessed 1 September 2022.

Z

F. Zandt, "Where Money Goes Mobile", *Statista*, available at: https://www.statista.com/chart/25713/mobile-money-accounts-by-region-in-2020/, accessed 1 September 2022.

Reviews

Trade is a powerful process shaping the global economy, leveraging development but also creating new tensions and social inequalities. If you want to understand how this works and how this should work, you have here a brilliant synthesis provided by an outstanding policy-maker in the world stage.
Professor Maria Joao Rodrigues, FEPS President

The FEPS Handbook on trade, co-authored by Arancha Gonzalez Laya and Yanis Bourgeois, is a must-read for any policymaker wishing to understand the modern global trading system.

The book smartly guides us through the underlying economic reasons for engaging in trade, the functioning of the international trading framework and key elements needed to facilitate trade.

While discussing various contemporary challenges to the world economic order such as rapid digitalization, reformulation of global value chains, increased geopolitical tensions and the effects of climate change, the authors do not shy away from elaborating on ways in which trade could help us tackle green and social transitions and create global common benefits.

This publication serves well as a source of knowledge, as well as an interesting introduction to the most actual discussions on the future of trade.
Prof. Dr hab. Marek Belka, former Prime Minister of Poland and Vice-President of S&D Group in the European Parliament

In this book, readers will benefit from Arancha Gonzalez's deep knowledge of all aspects of international trade. It is both a reference book and an inspiration. Trade will always lead to discussions, this book will make the discussion more factual and knowledgeable. The next step is a Feminist Trade Policy!
Ann Linde, Former Foreign Affairs Minister of Sweden

"A victim of the populist tide that has engulfed large swathes of the planet, multilateral trade is struggling for legitimacy amidst the revival of protectionist walls. Arancha Gonzalez's Handbook on Trade puts the intellectual and policymaking expertise of its author in best use, and articulates a 21st trade vision that has been sorely missing.

In a mesmerizing tour de force that takes the reader through the ebbs and flows of the intellectual and empirical evolution of the trade adventure, Gonzalez Laya articulates a fresh vision with courage and conviction. That vision consists of a new trade settlement that builds on its anti-poverty and growth success but also addresses the agonizing challenges associated with a laissez faire attitude harmful to workers, communities, and the planet. It is time to heed the call."

Dr. Dimitris Tsarouhas, Adjunct Professor, Georgetown University Research Director, Virginia Tech Consultant, World Bank Member of FEPS Scientific Council

About the Authors

Arancha Gonzalez Laya is the Dean of the Paris School of International Affairs (PSIA) at Sciences Po and first woman to lead the world's third school for Politics and International Studies.

Prior to joining PSIA, Ms Gonzalez served as Spain's Minister of Foreign Affairs, European Union and Cooperation (2020-2021). She previously was Assistant-Secretary-General of the United Nations and Executive Director of the International Trade Centre (2013-2020). Between 2005 and 2013 she served as Chief of Staff to the Director-General of the World Trade Organization. Before that she held senior positions at the European Commission in the areas of international trade and development. Ms Gonzalez started her career as a lawyer in the private sector.

A Spanish national, Ms Gonzalez holds a degree in law from the University of Navarra and a Master in European Law from the University Carlos III of Madrid.

Yanis Bourgeois is an Economic Affairs Officer at the World Trade Organization, in the Council and Trade Negotiations Committee (CTNC) Division. He specialises in e-commerce related issues at the WTO, both under the Work Programme and the ongoing negotiations in the Joint Statement Initiative.

Mr Bourgeois regularly provides technical assistance to developing and least developed countries on a variety of WTO issues, including on e-commerce, Ministerial Conferences and General Council matters, negotiations, plurilateral initiatives, and WTO reform.

He is a French national who holds two Masters' degrees, a Master 2 in English and North American Business Law from Université Paris 1 Panthéon-Sorbonne and an LL.M. in International Law from the University of Glasgow.

Acknowledgements

In this section, we wish to express our profound gratitude to the key contributors to the Trade Handbook: Making trade work for prosperity, people and planet.

At the outset, we are extremely grateful to the Foundation for European Progressive Studies (FEPS), for their initiative to focus attention on international trade and for continuously providing a forum for innovative ideas to be communicated and for progressive voices to be heard on the value of international trade, trade agreements and trade multilateralism. They have once more demonstrated this feat by supporting the Trade Handbook project from its inception.

We are also extremely grateful to Matthew Wilson, Ambassador and Permanent Representative of Barbados to the United Nations Office and other international organizations in Geneva; Victor do Prado, Professor at the Paris School of International Affairs, Sciences Po, and former Director of the Council and Trade Negotiations Committee Division at the WTO; Trineesh Biswas, Speechwriter and Communications Advisor to the WTO Director-General; and Michele Ruta, Deputy Chief in the Strategy and Policy Review Department at the International Monetary Fund. They have shared their invaluable trade-related knowledge, experience and insights. Their substantive contributions have significantly enriched the content of the Trade Handbook.

We also wish to highlight the wonderful work accomplished by the editor, Dietz-Verlag, and the team of graphic designers. They have truly been instrumental in the materialisation of this project.